T E
S C

A WORKING BIOGRAPHY

Gary Wharton

lushington **PUBLISHING**

For Aubrey and Philip.

© 2016 Gary Wharton
All Rights Reserved.

ISBN 978-0-9542187-9-9

Design: gary wharton

vetchbook@yahoo.co.uk

Printed by Beacon Printers Ltd.
Leyshons Buildings
Cornerswell Road
Penarth
Vale of Glamorgan
CF64 2XS
Tel 029 2070 8415

lushington PUBLISHING

As a toddler the theatrical bent of young Owen John Scott was apparent; at the age of three he offered his family his "plate on the head" comedy turn and a year later he had developed his "mud pie down my trousers" presentation. By seven he was creating his own little plays but was seemingly not encouraged and he was at this point a member of his local church choir at St James's. At eight he was playing Mr Bumble in Oliver Twist at school and by eleven he won a scholarship to Watford Grammar School where he would enjoy performing in the drama society.

"I knew him when we were boys living in adjoining streets in the area of Watford known as Watford Fields." reflects Fred Richardson in a letter to the author, "The rear of the houses on Tucker Street had gardens which back on to the playgrounds of the junior school we attended. Owen was a few years younger than myself but we both sang in the local church choir; St James's Church. The church and the school had connecting areas. Adopting the name Terry he performed at the Watford Palace Theatre at one time [post-war]...."

He lived next door to my grandparents - who were great friends with his mother. When he became famous, he bought his mother a house in Carpenders Park." Anonymous correspondence with the author.

His parents, Frederick and Beatrice (known as Mabel) had persuaded him to take an accountancy course but he devoted his spare time to Watford Amateur Dramatic Society; something he had been involved in for a number of years, before joing the Navy.

At the close of WWII, an eighteen-year-old Terry was also based at Glenholt Signal Camp during his National Service days and at some point he appeared in cabaret and variety shows for them. Registering with with Combined Services Entertainment, formerly known as Central Pool of Artistes, the CSE had superseded ENSA and at this time had offices in the plush Upper Grosvenor street, London W1. He was in good company as Terry-Thomas, Peter Sellers, Bill Pertwee, future comedy partner Hugh Lloyd and Frankie Howerd would all be involved with them after being demobbed. In the case of Lloyd, he and Terry would later become a popular team across theatre, film and television. It would also be at the CSE that both would come to work with a twenty-six-year-old Colonel Richard Stone, later to represent both.

Given a £39 demob gratuity, Terry started an act in pubs and clubs at 25 shillings a gig whilst continuing acting and developing his little boy 'Knocker' character/ act based on his cousin. It was around this time that he attended Watford Dance Academy, where he met a certain Thelma Terry Howard.

Quintin Butcher, Terry's cousin, known to him as "Tiny", in repeat correspoindence with the author, elaborates, "His sister Joan was a district midwife who lived in the nurses' home in Granville Road, Watford. One evening there was a knock at the door. W.Barrington Dalby, the famous BBC boxing commentator, who lived opposite was asking for help as his wife had been taken ill. He and Joan subsequently became good friends and he saw some of Owen's (Terry) performances. Mr Dalby suggested and arranged auditions for him at the BBC, which he passed. They advised him to change his name to a more acceptable stage one. It was from Thelma's name of Terry, that he chose; changing it by deed poll to Terry Scott."

Marriage for the couple followed in 1949 and they moved in first to a a friend's house before another in Kenilworth Drive. "This he converted into two flats; 32 Tucker Street (where Terry was born) was sold and his parents moved to number 9 to look after the house whilst Terry was away on tour." A blue plaque at Tucker Street was unveiled on Sunday 18 March, 2003, by Sir John Mills commemorating its role in the early life of Terry Scott.

Terry and Thelma had a son, Philip, who tragically died at about twelve months of age after choking on a meal. The event resulted in divorce. Back in 1933, then aged aged, Terry's own brother, Aubrey, had passed away due to bronchitis.

Grange-over-Sands was the location at which Terry obtained his first professional, paid role in the punishing world of repertory theatre. He worked as a stage manager booking and organising shows, "Doing everything from make tea to painting scenery".

By 1948, still known as Owen J.Scott, the man that we will come to know as 'Terry Scott' joined the Denville Players on Jersey, Channel Islands. "He was indeed a likeable character," remembers fellow company member Michael Dubras, whose father knew the Denville family well, "Terry certainly had talent and although relatively quiet, he was well-regarded." The two got on well together and Michael even had a variety script written for him by the visitor from the mainland (which truthfully, he didn't much care for). Both appeared in The Case of the Frightened Lady, which played from 12 October at the Playhouse theatre, St. Helier, home of the Denville Players, with Terry cast in the role of Sgt. Farraty. Originally a crime drama novel by Edgar Wallace, the play had been made into a 1940 film and is still performed theatrically today. Even early on, Terry was typecast and would play many police officers/ army people throughout his career.

"The Denville Players were so called because the founder member of the professional repertory company's name was Marjorie Denville and her husband was Len Laurie, "remembers Carole Owens in a letter to the author. "They were not Jersey people and they brought over young actors from England each year. Back in the 1940s and 1950s, the Playhouse was very popular (before television) and they produced a play each week. "Back then, my father, Jack, was a regular theatre-goer, and loved the Playhouse and the Denville Players. He used to take me to the comedies, I must have been nine or ten years old, and I loved it too. My dad got to know the players over the years, and he would invite Terry to our home to meet my mother, Marie, and me. He was very amusing all the time and my parents never knew whether or not to take him seriously. Being young in those days meant that I was sent to bed early, so my memories are only brief. But I recall Terry lying on the floor of our front room (which was at 1 Dorking Villas, Apsley Road, St.Helier), with one hand up in the air, playing odd notes on our piano. He was talking about the funny things children said and years later he produced the famous record *My Bruvver*.

These were not drunken nights, for my parents were staunch Methodists, so no alcohol; they would play cards, apparently my father took the game very seriously. Terry and my mother used to cheat and laugh, of course I didn't witness that, but they told me afterwards. Terry used to tease my parents by telling them all sorts of stories about a wife or girlfriend he had back in England and he would bring out photos from his wallet to prove whatever tale he was telling at the time! My one recollection of him acting on the Playhouse stage was, it must have been a melodrama I don't remember, but he was alone in a prison cell awaiting his hanging, all frightened and cowardly and he said, very dramatically 'The valiant taste of death but once, the coward many, many times over' (not those words, exactly) but it was a chilling moment that I've never forgotten. What an interesting man, I wonder what he was really like?"

Returning to Michael, he also remembers that Terry joined the Trinity Church Choir whilst resident on Jersey.

The Playhouse eventually closed and is no longer a working theatre, however, the building itself has remained: if you were to go looking for it, its exterior will give you a few clues, the Playhouse name has been removed but high above the entrance the year '1937' is set in stone, only now it is known as the 'Playhouse Apartments'.

"Everybody on Sunday night, when it was Variety Bandwagon, everybody was listening to it." said Eric Sykes.

By January 1949 Terry was on the radio in the live Sunday evening show Variety Bandbox but by the same time the following year, his name was forgotten or at least he felt that it was.

Bandbox was a half-hour programme variety show which saw early exposure for a great many performers including Peter Sellers, Frankie Howard, Terry-Thomas and Bill Kerr. Transmitted by BBC Radio on the Light Programme, it would feature a mixture of comic performances and music. First broadcast in 1941 and, presented by Philip Slessor, it soon became popular weekend listening until the early 1950s. But sadly little remains of the broadcasts today.

It was this year that Terry would sign a one year contract with the BBC to appear in a radio show with new comic writer Bob Monkhouse called It's in the Bag. Bob had completed his National Service by 1949 was given a two year deal to be tied exclusively to the BBC on an annual salary of £500. Terry was recorded as being, alongside Monkhouse, the first contracted comedian for the corporation but his salary is unknown. The BBC had a unique system of marking prospective performers, to gauge their suitability for the corporation; for which Terry recorded the highest-ever marks. Back to It's in the Bag, "The show was meant to be funny but the studio audience sat there quieter than a mouse peeing on a blotter,[1]" remembers Monkhouse in his autobiography.

Gaining in both confidence and experience, Terry was given another chance on radio, working alongside favourites such as Charlie Chester and Frankie Howerd.

Terry in the 1950s

By the late-1940s, music hall was struggling whilst summer shows were booming and so Richard Stone began organising the latter and had Terry and Hugh Lloyd replace Norman Wisdom and magic man David Nixon at the Jolly Roger theatre situated at the far end of Clacton pier. Meanwhile, an unknown Tony Hancock was starring in The Ocean Revue at the Ocean theatre, also on the pier but located at the shore end in a far more lavish production.

Terry had been recommended to Stone by a lady called Evelyn Norris who at the time was performing agent duties, on behalf of Terry, prior to Richard taking over. Stone recounts in his autobiography that Terry was auditioned in front of himself and actor Ian Carmichael, whom like Terry later, would also appear at the famous Whitehall theatre, London. Ian was involved with Stone professionally, "he had two main 'turns', firstly the horrid little boy, in which character he had done a few radio variety shows, and...a quick-change routine. He was funny and we engaged him."

"Clacton pier for healthy happiness."

Back in the 1940s, the area was one of the most popular resorts in the country and its pier added a theatre in 1928 to cater to the needs of visitors. The iconic Clacton pier had seen loads of visitors from both London and Norfolk, and it was here that celebrity Sunday concerts were very well received by its patrons. The pier had a huge ballroom and theatre at one time called the

Ocean Theatre, which it was known as in 1950. Two shows ran concurrently on the pier; one, an all-singing-all dancing extravaganza starring a Tony Hancock at one end and playing down the far end of the pier was another, the Jolly Roger. It would be there that a then-novice Terry got a break. Aged 23, he attended an audition for Richard Stone, then running summer shows, for a concert party show, Lagoon Follies, destined for the Jolly Roger. A tricky venue to play as upon occasion, the audience would be distracted by events occurring outside; with the lifeboat launched, and glimpsed through the glass walls of the theatre looking out.

Despite only having developed his cheeky schoolboy character (as seen below, right) and little else to call an act, Terry got the job at £10 a week (or £14 depending on another source); reduced by a nicker to pay for the costume he should have supplied himself. "But he was a funny man who could get laughs in even the feeblest of sketches," reflects David Croft, then a producer of the show. He would subsequently work with Terry on a great many projects, predominantly Hugh and I but more of that later.

Terry joined Mollie O'Connor, Lucille Gaye, George Clarkson, Gail Leslie and Herbert Armitage in the list of performers. Here he further developed his crude little boy act, something he had taken from his cousin Ron, known to all as 'Knocker'. Once described by someone as a "snotty-nosed, unkempt school boy, legs bulging and twisting beneath his short trousers."

He then played various theatres doing variety gigs.

Also said to be this year, Terry appeared in a comedy show called The Centre Show and made his debut as a theatre dame in panto.

Terry was employed for the summer of 1951 at Butlin's, Skegness backed by future comedy partner, Bill Maynard, as 'second assistant feed'. His salary was £13 a week, enhanced by an additional 10 shillings by doing the company's laundry together. This Bill would later recount with glee on Terry's This is your Life tribute show in 1978. "I met Ian Carmichael who produced shows for Butlin's and he paired me and

Terry Scott as a double-act," recounts Maynard in an interview with the Daily Express, "...Terry and I later made a TV series together called Great Scott, It's Maynard in 1955, with sketches and guests...it was a huge hit." Coincidentally, Bill's audition for Stone/ Carmichael took place in the exact same drawing room as Terry had been in a year later.

David Croft had been employed by Richard Stone to produce the shows for the chain which had poorly devised acoustics in most of their on-site theatres. They were large venues made of concrete, but with no surface to absorb sound, they echoed madly and often caused problems for the performers. Croft had detailed the fact that he would work directly with Terry and his then-acting partner Hugh Lloyd at both Yarmouth and Weston-super-Mare. Although researching into the history of Butlin's holiday camps, they never had a site in the latter, but there was a Pontins camp there, so perhaps he meant this?

At the enormous Skegness site, they had their Butlin Theatre, later renamed the Gaiety, found next to the main road and made available to residents and visitors. For balance, here's an alternate view from the Butlinsmemories.com, "Some of the main theatres were huge, seating 2,000 or more people, and boasted superb West End style facilities. In fact, the Gaiety Theatre at Filey, built in around 1960, was the largest theatre in Europe seating 3,000 on one floor. A lot of the shows were highly professional and many later stars of TV and stage had their first taste of fame here. Shows were run throughout the day although the main events were always scheduled for the evenings. The Sunday Night Showtime became one of the big events with top line stars brought in to entertain. Other shows included those by the resident repertory company, Redcoat shows, talent contests and even some highbrow entertainment in the form of visiting operatic and ballet companies." The theatre has since been demolished.

In his first-known television appearance, Terry was on The Services Show, hosted by John Hewer, a man remembered for his TV ads promoting Bird's Eye fish fingers. Singer/ actor Teddy Johnson also featured, as did regular Steve Race and pianist Norrie Paramor was another guest. London-born Lorrie would furnish the music on 3 films that all offered roles for Terry Scott between 1961 - 1964: No, my Darling Daughter, A Pair of Briefs and Father Came Too! Terry's contribution to The Services Show was broadcast on 14 March.

On Terry's This is your Life tribute from 1978, Bill told of their time together which saw them performing a naval-themed sketch which involved wearing white uniforms. The duo earnt themselves an extra 10 bob by doing the laundry! Also, Bill made the point of saying that whilst they worked together, they never argued with each other, with everyone else but not together!

By 1952, Terry returned to work at Butlin's Filey holiday camp, north Yorkshire, for another summer season.

Dame Helen Mirren has confessed that she was first drawn to a life in the entertainment industry after seeing Terry in a summer show at Southend this year. The author is not sure if she meant 1955 (see the incoming review) but as a production, Out of the Blue was a regular variety production which ran for many years so, Terry could have been there 1952 and/or 1955. According to www.arthurlloyd.co.uk he was there in 1955.

A certainty was that Terry met Hugh Lloyd for the first time in Weymouth, Dorset, where both were on the bill for a week of variety there in 1953. Top of the pile was the bizarre but devilishly popular, Morton Fraser's Harmonica Band. "I shared digs with Terry and his first wife Thelma and I can remember we just couldn't stop laughing all that week," remembers Lloyd in his autobiography. Some years later Terry would play Weymouth once again, without Hugh, in a stage farce.

Terry was a guest comedian on the BBC TV variety series Show Case. Hosted by comedian Benny Hill, he was joined by Charlie Drake and others in a programme broadcast on 24 May 1954. According to the linear notes in the subsequent 1966 Cinderella pantomime, this year saw Terry's first TV exposure. It came after he drew success from his 'little boy' act in a summer season at Clacton. This followed on after he had acted in a number of radio programmes, the last of which did him no favours; only delivering him six months of unemployment before the Clacton engagement (the author is assuming that this was It's in the Bag).

He would also appear on the live television variety show Garrison Theatre, alongside the Beverley Sisters, Joan Savage, Ken Morris, Joan Rhodes and Jimmy Wheeler. Broadcast on 15 November, the show originally started out on the radio in 1939 to entertain wartime audiences before giving small screen exposure to the likes of Bill Maynard, Bob Monkhouse, Dick Emery, Nicholas Parsons and Bill Kerr. Ernest Thomson noted Terry's burgeoning reputation as a performer, "Being funny, as any comedian will tell you, is no joke. Television, always on the look-out for new comics, has found one in Terry Scott, a tall young Londoner who even made the orchestra laugh in a recent Garrison theatre performance."

Sometime during the year, Terry and Hugh performed in a revue called Into the Sun at the New Theatre, Narrowcliffe, Newquay. John Trembath saw that very show, "I think at that time they worked as a double act," he reflects in a correspondence with the author, "This was of course before they both became famous in their own right. Many later stars started their careers way down here in Cornwall. The old summer shows were excellent training grounds, as they all had to muck in and do everything: sad that they no longer exist."

The theatre was originally known as the Astor and opened in 1938, showing films and presenting concerts. It would switch to offering films-only in 1953 and had a seating capacity of 610.

Sadly demolished by 2009, James on Flickr remembers it as, "a nice, if somewhat plain auditorium with a large, rectangular proscenium surrounding a large screen and decorative elements of playing card symbols on the side walls. The tabs were maroon velour which had gold, appliquéd bands towards the bottom and were lit by footlights (red when I was there). Altogether a welcoming and impressive cinema which also used to present live shows despite having no fly tower..."

It would be whilst they were playing in Newquay that veteran summer season producers and married couple, Ronnie Brandon and Dickie Pounds decided to book Terry and Hugh for the next three seasons at Southend 1955, Felixstowe 1956 and Hastings 1957, respectively.

At some point during this year Terry played the Empire theatre in Dewsbury, west Yorkshire. On stage "Twice Nightly" he was on a bill alongside pianist Semprini, Harriott and Evans, Carol Levis and lots of others. A large capacity venue, it was famous for its pantomime since opening to the public back in 1909 with bill of variety. (However, by 1955 the independently-run Empire closed and was demolished in the 1960s).

For the pantomime season Terry played the role of Simple Simon in Jack and the Beanstalk at the Connaught Theatre, Worthing. He would garner very positive reviews in a show which commenced its run on Christmas Eve. The cast was made up of Hazel Bainbridge, Michael David, Marion Sanders, Peter Byrne (as Alfy), John Faassen, Anne Bishop (as Princess Christabel), Cherry Lind, Richard Gilbert (as Dame Trot), David Howard and Tony Fletcher (as Daisy the Cow), Norman Stevenson, Richard Coleman, Camilleri, Gay and Gay and director duties were taken by Jack Williams.

The Art Deco Connaught theatre opened in 1914, but was originally called the Picturedrome. For 20 years it functioned as a cinema, until

1935 when the Worthing Repertory Company outgrew its own premises and came in to the venue, bringing with it the name Connaught Theatre.

The original Connaught Theatre is now known as the Connaught 2-Screen Cinema. The company added a stage and fly tower, and the venue began to trade as a theatre. In 1987 projection facilities were added and a full cinema programme now runs alongside the live shows. One visitor commented "this is a cosy theatre not very large but [it] has a nice warm feel to it."

Although the author is unable to document the exact year of the following stage appearance by Terry in Brighton, I feel it is of interest to include after discovering the comments on the My Brighton and Hove website. Reflecting on mybrightonandhove.org.uk, Sussex resident David Eldridge remembers visiting The Grand theatre, North road, Brighton on a number of occasions in the early 1950s and seeing Terry on stage there, "My sister was in the chorus line." John Wignall, then an eight-year-old, attended that same production, "they were putting on the pantomime Dick Whittington when volunteers were asked to go on stage and meet Tommy the Cat. Terry Scott was the comedian in this show and all stage fright went as he talked to us like a benevolent uncle and got us to impersonate various characters. Mine was a spiv trying to sell black market food. After this we sang a song. I don't remember what it was but the experience and the handful of toffees were enough to capture my imagination for the rest of my life."

Pictured above, the venue when Terry would have known it back in 1950. Courtesy of the Connaught theatre.

The building had been converted into a theatre in 1894, and by 1904 it became known as the Grand Theatre. With its large stage and enough seats for 2,000 patrons, it switched to showing films-only in 1931 but by the start of the next decade, it would convert back to a working theatre, offering pantos (for which is was rightly famous), musicals and variety shows through to the early 1950s which is when Terry would have played there.

Sadly the Grand closed permanently in 1955. John Desborough also reminisces, "My mum and dad took me to most theatres and picture houses in Brighton but The Grand stands out in my mind. Queuing outside this very grey building, the excitement of what was to come, I must have been only nine or ten (circa 1952). We saw Max Miller, Arthur English, Max Wall to name but a few." The venue was destroyed by fire in 1961 and was subsequently demolished.

Terry was a guest on It's a Great Life, a one-hour dancing/ variety TV show filmed in black and white and encompassing a plethora of talent including singer Betty Driver and the King Brothers. It was broadcast on 22 January, 1955. Curiously, IMDB film website lists a project where Terry plays a character called Sammy, in a script that he had written himself, produced and directed by Dennis Robertson. I think that the project in question is the aforementioned It's a Great Life. I believe that Terry participated in a sketch interlude with the show introduced by Ralph Reader, known for staging the original Gang Show which had offered Tony Hancock, Peter Sellers and Dick Emery early experience.

The aforementioned Dickie Pounds put Terry into his show Out of the Blue, at Southend this year. According to Hugh Lloyd, in his autobiography, it was Pounds that discovered both of them as well as the likes of Bruce Forsyth and Roy Hudd. A review from back then reads, "It's no laugh being in Out of the Blue. Appearing... at the Pier Pavilion, are a hard working band of talented artists, but it is no joke trying to raise a laugh with row upon row of empty seats. These artists, led by comedian Terry Scott, set out to entertain, and they achieved their purpose on Monday, when they presented their third edition. Alec Halls tried in vain to make the audience sing. His performance needed drastic trimming. The artists - and the audience - lacked the spark that brings free and easy entertainment. The sketch, Unnecessary Remarks, we have heard before, and, in fact, was indeed unnecessary. The first half finished with Egypt; a riot of colours, grand costumes, and with Terry Scott, Hugh Lloyd and Marjorie Wieland.

The second half began with a high note, and never left it. A scene, The Show Must Go On, hit the right spot. It was colourful, tuneful and it had zest and life...Freddie Lloyd and Roberta, the dancing pair, gave another excellent presentation. In his solo number Terry Scott Presents The Play's the Thing and had the audience laughing at his antics."

Out of the Blue, devised by Dickie Pounds had began its life as far back as the mid-1930s with Pounds himself a performer in the original concert party/summer revue project. This show saw the music and lyrics composed by popular1950s singer Ronnie Hill.

With eighteen inserts, Terry and Hugh Lloyd first appear in the third piece, Unnecessary Remarks, with Terry playing a husband to Marjorie Wieland and Hugh, a Curate. Following a quick change, they returned as school girls in a sketch called Goosey Gander. Closing the first half, the boys featured as a pair of tourists in Egypt - in exotic Mood. Following the interval, The Show Must Go On commenced proceedings, seeing Terry as "The Lad" amongst seemingly the entire company. After a solo spot from Hugh Lloyd, Terry featured in ensemble piece Voice that is still before returning after the next insert, enjoying his own moment in the spotlight in a little something called The Play's the Thing. That was the penultimate offering from the company before they returned for the traditional farewell and a rendition of God Save the Queen. The production managed to be the recipient of an award for best summer season, much to the surprise of those appearing in it!

The Pier Pavilion was built on the shore end of the Southend Pier, the longest pier in the world and its location proved a problem for any artistes appearing there. Terry and Hugh definitely had their concerns, as documented in Lloyd's autobiography, "...the distinct drawback was that it was directly over the station from which the pier train started. Apart from the usual intricacies of timing that we had to work out, we found ourselves having to allow for the trains arriving or departing, to coincide with the punch lines. It didn't always work but it presented us with a marvellous excuse if we didn't get a laugh."

Sadly the Pavilion was destroyed by fire in 1959 which trapped around 500 visitors at the end of the pier who then had to be rescued by boat. The Pavilion was replaced by a bowling alley in 1962 which was itself destroyed by fire in 1995. The site is now just decking.

On BBC Radio, a live show was broadcast in September from Margate titled Wish you were Here. Introduced by Bill Maynard, Terry and Hugh performed together from the Winter Gardens. Still on the radio, Terry acted in the thirteen-part BBC radio serial All My

Eye and Kitty Bluett with Stanley Baxter and Patricia Hayes. Scripts were provided by Terry Nation and Dick Barry, the former wrote probably best-known for creating the dreaded Daleks in Doctor Who.

Live work took him to the Odeon, Romford, then being used for Sunday concerts, with Terry billed as "TV's Little Boy". Headline act was Frankie Vaughan, with the Ken Mackintosh Band Show taking up much of the concert on 10 April. Presenting live Sunday shows by 1955, its auditorium could facilitate more than 2000 patrons. Opening as a cinema in January 1936, the building has remained but is now in use as not one but 2 nightclub venues.

After working hard in developing his career, Terry got a break on television with Great Scott, It's Maynard. Three series consisting of a total of 17 episodes were made across a little over a year of this ground breaking show which combined variety with lengthy sketches introduced by Terry and Bill Maynard, whilst also participating across each half-hour show set in their flat share. Produced and possibly directed by Duncan Wood, later to work with Terry and Hugh Lloyd in Hugh and I, Wood was a well-respected name at the BBC for many years and thereafter upon moving to Independent television.

Dave Freeman, Eric Merriman, Lew Schwarz and Johnny Speight helped shape the opening episode broadcast on 4 October before Speight dropped out (he had offered sketch material for the opening show only). The Golders Green-born Merriman would supply scripts for Happy Ever After and Terry and June, which would cement Terry's place as television's epitome of the middle-class man. Also a great radio scriptwriter, elsewhere he provided the words for Morecambe and Wise and Frankie Howerd.

Lew, originally credited as Lewis Schwarz, was a Glasgow-born taxi driver writer who originally started out as a radio gag writer but television would prove his forte. Becoming a part of the Sykes/ Milligan/ Galton and Simpson/ Speight writers stable in Shepherd's Bush, he partnered the more-experienced Merriman to create Great Scott, It's Maynard! Joining Bill and Terry each week were Shirley Eaton, Hugh Lloyd, Marie Benson, The Cornets and Gary Wayne.

Broadcast live, Great Scott proved an instant popular success across its initial run that concluded on 13 December. Bill Maynard's life was changed by the show, "Comedy, that's where the skill lays...it turned me into a superstar...[2]"

At Christmas time, Terry enjoyed a spell at the Theatre Royal, Leeds in their seasonal production of The Sleeping Beauty.

Cast

Anne Boobier...The nurse

Eric V. Marsh...The King

Billy Whittaker...The Queen

Patricia Somerset...Princess Beauty, their daughter

Charles Wlaat...The Chef

June Campbell...Lady Hermione

Ruby Wlaat...Baroness

Moyna Cope...Prince Florisel

Albert and Les Ward... The Two Jesters

Terry...Osbert, the Orphan

Stephanie Dane...Fairy Stardust

Robert Hargreaves...Furiosa

Plus Joan Davis Corps De Ballet, Betty Hobbs' Globe Girls, The Twelve Little "Sunbeams", Ruby and Charles Wlaat & their Live Comedy Dog.

Terry also featured on the BBC special Christmas Box, a festive evening show. Radio Times offered prospective viewers a glimpse of what they could expect; "...BBC Television takes you out to join in the fun and games at Christmas parties in Sheffield, Bournemouth and London. [With] Shirley Abicair, Eve Boswell, Carl Brisson, Charlie Chester, Sooty with Harry Corbett, Jimmy James, Bill Maynard, Bob Monkhouse, Jon Pertwee, Edna Savage, Terry Scott, Shani Wallis." Coincidentally, one of the hosts was Macdonald Hobley, an actor/presenter who would work with Terry and June Whitfield in A Bedfull of Foreigners many years later.

For three pence, TV viewers could buy a copy of the Radio Times and seen on the cover of the 6 April, 1956 edition of this "Journal for the BBC", they would have found Bill and Terry. The duo were promoting the second series of Great Scott, It's Maynard. With six new episodes offered, beginning on 10 April and running through to 15 May, writers Eric Merriman and Lew Schwarz used the same cast but episode two had the bonus of finding Pat Coombs in it and she would continue through to episode six.

"After 2 series, it began to flounder as it became less clear who was the star," Recollects Richard Stone, "At first Bill accepted the seniority of Terry, and was happy to 'feed' him. As Bill's reputation increased rather rapidly, the situation became fraught."

Their profiles were increasing vastly, with Bill and Terry featured in the 15 December issue of TV Mirror magazine, along with other names of the day. Co-star Shirley Eaton would also join them on the cover of the debuting TV Fun annual published for 1957.

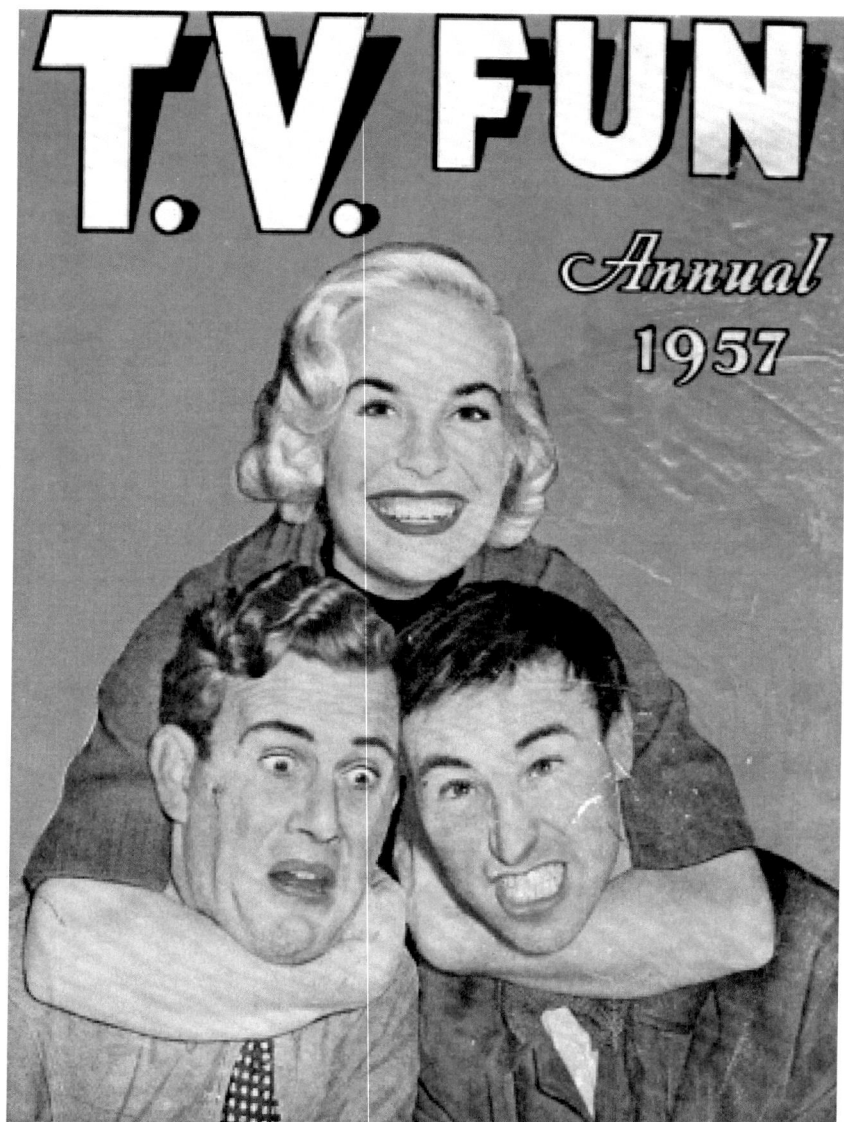

TERRY SCOTT ★ SHIRLEY EATON ★ BILL MAYNARD

★ LAUGH WITH THE STARS ★

Despite the issues, their partnership continued through to a third and final series of Great Scott, It's Maynard which commenced its run of five episodes from 25 October - 20 December. One at the end of October featured future Carry On face Liz Fraser.

For this batch of shows, the lads were buoyed by the return of Ms. Eaton, Ms. Fraser, Norman Vaughan, Hugh Lloyd and Pat Coombs for episode three: all of them had Terry connections. Additional artistes included Dennis Chinnery, Peter Haig, Graham Learman, John East, Ann Lancaster, Ian MacNaughton, Roger Ostime, Ivor Raymonde, Desmond Rayner, Totti Truman Taylor, Patti Lewis, Lillemor Knudsen, Bruce Seaton and Johnny Vyvyan. The latter would work with Terry in a 1957 episode of Scott Free. Ms Olrich would see Mr Scott in an episode of 1970s TV panel show Whodunnit? Hugh played a Native American chief in one episode and had to say "Ugh" which proved most amusing to the audience. So much so that Maynard asked if he could be the one to say it even though he was playing a cowboy in the said story! It would seem that possibly only Terry and Bill Maynard featured in the final programme of the series.

Remaining in 1956, Terry co-presented a Midday Music-Hall show radio show from Felixstowe, broadcast on BBC Radio in September. Also on the bill was the BBC Variety orchestra, George Firestone and his Quintet and others. At the time, Terry was appearing in Out of the Blue at the Spa Pavilion, also in Felixstowe, Norfolk.

The venue, dating back to 1909, has survived and had a change of ownership in 2015, according to the Spa Pavilion website, "It originally opened as 'The New Floral Hall', a true seafront pavilion...and soon became known as the "Spa Pavilion".

Completely re-vamped and extended in the late 1930's, it re-opened as a large theatre and music hall in April 1939. Sadly the outbreak of war ensured that it was hardly used before a bomb demolished a large part of the new building in 1941, rendering it derelict. Re-built again, from it's re-opening on 26th May 1950, The Spa was a thriving seaside venue right up until the 1990's. A gradual decline...led to the closure of the theatre in 2013[3]."

Another panto booking for Terry saw him in Robin Hood at the Finsbury Park Empire, London. Patricia Burke, an Australian actor-dancer and singer with extensive theatre experience, played the title role. The 'Twinkling Tappers' duo of Syd and Max Harrison were cast as the Robbers, whilst Terry and Joyce Golding were also on the bill. In her obituary printed in The Stage, Joyce was remembers as "one of the few women who played the pantomime dame".

The Finsbury Park Empire was built for Moss Empires Limited and opened on 5 September 1910. A huge Frank Matcham house, it was second only to the London Palladium as the major theatrical venue. Astonishingly, it closed in May 1960, with seating removed to allow scenery to be stored there and a rehearsal space accommodated in the former theatre. If you want to see it in its final days, watch the Cliff Richard film The Young Ones, which utilized the Empire for its theatre sequences. Located on St Thomas' Road, sadly the building was demolished in 1965 and flats now stand on the site.

Still in this year, Terry performed in A Season of Variety at the prestigious Prince of Wales theatre in the West End. It was during this decade that the venue mostly put on revues and variety acts and his name joined a strong list of talent to have played in variety bills there previously; including Norman Wisdom, Peter Sellers, Bob Hope, Terry-Thomas, Dickie Henderson and Morecambe and Wise.

Richard Stone got two of his clients on the bill, Jon Pertwee closing the first half (a much sought-after spot) and Terry, then somewhat unknown, filling the trickier second spot. A playbill can still be found in the theatre today, listing the season commencing on November 19 for two weeks with headliner Gracie Fields followed in the pecking order by Pertwee, Terry, Stan Stennett, Daisy May (assisted by Saveen), Cin and Peres, Ravic and Babs, The Kelroys and Warren, Devine and Sparks.

From 3 December, Lonnie Donnegan and Anne Shelton headlined with a big supporting bill also promised. Terry would make 2 appearances on Ms. Shelton's television show in 1951.

Stone recounts Scott being involved in a car accident at the time of playing there but being a trooper; he turned up to perform right from Watford hospital! Still in a confused, possibly concussed state, he proceeded to showcase his full act, running at close to a half-hour rather than the eight minutes scheduled. This meant that the headline act, Miss Fields had to cut two of her songs and those in authority at the theatre were furious and wanted Terry sacked. The agent removed two of Terry's stage costumes and saw his client remain on the bill.

Looking at a photograph in the Alamy library, it featured a grinning Terry Scott in a Mayor-type costume being given the 'bumps' by a group of giggling chorus girls at the theatre, it was dated 1 January 1957.

Originally an 800-seater venue, the current theatre is not the first structure to be built on the Piccadilly plot. It was rebuilt and reopened in October 1937 with, coincidentally Ms Fields laying the foundation stone to commemorate the occasion (it is still there). Today, the Prince of Wales comes under the Delfont Mackintosh Theatres branding.

After his partnership with Bill had ended, Terry took on his own show, as did Maynard. Written by Lew Schwarz, the Scott Free series aired on BBC in early summer 1957. The show has the premis of resting actors Terry and Norman Vaughan, recently seen in episodes of Great Scott, It's Maynard, being sent to dowdy seaside resort Bogmouth-on-Sea by their agent. A total of six half-hour episodes were made and directed by Eric Robinson and just like Bill's solo show, Mostly Maynard, their agent remembers that both shows "were unqualified disasters". It was Schwarz's first independently-written series but he would soon return and later scripted projects for many Terry associates, including Dora Bryan and Ronnie Barker. He also worked on the Carry On Laughing series in 1975. Finally, he taught creative writing, and his introduction to his book The Craft of Writing TV Comedy, gave us a glimpse into his working life, "Writing comedy for television is not as easy as it looks. It is a craft, as wood carving and pottery are crafts. Talent is essential, but without an understanding of the materials and a mastery of the tools, success will tend to remain elsewhere." Schwarz died in 1999.

Returning to Scott Free, the cast was as follows:

Wallas Eaton...Gribble

Henry B.Longhurst...Councillor Bland

Marcia Ashton...Bland's daughter

With single appearances from Percy Edwards, Mario Fabrizi, Gilbert Harding, Brian Johnson, Billie Love, The George Mitchell Singers, Bruce Trent, Stanley Unwin and Johnny Vyvyan.

Remaining in 1957, Terry appeared live, as second support to singer-song writer Russ Hamilton. This was on another peculiar bill and it included Walters Dogs and Monkeys, magician George Braund, Oliver and Twist, Ballet Montmartre, Nordics and Donovan and Hayes. The show played the imposing Chiswick Empire theatre on 21 October for one week.

Designed by cinema architect Frank Matcham, a name that crops up through much of the text, the Empire at Chiswick, found on the High road, had opened to the public back in September 1912. With an auditorium able to accommodate 1,950, across the years, variety, revues, plays and opera all played to responsive audiences before the venue switched to screening films. Sadly, it would be demolished a couple of years after.

Released in cinemas towards the end of the year, Blue Murder at St Trinians was made by British Lion Films. Inspired by the cheeky Ronald Searle comic strip illustrations, writer-director team Frank

Launder and Sidney Gilliat turned the work into the St Trinian's format resulting in a series of feature films between 1954 - 1980.

The amusing thing about the girls at this anarchical boarding school is that the sixth formers all look so terribly grown-up, in Blue Murder, for instance, Dilys Laye was 23 and Rosalind Knight, 24. But at St Trinian's we are not to be concerned with such actualities as the institutionalised young women rule the roost, only causing conflict when confronted by the outside world or in this case, the army!

Written by the Launder/ Gilliat/ Val Valentine trio, Blue Murder was the second in the series, favouring a black and white world and released in December 1957.

Launder generated a massive CV stretching back to the late-1920s and he would also contribute to The Bridal Path (1959) screenplay and direct the Terry-related film.

The role of the inimitable 'Flash' Harry in the series is ingrained in British film history as a true comedy gem. George Cole, later of Too Many Crooks, makes the part his own, a Cockney spiv, all sharp suit, pencil-thin moustache and ubiquitous hat attire presented in a shifty but brilliant manner. Each time his character appears on screen, pianola-type music plays, never failing to bring a smile to the viewer, no matter how many times you might have seen it.

4 DISC COLLECTION

Sidney Gilliat and Frank Launder Present

The St. Trinian's Collection

The Belles of St. Trinians • The Pure Hell of St Trinian's • Blue Murder at St Trinian's • The Great St Trinian's Train Robbery

The plot is never that important in a St Trinian's film, so let's be brief; the girls break into the Ministry of Education building to view a schools competition paper for a UNESCO contest where the first prize is an escorted trip to Europe. Many of the nubile sixth formers want to go to Italy as Harry (Cole) a bookie and proprietor of a marriage bureau, plans to introduce many of them to the bland Price Bruno (Guido Lorraine) who is seeking a bride. This they do whilst the school is under siege, with the exhausted army, led by Major Whitehart (Thorley Walters) and Captain Cyril Chamberlain. Whilst the men at the ministry, trusty faces Richard Wattis, Peter Jones and Eric Barker faff about upon discovering that St Trinian's has won the competition and that they need to control them when they do go abroad. Incidentally, in the following year Barker and Terry would both act in Carry On Sergeant.

Back to the story, down-trodden Captain Ricketts (Terry-Thomas, a trifle underused) is approached to transport two bus loads of rowdy young women across Europe. It is also the point where middle-age sweethearts Bird (Lloyd Lamble) and Sgt Gates (a luminous Joyce Grenfell) come in to the story, as does Terry, here as a desk sergeant at the local police station. He initially comes on screen at around thity nine minutes in, featuring in a couple of perfunctory scenes.

Renowned diamond thief Joe Mangan (Lionel Jeffries) ventures to visit his daughter Myrtle (Lisa Gastoni) at St Trinian's having just completed his latest job, unaware that a £10k reward has been issued for his arrest. Ruby (Grenfell) despite her previous association with the school, agrees to go undercover as an interpreter accompanying the school party to Europe. But she proves to be most inept in this role, immediately being 'clocked' by Harry as the trip commences. (Her character having already featured in The Belles of St Trinian's, in 1954). He leads the coaches in his 'bubble' car, seen in a number of British film of the period (see Double Bunk and I'm All Right Jack).And whilst preparing for the trip, Mangan stashes the stolen jewels in a water polo ball which forms part of the sports equipment packed by the girls. Only, he doesn't realise that he has been observed doing this and so the girls pressure him into completing the trip with them, forcing him to dress up as their new headmistress after incapacitating the real one, as personified by actress Judith Furse.

Terry-Thomas drives one of the buses and gets close to Ruby after she tells him that in time, she will be inheriting some money from her grandmother. He begins manipulating her affections until blubbing to him her true identity and that she has just spotted the jewel thief (Jeffries). The girls annihilate all their European sporting counterparts as the tour makes its way across France, Germany, Austria and eventually arrives in Italy, and its capital, Rome.

Back at the station, Sgt Scott announces that the real Dame Maud has escaped from the bell tower at St Trinian's after being pounced upon by her new charges, previously. And this is the last we see Terry

A B C 1 2 3 4

Cast

Terry-Thomas... Captain Romney Carlton-Ricketts

George Cole...Flash Harry

Joyce Grenfell... Policewoman Sergeant Ruby Gates

Alastair Sim...Miss Fritton

Sabrina...Virginia

Lionel Jeffries...Joe Mangan

Lloyd Lamble...Supert Kemp-Bird

Raymond Rollett...Chief Constbale

Terry...Police Sergeant

Ferdy Mayne...Italian Police Insp.

Thorley Walters...Major Whitehart

Cyril Chamberlain...Capt

Ronald Ibse...Lieutenant

Judith Furse...Dame Maud

Michael Ripper...Eric, the liftman

Kenneth Griffith...Charlie Bull

Richard Wattis...Manton Bassett

Peter Jones...Prestwick

Lisa Lee...Miss Brenner

Guido Lorraine...Prince Bruno

Alma Taylor...Bruno's mother

Peter Elliott...Equerry

Charles Lloyd Pack...Henry

Lisa Gastoni...Myrna

Jose Read...Cynthia

Dilys Laye...Bridget

Rosalind Knight...Annabel

Patricia Lawrence...Mavis

Marigold Russell...Marjorie

Vicki Hammond...Jane

Nicola Braithwaite...Daphne

Janet Bradbury...Mercia

Mandy Harper...Tilly

Moya Francis...Bissy

Eric Barker...Culpepper Brown

Carol White...school girl

until 1967's The Great St Trinian's Train Robbery, where he again plays an officer of the law. The story reaches its climax in a witty sequence set initially at a water polo match between local opposition and St Trinian's before advancing to the notorious Colosseum. In a joyful mix-up, during the match, the lanky Mangan, Mr Jeffries resembling Old Mother Riley, grabs the valuable ball and runs off with it. Pursued by Harry and the girls, he is eventually caught after a chase at the infamous landmark, in a beautifully shot moment.

There is not too much to get excited about in Blue Murder, and Terry-Thomas is not in it enough but both Joyce Grenfell and George

Cole are fun. Such was the reputation of the esteemed Lauder/ Gilliat team that the St Trinian's series would offer many now much-loved character actors supporting roles; Blue Murder continued the trait.

"After Cinemascope started, there was a drop in the number of live shows. Pantomimes were suffering from the changing times. Robin Hood at Tooting, Woolwich and Sutton in 1957 proved to be the last of the Tooting Granada pantomimes. Robin Hood starred Terry Scott and David Hughes. At Tooting they were joined by the "Queen of the Keyboard, Winifred Atwell as guest star, and continued to Sutton, Slough and Woolwich." Today, this incredible building remains but is in use as a bingo club.

A busy Terry and Hugh also appeared at the glorious Chelsea Palace, a huge 2,500+ venue that was on its last legs as a working theatre in what Richard Stone termed "a sort of summer show". ". The London Revue could not prevent the Granada-owned venue stem closure and by October prior to it becoming 'Granada Studio 10', a television recording venue.

It was during a summer season in Scarborough this year that Terry experienced a whirlwind romance with a dancer called Margaret Pollen and on 20 December 1957 they were married at Morden Registry Office.

By the following year Terry was contracted to make live appearances at Moss theatres around the country. One engagement being at the Birmingham Hippodrome on 10 March, supporting "the glamorous radio, TV and recording personality" headliner Alma Cogan. This Monday evening show played at 6.15 and 8.30 and saw Terry labelled "from TV's Great Scott - It's Scott".

He was joined on a rather unusual bill by teenaged rockabilly singer Terry Wayne, who would coincidentally, record on the Parlophone label, as Terry would later. Desmond Lane aka 'The Penny-Whistle Man', McAndrews and Mills and The 3 Ghezzis completed the line-up.

The Birmingham Hippodrome, still functioning today, has a mammoth seating capacity of some 1,800 and had opened to the public back in 1925.

Monday 24 March found Terry performing twice nightly, 6pm and 8.15pm, in another show, this time at the Leeds Empire, with the headline act being "Mr Personality" Jimmy Young. Then a TV, radio and recording success, Young would later become a Radio 2 stalwart. Also on the bill was a diminutive singer called Billie Anthony (known for her original hit single This Ole House), dance partners Jean and Julie, illusionist Granville Taylor and his wife, Valerie, with "music and

MOSS' Hippodrome
BIRMINGHAM

6.15 · **MONDAY, MARCH 10th** ★ **8.30**
TWICE NIGHTLY

THE GLAMOROUS RADIO, TV AND RECORDING PERSONALITY

★ **ALMA COGAN**

COLUMBIA'S 16 YEAR OLD PERSONALITY SINGING STAR

TERRY WAYNE

WITH HIS GUITAR & RHYTHM BOYS FROM TV'S SIX-FIVE SPECIAL

TERRY SCOTT
FROM TV'S GREAT SCOTT - IT'S SCOTT

McANDREWS AND MILLS
RICHMAN & JACKSON
BOY MEETS GIRL

THE THREE GHEZZIS

DESMOND LANE
THE PENNY-WHISTLE BOOGIE MAN

Above: one of the many typical stage shows that Terry would be a part of during his long career.

movement" provided by the Kendor Brothers. Comedy performer Victor Seaforth, known for his many voices, completed the eclectic line-up. These types of shows, one nighters or weekly slots, were the norm in the period for such acts.

Granville Taylor made his stage debut as a boy magician in 1945. He went on to perform at many of the Empire theatres across the country, including Leeds where Terry was on the same bill.

Now 86, he turned professional in 1957, it was whilst appearing at Collins Music Hall, London that he learnt that a certain Cissie Williams, the booker for Moss' Empires Ltd., was in the audience. "She must have liked my act, because a few weeks later I received a contract from my agent to appear at the Empire Theatre in Leeds for week commencing 24 March, 1958." "Well, remembers Granville in a letter to the author, "we did get booked again and at most of the other theatres on the Moss and Stoll circuits. The big theatre circuits like Moss' Empires and Stoll Theatres, made them number one theatres to play, as distinct from all the others, was that they gave the artistes the best possible working conditions; such as a 16-piece orchestra to play the music for your act.....what a thrill to hear it played to perfection from start to finish. Also a big stage and excellent lighting conditions."

The Yorkshire Evening News (March 1958) said of Terry's performance, "...wearing a schoolboy cap and bothersome tight trousers, (he) puts over some juvenile delinquent gagging and later gives an alleged soliloquy from Macbeth that sounds like a mumbled rock'n roll lyric; only the costume was convincing." That outfit may well have been the one purchased for Terry by agent Richard Stone, back in the late-1940s when he auditioned for him and Ian Carmichael for a job in a revue on Clacton pier. Terry had to pay £10 for it and would have a pound deducted each week from his salary to repay the frugal Mr Stone!

Back to Granville, "All the Moss and Stoll theatres were very impressive buildings, and by having a top star, often from America, with six or seven top-class supporting acts, the theatres were very well attended." Moss owned Empire theatres including Birmingham one, Finsbury Park in London, Newcastle, Swansea and others.

The Leeds Grand theatre, built in 1878, could accommodate 1,550 theatregoers per show and was able to offer a broad range of productions for audiences to enjoy. Accordingly on its website, the Grand self-aggrandised, "It is widely regarded as a major milestone in Victorian theatre building."

On 23 June Terry featured in an edition of This is the Henry Hall Show with pianist Winifred Atwell, actress Evelyn Laye, clarinet player Donald Purchese and actress Barbara Young. Produced by Ned Sherrin, Henry Hall was a London-born dance band impresario who enjoyed a series of his own show across 1957-1958. He was able to draw many performers that would subsequently work with Terry elsewhere during his career.

Terry also made an appearance on the BBC entertainment show The Good Old Days; the idea seeing contemporary performers recreating the songs and sketches from the music hall era. The premise proved an immediate success with the television viewing public and the invited-theatre audience (with many of them getting in the spirit of things by wearing period costumes). Terry was on a show that was hosted by Leonard Sachs, included actress Rose Alba (whom he would be associated with in the 1961 film Mary had a Little...), Leon Cortes and comedian Ken Dodd. The show had originally aired back in 1953 and would run through to 1983. Terry would make his second and final appearance on the programme in 1981.

Presenter Pete Murray introduced the very first Six-Five Special like this: "Welcome aboard...We've got almost a hundred cats jumping here, some real cool characters to give us the gas, so just get on with it and have a ball." As himself, Terry was in two shows of this early Saturday evening music show written by Jeremy Lloyd and Trevor Peacock. His debut came on 19 July and was followed on 30 August. Carry On actor/ singer Jim Dale hosted and another name forever associated with series, Barbara Windsor, was a guest.

"Get 'Fell in' for an assault course in laughs."

That was the poster strap line for Anglo Amalgamated's new comedy hit Carry On Sergeant. 24 March marked the start of shooting for this the first ever Carry On feature film and who'd ever have imagined that Carry On Columbus, in 1992, would be the final entry?

WILLIAM   BOB
HARTNELL • MONKHOUSE
SHIRLEY EATON • ERIC BARKER
DORA BRYAN • BILL OWEN
KENNETH CONNOR

CARRY ON
SERGEANT

ANGLO AMALGAMATED FILM DISTRIBUTORS LIMITED

Certainly Producer Peter Rogers did not, "we thought it would be a one-off...⁴" A 'U' certification, Sergeant, shot in black and white, cost under £78K to make but proved popular at the box office; becoming the third highest grossing film of 1958 upon its August-release (Bridge over the River Kwai and Dunkirk were first and second, respectively). Sergeant earned its money back in two weeks and by 1965, the film had made 500k with director Gerald Thomas adhering to a strict, six weeks filming schedule. For this one, he was required to complete three minutes of film each day.

The screenplay by Norman Hudis was based upon The Bull Boys, written by novelist and ex-journalist R.F. Delderfield. As a project the idea had been around for some time before former R.A.F man Hudis gave it his attention and turned a serious story into a comedy. It would be the first of six Carry On scripts that he furnished between 1958 - 1962. John Antrobus, one of the writers of The Army Game, a popular TV series of the time and featuring a few of the Sergeant cast, was credited for additional material (he's also an extra).

Terry played Paddy, one of the sergeants at the Heathercrest National Service Depot; within which the latest bunch of motley recruits arrive for ten weeks of training. Wearing his army uniform, Scott is first seen a mere four minutes into the film, in the officer's mess with Sergeant 'Grimy' (William Hartnell) and others, with the latter hoping for a decent final training platoon before retiring from the Army. A £50 wager is set between himself and his colleagues, including Terry, sounding quite posh here, as to which of their group can finish top of the rankings, come the close of the training period.

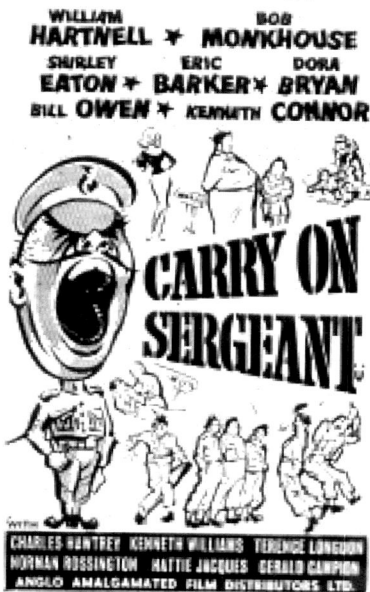

The film begins with Bob Monkhouse and Shirley Eaton on their wedding day, rudely interrupted with call up papers notifying him that he has to do his National Service starting that same day! On the way to the centre he meets a sickly Kenneth Connor whilst Captain Potts (an under-used Eric Barker) soon laments the poor showing of the latest 'Able platoon' which also contains a bolshie Kenneth Williams, dozy Charles Hawtrey, a pining Monkhouse and hypochondriac Mr Connor. Queen's Barracks, Guilford was utilised for exterior filming locations seeing the cast marching endlessly, bayoneting, run and jumping and generally prove inept at most of the tasks. As the weeks pass, the collective performance of 'Able' platoon, a joke in itself, worsens and it seems that this bunch are likely to be the worst ever. Within the barracks, Monkhouse and Ms Eaton swoon as newlyweds whilst Dora Bryan proves amusing in her instantaneous love for the whiny Strong (Connor). It is the first time that we see subsequent favourites Hawtrey and Williams and Hattie Jacques in this brisk introduction to a much-loved series.

Terry's character is only seen a second time, some minutes before the end, on the training ground where the platoon turn things around and produce a winning presentation to the delight of Captain Potts and Sgt. Grimshaw. Realising that he and his colleague have lost the bet, Paddy (Scott) utters, "Cor Blimey!" Carry On Sergeant would be his first role in the series with several more following: Khyber, Camping, Jungle, Loving, Henry and Matron, as well as the Christmas television entries in 1969 and 1970. William Hartnell, as the seemingly brisk Grimshaw, was an actor known for being Dr Who and he would also have a major role in And the Same to You (1960), a film which also gave a part to Terry Scott. Charles Hawtrey would be in What a Whopper (1961) alongside Terry and in a number of memorable Carry On moments.

Dulwich-born Anne Shelton had been a forces sweetheart much like Vera Lynn and a singer that had appeared on Variety Bandwagon, previously. Terry makes the first of two appearances on the Anne Shelton Variety Show, the first being on 26 January, 1959, in a programme that also included Deryck Gyler, Dickie Valentine, Joe Lynch and others. Lynch would work with Terry on another television project, a 1970 episode of sitcom Happy Ever After.

It was followed by another on 6 April which included future Carry On co-star Peter Butterworth and former child actor Harry Fowler in the show. Bill Maynard, Irene Handl and Kenneth Connor also featured in separate broadcasts.

"Briskly done and cleverly plotted with a number of great comic performances large and small: a real gem. Had to raise half a star after considering it overnight and realizing how funny it must be to make me laugh audibly alone at 12:30 in the morning. It must have been a riot with a crowd in the theatre." Goodwin, writing on letterboxd.com

The trailer for Too Many Crooks may have laid claim to it "starring the greatest comedy cast ever…" but the film proves breezy viewing and jolly good fun. Michael Pertwee's efficient screenplay plants all its plot details clearly and ticks all the boxes when bringing its strands together. From a story by Christiane Rochefort and French novelist Jean Nery, Crooks was produced and directed by Italian creative Mario Zampi and is beautifully photographed in glistening black and white by Stanley Pavey. Pertwee, brother of Jon, along with their father, Roland, had co-created a number of stage farces.

Returning to Crooks, working on a Zampi project often proved exhausting for his actors, with the director known for his multi-takes. A youthful George Cole stars as Fingers, the uncertain leader of a luckless gang consisting of embittered Sid (Sidney James), the child-like Snowdrop (big Bernie Bresslaw), Whisper (Joe Melia) and the red hot Charmaine (Vera Day).

After bungling their latest robbery, Fingers (Cole) tells the others of his plans for the "big snatch, the crime of the century." He has the idea of kidnapping the daughter of the rakish Billy Gordon (the quintessential "silly-ass Englishman" Terry-Thomas, here on blisteringly good form), a rather unscrupulous businessman and cad with a low moral compass. They target him as he is a man with a disdain for banks, preferring his own office safe or stashing his loot at home, well away from prying eyes. More concerned with his public image, Billy pays scant attention to his doting wife Lucy (Brenda de Banzie, in one of her best roles) preferring the charms of younger women such as his secretary Beryl (Delphi Lawrence) or a visiting journalist (Vilma Ann Leslie).

The gang had already unsuccessfully attempted to rob Gordon's office, having their bluff called by the sharp-witted bounder. Returning home, the rightly paranoid T-T sets about hiding his wads of cash under the floorboards, only to be disturbed by his daughter Angela (Rosalie Ashley) introducing him to her new fiancé, Nicholas Parsons, who tells him that he is a tax inspector! This outrageous his sensibilities and Billy will not entertain the notion, saying that in his view such people are worse than the police.

They begin their action to enter the house and almost succeed in pilfering his funds until an irate T-T returns home unexpectedly and kick them all out. Undeterred, they return at night, each dressed up in top hat and tails as pall bearers using a stolen hearse as cover. They plan to utilise a coffin as a means of getting the girl away in what proves to be the funniest part of the film.

The deed is done and they make their escape but unfortunately, "the most valuable rabbit in history" is revealed as actually being Mrs. Gordon, Lucy (De Banzie) and not the intended daughter! This reality becomes apparent after the "bungling clot" Fingers and company manage to lose the hearse with their captive inside, terrifying a passing vicar and tramp in the process. Subsequently they recover the vehicle and its contents and return to their hideout.

George Cole is most amusing in Too Many Crooks, adopting terribly faltering accents to disguise his identity when attempting to extort a ransom from Gordon. Oddly, he proves delighted at the mix-up and refuses to pay anything, even after Fingers knocks down his price.

Lew & Leslie Grade Ltd presents

ROBIN HOOD

programme sixpence

Away from Crooks for a moment, for the pantomime season Terry was in Robin Hood at Adelphi theatre, Slough. Headlining the cast was singing star David Hughes, Joyce Golding, who had enjoyed an early career as a very popular variety act, Leslie Noyes, Ted Carson, Grace O'Connor, Peter Hardy and a number of supporting roles involved across eighteen scenes. Originally opening in 1930, in its heyday the Adelphi could facilitate a little over 2000 seats in the main auditorium, stalls and balcony.

A large building, it was designed by cinema architect Eric Norman but taken over by Grand Theatres in the 1950s with the stage seeing appearances from Jerry Lee Lewis, The Kinks, Cliff Richard, The Beatles, Billy Fury and others. Closed as a working cinema by 1973 to be converted into a bingo hall, since 1991, it has been under the Gala Bingo banner since 1991. Circle seats remain from the days when Terry played to audiences there.

Returning to Too Many Crooks, George Cole was not the first choice for the role as it was meant for Peter Sellers and later, Tony Hancock was also offered the part but Cole does a fine job here as a 'crim' out of his depth. Terry had a part in Blue Murder at St. Trinian's (1957) and again both men feature in The Bridal Path (1959), the latter released in the same year as Too Many Crooks but very different in its style. Both actors would later have roles in The Great St.Trinian's Train Robbery (1966).

Returning to the story, Lucy overhears Fingers telling the others what happened and is distraught to hear her husband's lack of interest in her well-being. This will prove to be the catalyst for much of the story from this point forth. Cole tries once more to get cash from Mr Gordon, wearing a tramp disguise but laughing T-T dismisses him before seeing a newspaper headline about a grizzly murder and convincing himself that the gang has killed her.

Meanwhile, upon his return to their hideout, Fingers (Cole) is usurped from being the gang kingpin by a bolshie De Banzie. Angry and humiliated at her husband's abandonment, she offers them a deal to get her half of his fortune, with a major cut for them if they help her. However, T-T is genuinely distraught at thinking that he has lost her. The group return to the house and remove all the hidden cash before one of them accidentally sets fire to some curtains during their hasty departure. Further jewels are taken from his mistress before he learns of the fire.

Attended to by leading fireman Scott, Terry makes his initial appearance on screen just before the hour mark as a fire policeman forced to rugby tackle a frantic Terry-Thomas and his attempts to enter and re-enter the house to remove his lolly.

A few minutes later on screen and Thomas is up in court, in front of Magistrate John Le Mesurier, defended by Sydney Tafler and present to face up to his alleged assault upon an actual tramp that he mistook for Cole, previously. Terry features again as a uniformed officer, next to the wronged individual.

Portraying "James Smith, PC 166m, S Division", Terry takes the stand and informs the court about his earlier dealings with T-T at the house fire. Fined £5, then £10, "Le Mes" says that he does not believe anything that the accused says and simply wants him to go away. But of course, the next case being called is another featuring Thomas!

The plot zips along at pace whilst the gang and Lucy are still not finished emptying the pockets of Billy Gordon, impersonating police officers in a further attempt to fleece him soon following. The seductive

Charmaine (Day) takes him for an additional £500 before he foolishly tells her that he has more stashed away at his elderly mother's home (played by an unsuspecting Edie Martin). Convinced that his wife is dead, T-T faints at the sight of his returning spouse before the gang head off, now at last successful criminals and some £50k richer. But good fortune fails them, as driving off in Billy's purloined sports car, the five of them crammed in, big Bernie carrying the suitcase full of notes, it pops open and all the money flutters out as they drive away unaware of their loss.

Made at Pinewood and released across the country in March, Terry's future theatre co-star and cast member here, Nicholas Parsons, aptly described Too Many Crooks as a "delightful comic thriller."

Terry performed in front of a live audience at the Pavilion, Torquay for the week commencing Monday 18 May, in a Richard Stone presentation of The Billy Cotton Band Show. Offering the usual twice nightly engagement at 6pm and 8.30pm, the Pavilion facilitated cheaper seats for the first house, with prices from 2/- to 6/- whilst the second house ranged from 2/6 through to 7/6-. The production featured eight sets, starting with dancers Nick Lundon and Pam, Bernie and Barbara, followed by another duo, Paul and Peta Page, before Terry performed the first of his two sets, sandwiched between Hungarian acrobats and the return of Nick and Pam. He finished with his familiar The Play's the Thing skit which was followed by Billy 'Wakey Wakey!' Cotton and company. Today, the Pavilion is in use as a shopping centre and no longer presents shows.

Monday 2 November, 6.25pm and 8.40pm at the Glasgow Empire saw 'The Hit Parade hat trick star of the keyboard' Russ Conway headline a show supported by nine other acts including Terry, Toni Lee, Three's Company, Johnny Wiltshire and the Trebletones, Alexis Troupe, the Agnes Duncan singers, Eddie Falcon, Victor Soverall and Rosa Goldi.

On to Monday 16 November at the ABC Regal, in Gloucester with headline act Conway supported by The Gay Girls, Three's Company, Terry, the legendary Wilson Keppel and Betty, Eddie Falcon, Saveen assisted by Daisy May and Toni Lee / Johnny Wiltshire with the Trebletones. The theatre programme cost 6d.

Good timing had been fortuitous for John Creese-Parsons, owner of the imposing Grand theatre, Llandudno, earlier in the summer, when composer/ pianist Mr Conway was scheduled to play there. Conway had been booked when he was still a largely unknown name, but his appearances happened to coincide with the release of his chart topping record Side Saddle. This led to his two daily shows being sell-outs each day, with crowds of fans queuing round the block in the north Wales seaside resort.

Devised by comedian Issy Bonn, The Russ Conway Show plays for two weeks, in separate stints in June and July. If you had have wanted to see the show, a ticket cost 3/- for the stalls; the Dress Circle was 5/6 and the Upper Circle started from2/-. Terry was third on in a programme consisting of a dozen skits. He came on to say Good Evening before returning after the Copa Cousins, for an act titled "Great Scott! It's Scott!" Following the interval, he returned to offer the audience an introduction to "the sensational piano star of television, stage and recordings...Russ Conway". After the star turn, Terry joined the whole company to say a "Good Night" to the crowd before the customary singing of the national anthem. Also on the bill were Ronnie Winters, Jessie Caron, The Peter Crawford Trio and the Dancing Debutantes.

Sadly, today, the Grade II star listed theatre lies in a state of disrepair with more than £1m required to make it safe. Its final theatre production having played there in 1985, back when Terry had performed there, it was a 4,000 seat venue. Conway died in November 2000.

There is something quite lovely to see established television actors such as

ⒶⒷⒸ①②③④

Cast

Terry-Thomas...Bunny Gordon

George Cole...Fingers

Brenda De Banzie...Lucy Gordon

Bernard Bresslaw...Snowdrop

Sidney James...Sid

Joe Melia...Whisper

Vera Day...Charmaine

Delphi Lawrence...Beryl

John Le Mesurier...Magistrate

Stanley Tafler...Solicitor

Rosalie Ashley...Angela

Nicholas Parsons...Tommy

Vilma Ann Leslie...journalist

Edie Martin...Gordon's mother

Tutte Lemkow...Gun seller

John Stuart...Insp. Jensen

Terry...Fire policeman

Sam Kydd...Tramp

Cyril Chamberlain...fireman

Gibb McLaughlin...vicar

Wally Patch....court usher

George Cole, Gordon Jackson, Terry and even Annette Crosbie as youngsters when we have come to know them as esteemed TV actors in their older years in Minder, The Professionals, Terry and June and One Foot in the Grave, respectively. This is the pleasure afforded from viewing The Bridal Path (1959). The Western Isles/ Highlands seen in the film look absolutely stunning, their wide, open landscapes photographed in colour and the film has a real period feel to it. Directed by Frank Launder, if you liked Geordie (1955) then you would enjoy Bill Travers here as Ewan, a ruggedly handsome yet naïve young man on a quest to find himself a wife. Armed with a list of desirable/ undesirable qualities of a rather dubious nature, examples consisting of her not being a Catholic, English/ Welsh or Irish but possessing firm thighs for all the working that she will be doing when living with him on Eigg, a little stretch of the Western Isles!

Terry, once more in uniform, is found in the film as a randy young local policeman more interested in the charms of Carry On lady Dilys Laye, here in a deliciously saucy role, than locating a troublesome Mr Travers, who somehow manages to get himself in a right pickle, thanks mainly to misunderstandings and fish-out-of-water shenanigans! He comes into the story at around the 40 minutes mark in the above mentioned scene. "At times like these, there's nothing like the strong arm of the law!" quips Terry, taking the married Isobel (Laye) into his arms. Discovering Ewan's trousers drying by the fireside, P.C. Terry aka "The big teddy bear" to Ms Laye's character, discovers Ewan and pursues him around the house before seeing him run off into the hills. Not bothered by this, he grins and turns back to the door and into the house. Although Terry utilises a soft Scots-type accent, he still sounds like the actor we all know and love.

The film uses the Nigel Tranter 1952 novel as its source, with a screenplay co-written by director Launder with Geoffrey Willans, the latter who worked with St Trinian's creator Ronald Searle.

In another scene, at the Highland games, Terry is distracted whilst about to 'toss the caber' (the task of running with a large wooden post and lobbing it as far as you can from the stomach region, with both hands). Wearing a little white vest and kilt, he stops upon seeing Ewan (Travers) in the crowd and chases after him. Donald (Scott) and the many other police officers competing in the games run after Ewan, upturning a table full of prized vegetables before losing sight of him. It was this scene featuring Terry that was used as one of the cinema lobby cards displayed to advertise the film.

The nature of the offences committed by Ewan are hugely inflated by others, which would create far more tension in the narrative if this was a Hitchcock film but here it is almost amusing as the audience is in on the joke: it's all circumstantial evidence. He doesn't quite realise how he is coming across to the people because he seems so amiable a presence.

The film was known rather more aptly as Mating Time for its American release and was well-received by the critics there. Esteemed magazine Time commented, "Recommended – Thoroughly charming," whilst the Chicago Sun Times offered, "Thoroughly delightful – Enchanting."

Look out for What a Whopper! (1961) actress Molly Weir as one of two waitresses; she would also be seen in the film spin-off of Bless this House (1972) and some years previously, Molly had a role in a 1963 episode of Hugh and I. Also, Joan Benham would later act alongside Terry in Happy Ever After and Terry and June.

A British Lion film release, much has been said of I'm All Right Jack (1959), a lively Boulting brother's satire concerning class and the role of trade unions in the British workplace of the late-1950s.

But it is the phenomenal cast that was exceptional here: packed full of vintage British actors, Terry is in the film fleetingly as 'Creepy' Crawley, a shop floor manager forever cajoling the workers to get on with their jobs.

Taken from the Alan Hackney novel Private Life, Frank Harvey and John Boulting shaped a screenplay with help from the author. And from the opening titles, the biting title song by Al Saxon proffers the intent; in actuality, the title of the film derived from the rather pithy phrase, popular of the time, of "Fuck you, Jack, I'm alright."

At Sunnyglades nature camp run by a mellow Miles Malleson, his onscreen son Stanley, (Ian Carmichael, once more making his acting appear effortless) is a youngish man fresh out of the army and finding it difficult to match his skills to a suitable professional role on 'civvy street'. After proving both disastrous and unrealistic in many areas, he eventually accepts a junior position at a company where his uncle is a board member (Dennis Price, playing a conniving bounder). Here the working lives of employees are heavily controlled by the unions, headed by the peculiar Fred Kite (a heavily mannered Peter Sellers in an award-winning role). Stanley decides to lodge at the Kites family home after meeting the nubile Cynthia (Liz Fraser from A Pair of Briefs and others) and her mother Irene Handl; coincidentally, both would appear in similar family roles in The Night we got the Bird (1961).

Terry and the delightful Liz are both in Double Bunk and Jack.

Life at the engineering factory proves an eye-opener for 'Stan'; with lots of workers seeming to do nothing at all and a strict one-man-one-job function and fixed bonus scheme. Shown the ropes by Victor Maddern, here offered a decent role with time on screen, Kite and his cronies including Cardew Robinson and others are immediately suspicious of the posh newcomer. Terry would have a professional association with many of them during his career.

Sellers puts in a method-like performance as a communist union leader; all eyebrows, sharp hair cut and peculiar use of language, effected by the shenanigans of slippery, self-serving business men like Tracepurcel (Price), Coxy (Richard Attenborough in delightfully despicable form) and a man caught in the middle, Major Hitchcock (Terry-Thomas worth seeing to hear him utter the classic "absolute shower!" line which according to former Servicea man Huntley, was taken from a real person).

ⒶⒷⒸ①②③④

Cast

Bill Travers...Ewan McEwan
George Cole...Sgt. Bruce
Bernadette O'Farrell...Siona
Duncan Macrae...H.Q. Police Sgt
Alex Mackenzie...Finlay
Patricia Bredin...Margaret
Fiona Clyne...Katie
Dilys Laye...Isobel
Eddie Byrne...Mike
Terry Scott...P.C. Donald
Gordon Jackson...P.C. Alec
Roddy McMillan...Murdo
Joan Benham...Barmaid
Nell Ballantyne...Jessie
Jameson Clark...P.C. @ Crossroads
Jack Lambert...Hector
Vincent Winter...Neil
Elizabeth Campbell..Kirsty
John Rae...Angus
Jefferson Child...Wallace
Eric Woodburn...Archie
Andrew Donnie...P.C. Hamish
John Dunbar...Sgt. MacConnochie
Robert James...Inspector
Joan Fitzpatrick...Sarah
Pekoe Ainley...Craigie
Annette Crosbie...waitress
Molly Weir...waitress
Russell Waters...Bank cashier
Lynda King...Clerk
Abe Barker...Poacher
Graham Crowden...Man

In to the frame comes the naïve Stanley, who is soon used as a patsy by others for their own nefarious ends. He innocently stirs up problems after showing a visitor, sly time and motions man Waters (a twitching John Le Mesurier) how much quicker he could do his job as a fork lift truck operator. This leads to a strike being called, Stan being sent to 'Coventry' by his work mates and unanticipated problems beginning for all involved. Compromise ensues before Windrush realises the truth and seeing the rampant self-serving interests of people such as his uncle, old army chum Coxy and others. This comes to a climactic head during a live television debate involving many of the protagonists, and includes a memorable speech by Ian Carmichael. He had a five film deal with the Boultings and Jack was his last picture for the "demanding and difficult[5]" brothers. Attenborough learnt a lot from John Boulting particularly, "from him I came to understand that good directors do not shout and stamp around.[6]"

As Crawley, Terry is not impressed by Stanley forgetting to charge the battery over night of his fork lift truck. Look out too for the ubiquitous Sam Kydd, amusing as a tramp startled by the actions of Sid James and the gang in Too Many Crooks (1959), he can also be seen here as a stuttering shop steward. Wally Patch, billed on the old variety circuit as the "film character comedian", is also in the aforementioned Terry-related film, The Night we got the Bird, Nothing Barred (both 1961) as well as appearing on Brian Rix's This is your Life tribute, as would Terry, in 1961.

The picture proved to be the major box office draw in the UK following its theatrical release in August, back when Cliff Richard was top of the Hit Parade with Living Doll. Some 2m UK cinemagoers saw it and I'm All Right Jack would also perform well in America upon its release there in April of the following year.

Cast

Ian Carmichael... Stanley

Terry-Thomas... Major Hitchcock

Peter Sellers...Fred Kite/ Sir John Kennaway

Richard Attenborough... Sidney De Vere Cox

Dennis Price... Bertram Tracepurcel

Margaret Rutherford... Aunt Dolly

Irene Handl... Mrs Kite

Liz Fraser... Cynthia Kite

Miles Malleson...Windrush Senior.

Marne Maitland... Mr. Mohammed

John Le Mesurier... Waters

Raymond Huntley... Magistrate

Victor Maddern... Knowles

Kenneth Griffith... Dai

Fred Griffiths...Charlie

John Comer... Shop Stew

Sam Kydd...Shop Steward

Cardew Robinson... Shop Steward

Tony Comer... Shop Steward

Bruce Wightman... Shop Steward

Esma Cannon...Spencer

Bill Rayment...Shop Stew

Ronnie Stevens...Hooper

Martin Boddey...Num Yum's Executive

Brian Oulton...Ap Examiner

Malcolm Muggeridge

John Glyn-Jones...Detto Executive

Pauline Winter...Miss Fosdyke

Maurice Colbourne... Missiles Dir.

Jeremy White...Chemist

Robin Ray...Chemist

Michael Bates...Bootle

Photographers: Arthur Skinner & William Dexter

Robert S. Young...Owens

Roy Purcell...Police Insp.

Terry...Crawley

Also: Marianne Stone/ Marion Shaw/ Wally Patch/ Alun Owen/ Muriel Young/ Frank Phillips/ Ian Wilson/ Margaret Lacey/ David Lodge/ George Selway/ Alan Wilson/ Basil Dignam & Harry Locke.

A number of actors appeared, uncredited: Victor Harrington, George Hilsdon, Juba Kennerley, Aileen Lewis, John Leyton, Jim O'Brady, Ernie Rice & E.V.H. Emmett (narrator).

Terry in the 1960s

Stepping into the next decade, Terry was again a part of the Russ Conway Show, touring the UK and on 2 May the show arrived at the Gaumont theatre, Southampton, for a week long residency.

With a slight change in supporting artistes, a dozen pieces were presented with Terry on stage three times; twice before the interval and finally as the penultimate act before the headliner. The troupe consisted of Peter Crawford Trio, Key Sisters and Kenny, Rosa Goldi, Bert Weedon, Mary Weston, Debbie Sisters and Eddie Falcon. A programme for the show set you back 6d, whilst seats in the former cinema auditorium ranged from 6/6 or 5/- in the stalls, 6/6 or 5/- in the Circle or 4/- in the balcony. He was on twice before the interval and was the penultimate act before the headliner in the second. The critics seemed to enjoy it, too, "Terry Scott is a capable compere. His sketch as a horrid school boy (scratching, wriggling, blinking) who talks about his sister's wedding I enjoyed very much. The show is...good, clean fun for the family." CW, 3 May 1960 review, Southern Evening Echo.

For the summer season booking, Terry was stationed at the Floral Hall, Scarborough in a show titled Make it Tonight. The venue was "a large, airy auditorium surrounded by a solid wall of lightly curtained windows," according to future Dad's Army creator David Croft. A writer/producer and director, he hailed from a theatrical background, with both parents being actors. Croft had signed up to be represented as an actor with Richard Stone, Terry's agent, just after the end of WWII. However his later career saw his acting roles subside with gems Dad's Army and Hi-De-Hi! co-created by him. David directed 1962 and 1963 Hugh and I segments of Christmas Night with the Stars episodes. He was also the producer of Hugh and I Spy/ Hugh and I and Puss in Boots (1965) with Terry.

Presented by workaholic agent Richard Stone, singing star/ actor Dickie Valentine received top billing for the show which opened on Wednesday 22 June and played twice nightly on the little stage.

Mr Valentine was followed by Terry and Dennis Spicer receiving equal billing, ably supported by Sally Logan and Jo 'Mr Piano'

Henderson. Also on the bill were Reco and May, The Twelve King Dancers and The Wish Mary Hunt Duo.

Dickie would open the show prior to being joined by Terry for a number called Make 'em Laugh. Five more skits would be played out prior to the interval, with Terry participating in one as "The Actor" in The Stand In.

Following on from the opening number of the second act, Terry performed in a three-hander scene, as his little boy character Knocker, alongside Valentine and Mary Hunt. He later got his own time in the spotlight to perform Making the Best of It prior to Valentine concluding the show prior to Valentine concluding the show before being joined on stage by the company to wish the audience a good night and for the traditional playing out of the national anthem accompanied by a band.

Wednesday 22 June at 8pm saw the season commence with Richard Stone presenting the 1960 Floral Hall Show. Dickie Valentine was the headline act, followed by Terry and Dennis Spicer receiving equal billing, ably supported by Sally Logan and Jo 'Mr Piano' Henderson starring in Make it To-night. Also on the bill were Reco and May, The Twelve King Dancers and The Wish Mary Hunt Duo.

BBC cameras recorded The Dickie Valentine Show from there in September that year but the author is not sure if Terry was featured.

"I was pleased to see that one of the foremost designers in the UK and probably in Europe as well had some kind words to say about the long-gone Floral Hall, which stood on Scarborough's North Side. The place...didn't get too many kind words during its latter days," offered Richard Seymour during a recent visit to his home town. He believed that the demolition of the Floral Hall had been one of the greatest sins committed in Scarborough in recent times.

The Floral Hall, "a fabulous thing," as Mr Seymour remembered it to for website thescarboroughnews.co.uk, "it was an unlikely theatre, it must be admitted. It was always more of a vast conservatory. A glass roof was very soon erected above the arena, and then the covered area was extended until the place became a full-blown theatre. By that time it had in fact ceased to be a "floral" hall at all, since huge areas of glass in the roof had to be painted over to help with stage lighting effects, and nothing would grow in the place any more. Despite its chequered early history...it was a successful theatre for many years. The place pulled in very big crowds in the decades after second world war, but by the 1980s had lost a lot of holidaymakers to foreign sun-spots. "

Located within Alexandra Gardens on Scarborough's aforementioned North side, lots of stars played there including Frank Ifield and Barbara Windsor would appear in a 1983 production of The Mating Game. However, these lively years of excited audiences and popular performances eventually took their toll on the venue. The concert pavilion became structurally unstable, as noted by Susan on the Stories from Scarborough Facebook page: "I worked there the last year it was open in 1986 and it was in need of some serious TLC".

By 1987 the Floral Hall had closed, and, with the reported £500k lacking for the necessary restoration work to make it safe, including addressing the corrosion of the main structure supports, it was demolished two years later and the site is now occupied by Scarborough Bowls Centre.

Radio offered an opportunity for Terry in the form of a Variety Playhouse broadcast from the BBC. He was one of the performers which also included the BBC Revue Orchestra, George Mitchell Singers and married actors Jack Hulbert and Cicely Courtneidge.

Broadcast on BBC TV on Thursday 21 July, they presented their Scarborough Show Parade, with Dickie Valentine in a sketch with Terry which saw the latter dressed as an old woman!

Filmwise, Terry advanced to a part in And the Same to You. "I'm on top of the world with a rosy view, jolly good luck and the same to you." That is a sample lyrics from the catchy theme tune to the film.

Sid James received a special guest star appearance credit amidst a large cast in a 'U' certificate feature led by Dr Who man William Hartnell. Whilst the sexy Vera Day, Brian Rix and a big, dopey Tommy Cooper all enjoy roles across a brisk 70 minutes running time. Vera has a more substantial part here, yet always the girlfriend of someone, she was also in Too Many Crooks before filming this. Sid is Sammy Gatt, a none-too-kosher boxing promoter and old associate of Wally. The amusing Leo Franklyn is the new vicar tasked with assessing the former's suitability to run a boxing club at the church hall.

Almost all those associated with boxing in this film seem corrupt, from manager/promoter Wally (Hartnell) to 'bent' prized fighter Perce (Tony Wright) and others. Only young Dickie (Rix, here taking a break from the northern prat that he usually portrays) seems to have some integrity and once his boxing skills are discovered after he floors the cocky Perce, he gets nobbled in his first fight! Only Cynthia (Day) sets about correcting things and gets 'Dickie Dreadnought' a shot at a fight with hotshot Chappy Tuck (Larry Noble). DD is a short notice replacement to fight Tuck; not prepared to throw the fight to a novice.

Terry comes on screen close to fifty minutes, in, yet another policeman role, here chasing after scene- stealing Sydney (Franklyn) out training with his nephew, Dickie (Rix), he manages to wreck his bicycle and as a consequence, has a broken light and ends up giving false information to the officer. Franklyn is the saving light in the picture and he's very funny in a sequence whereby everyone denies knowing him to the condescending officer. Hartnell is ever-dependable as a shady promoter prepared to do whatever it takes to be successful. His team includes simpleton Horace (a young Tommy Cooper) and trainer Arthur Mullard in a minor role.

Everything goes wrong on the night of the big fight, with the regional Archdeacon and his wife paying a visit to the youth club / boxing club but being tricked by Hartnell and the others. Renee Houston is amusing as Mildred, wife of the V.I.P. and a keen sports gambler who wants to stay and watch the bill. Both boxers end up drinking from a water bottle spiked with alcohol and the evening ends in mayhem.

Consequently, it seems Rix will not be furthering a vocation into the priesthood and his uncle has also been asked to resign. Accepting the decision, Uncle Sydney offers that his nephew could well have been a winner, with Dickie jabbing at a post inside the hall, much of the roof comes crashing in around them! This gives his uncle second thoughts, as the whole purpose of their involvement in boxing was purely as a means to raise funds for a new roof for the church hall.

45

Jennifer Phipps went from being secretary to Sid James here and straight on to The Night we got the Bird (1961). Whilst Dick Bentley would appear on June Whitfield's original This is your Life tribute, as would Terry. Big Arthur Mullard would work on 1964 and 1965 film projects with Terry, too. The excellent William Hartnell also enjoyed screen time with Terry in Carry On Sergeant (1958). They shared a scene in You where Terry comes rushing in to the hall in search of Sydney (Franklyn).

"The results of our efforts was a very funny, albeit simple, film... unfortunately, the critics loathed it. I think the fantasy elements about a man reincarnated as a parrot got their collective wicks.[7]"

That was Brian Rix in 1961 reflecting upon his film The Night we got the Bird in his autobiography. Made at Shepperton studios at the end of February, this energetic farce was co-written by Tony Hilton and Ray Cooney, freely adapted from The Lovebirds by Basil Thomas.

Rix and Dora Bryan were top-billed in this film which sadly, despite the efforts of a sterling cast proves to be a real turkey.

Terry is seen very early on, as P.C. Lovejoy, out on his beat along the street where he stumbles upon the charisma-free Ronald Shiner returning to whining wife Julie(Dora Bryan) after being out all night.

Cecil later gets killed in a road accident, in a vehicle driven by soft-lad Bertie (Rix) who subsequently marries Dora and we follow the characters as they attempt to go on their honeymoon in this Brighton-set comedy with few laughs despite the endeavours of a strong cast.

Terry is next seen outside the house where he spots Rix attempting to enter his new wife's bedroom via the window above the front of the house (circumstance decrees he does it this way!)

Then a few moments later, we again see Terry, this time reacting to the mix-up inside and chasing after Rix who is carrying a covered bird cage which he happens to believe is the reincarnated Cecil in parrot form. As an aside, the concept does not read too well, does it?

They dash towards the promenade and onto the now-lost West Pier (back when it was still open and not the skeletal remain of the present day). A chase along the deserted boardwalk ensues and he catches up with Rix just at the moment he is about to throw the cage over the pier top. All this occurs almost an hour into the film whilst the two actors are obviously replaced by stunt performers as both men end up in the water!

We get to see more of Terry in the very next scene, in front of a dotty/hearing-impaired J.P, W.D Warre-Monger (Kynaston

Ⓐ Ⓑ Ⓒ ① ② ③ ④

Cast

Brian Rix...Dickie
Tommy Cooper...Horace
Cynthia...Vera Day
Leo Franklin...Rev Sydney
Tony Wright...Perce
Renee Houston...Mildred
Dick Bentley...George
John Robinson...Pomfret
William Hartnell...Wally
Miles Malleson...Bishop
Ronald Adams...Butch
Shirley Anne Field...Iris
Tommy Duggan...Mike
Arthur Mullard...Tubby
Rupert Evans...Butch
Terry...policeman
Lindsay Hooper...Bert
Jack Taylor...M.C
Micky Wood...referee
Larry Taylor...Chappy
George Leech...Jake
Jean Clark...manicurist
Jennifer Phipps...secretary
Bob Simmonds...boxer
Sidney James...Sammy

Reeves). Alas the older man mishears an earlier case involving another couple, to the bemusement of barrister John Le Mesurier. P.C Terry Scott is accused of wrongful arrest before the judge dismisses Bertie without charge.

About to set off once more on their honeymoon, Bertie is disturbed by the arrival of Wolf (a menacing John Slater) who threatens him into locating a genuine Georgian, four-poster bed that his former colleague Cecil (Shiner) duped him over.

Speaking to his former employee Charlie (Reginald Beckwith) Bertie wonders how he could do this. Naturally, he pays a visit to a local RSPCA aviary and sounds out the parrots there, reasoning that one of them might be Cecil!

This is where Terry's character comes back into the story, by now getting rather silly, when Rix pinches his bicycle whilst in pursuit of the escaped bird. Moments follow with the constable (Scott) hot in pursuit but never quite catching his man.

Sometime later, having gotten rid of the pesky parrot, whilst seeming quite insane to his new in-laws; the appealing younger daughter Liz Fraser, a dab hand at light comedy here and parents Irene Handl and Leo Franklyn, newlyweds Bertie and Julie finally set off in their car to enjoy their honeymoon in Weston-super-Mare.

It seems that Cecil has ended up being launched into space as part of a British atomic rocket project and Rix winks at the camera as this is revealed on the car radio!

Bird is not without some amusing moments, particularly in its word play but it suffers from being a little narrow in its staging. Chapman was at the time an actor within the Rix stock company branching out into writing and it does show. However, if you are a lover of old Brighton, the film will prove to be a treat.

Terry is a guest on colleague Brian Rix's This is your Life tribute show which was broadcast on 23 October after initially reading for him at an audition and proving to be "easily the funniest..." Mr Rix would later appear on Terry's own tribute in 1978 and would add, "I can safely say that he's one of the funniest comic actors in the business. But he's certainly one of the very worst gigglers!"

The year proved a hectic one for both men, what with Rix involved in three films and a television farce. A grateful Terry was cast in three of them: The Night we got the Bird, Nothing Barred and TV comedy Will any Gentleman?

Shot at Shepperton studios end of February, The Night we got the Bird is an energetic farce co-written by Ray Cooney and Tony Hilton and adapted from The Lovebirds by Basil Thomas. "The result of our efforts was a very funny, albeit simple, film…Unfortunately, the critics loathed it – I think the fantasy element about a man reincarnated as a parrot got on their collective wicks…[7]"

"Frantic antics on land and sea! It's a monstrous riot of fun. Don't see a doctor! Go to sea…."

After a stuttering start, Terry's next film release proved to be quite a curiosity piece: What a Whopper.

Little Adam Faith stars and sings the Buddy Hollyesque title song to a light comedy written by sci-fi legend Terry Nation. From an original idea by actors Jeremy Lloyd and Trevor Peacock, Whopper was directed by former documentary man Gilbert Gunn, and would seem to have been his final film work.

The wooden Mr Faith plays the achingly hip Tony, a struggling author living at a desireable Chelsea address full of creative types: there's composer Vern (Carry On Sergeant's Terence Longdon), dizzy Charlie (a lovely Carole Lesley, providing much fun), Arnold (Charles Hawtrey) and one other.

The story opens with Clive Dunn doing his best old man shtick, attempting to serve an eviction notice on the group which forces Tony to come up with a plan. He ropes in his pals to fake a sighting of the Loch Ness monster, one of the subjects of his writing projects, to drum-up some much-needed funds.

He does this by recreating a sighting of 'Nessie' and photographing the said results to take with him on a publicity trip to Scotland and to the world famous loch. Their attempt to do this in a local London park early one morning is almost thwarted by the appearance of tramp Spike Milligan, here in a memorable little cameo. He awakens to see that he has 'caught' the monster on the end of his makeshift line and runs off in fear, whilst the pals also make a swift exit as their smoke bomb creates havoc!

Joined by Charlie, Tony (Faith) and Vern (Longdon) set off for Scotland in a recently purchased hearse, needed to transport all their gear, in another comedy outing for the said vehicle (see also Too Many Crooks). On their way they pick-up pretty French hitch hiker Marie (Marie French) and for a plot contrivance, somehow manage to give Charlie's parents the impression that she is eloping to Gretna Green and so they pursue her in a car driven by a permanently sloshed Gilbert (Freddie Frinton).

ABC 1234

Cast

Brian Rix...Bertie
Dora Bryan...Julie
Ronald Shiner...Cecil
Leo Franklyn...Victor
Irene Handl...Ma
Liz Fraser...Fay
John Slater...Wolf Mannheim
Reginald Beckwith... Chippendale Charlie
Terry...P.C. Lovejoy
Vincent Harding...Ben
Dennis Shaw...stooge to Wolf
Ray Cooney...man with cartwheel
Gerald Cross...Uncle Arthur
Vera Pearce...Aunt
Grace Denbigh-Russell...Aunt
Jennifer Phipps...Mrs Jackson
Kynaston Reeves...Warre-Monger
John Le Mesurier...clerk
Gilbert Harding...2nd clerk
Thomas Muschamp... RSPCA officer
Tony Hilton...passerby
Merilyn Roberts...girl in punt
Toby Perkins...young man
Henry Longhurst...vicar
Hazel Douglas...bespectacled lady
Frank Atkinson...bald-headed man
Beryl Ede...his wife
Geoffrey Colville...curate
Charles Cameron...military gent
Elspet Gray...woman with dog
Wally Patch...ticket collector
June Wyndham...lady
Roberta Tone...little girl
Robertson Hare...doctor
Lionel Ngakane...porter
Hubert Cross...man servant
Wynne Clark...Miss Hawkesworth
Sheila Mercier...school mistress

When they arrive, Marie suggests that they stay at the Claymoor hotel on the banks of Loch Ness, which is run by proprietors Sidney James and Jimmy (Ewan Roberts). This dodgy duo has a sideline in salmon poaching, which plays a major part in the story. Mistaking a puzzled Tony for their London buyer, the twosome put the purloined fish in the back of the hearse whilst avoiding the attentions of a local P.C (Gordon Rollings). The aforementioned quarry provides much humour, beginning with Tony and his pals removing it from the vehicle and placing into another one nearby.

The plot of What a Whooper is a little weak, as the dozy copper dashes off and returns with his boss to show him the found evidence.

A little over half hour in, Sgt Terry Scott arrives with him, both on bicycles, only to discover that the fish has since vanished. Terry employs a somewhat dodgy Scots accent, a bit like the local postman, a funny Wilfrid Brambell, does.

Fortunately, the officers discover the fish elsewhere and step into the hotel bar to interview the owner of the car (Frinton) whilst observed by the proprietors. It is a pleasure to see Sid and Terry in a scene together, however briefly.

Terry and his associate decide to secrete themselves outside in an attempt to catch the poachers, "We're on to something here. I think we'll keep it under surveillance."

"I've got a better idea, why don't we keep a watch on the place?" replies his subordinate in a gag that falls flat but sounds funny.

Still perpetuating the scheme to publicise the monster, Tony tasks Vern with running audio cable outside the hotel to play the sound loop they manufactured of the creature. Unfortunately, he is discovered by the two policemen but manages to make his excuses to leave. With the day drawing in, some of these exterior scenes are shot in daylight whilst others are darker: all disconcerting but ultimately not that important. The police duo continue to chase after anyone that comes outside before Tony (Faith)is seen in the bar, carousing the locals over a drink to talk about the sea creature. Then on cue, Vern (Longdon) plays the clip of the beast. Sgt Terry and his constable hear it whilst outdoors and the former sprints away back to the station in fright! And that is the last time we see Mr Scott.

Amid a media frenzy, Tony manages to disappoint everyone by losing the photo that he fabricated and in a surreal moment, he and Marie hear a singer introduced on the transistor radio (I don't dare to

Ⓐ Ⓑ Ⓒ ❶❷❸❹

Cast
Adam Faith...Tony
Sidney James...Harry
Carole Lesley...Charlie
Terence Longdon...Vern
Clive Dunn...Mr Slate
Freddie Frinton...Gilbert
Marie French...Marie
Wilfrid Brambell...postie
Fabia Drake...Mrs. Pinner
Harold Berens...Sammy
Ewan Roberts...Jimmy
Archie Duncan...Macdonald
Terry...Sergeant
Anna Gilcrist...Grace
Gordon Rawlings...P.C.
Bernard Hunter...Legree
Lloyd Reckord...Jojo
Lance Percival...P.C.
Molly Weir...teacher
Fyfe Robinson...
commentator

use the term "tranny" which would be historically correct) and it is none other than...Adam Faith. He then proceeds to sing-along to the record, The Time has Come.

The hoax is revealed to the furious locals resulting in Tony being chased off before returning to find Marie. Jumping in a rowing boat and drifting out onto the loch, panic ensues as behind the youngsters is a full-sized Nessie. Not to worry, the creature winks and at the camera and says, "Oh, what a whopper!"

Sid James puts in a by-the-numbers performance, complete with trade mark yak!yak!yak! laugh in a film shot on location in Scotland and at Pinewood studios. Goodness knows what 1961 audiences would have made of it all; it certainly is no Ealing-type gem but is worth a look to see Terry and Sid onscreen together following on from roles in And the Same to you (1960), Double Bunk (1961) and Too Many Crooks (1959). Look out for blink-and-you'll-miss-them cameos from Amanda Barrie, Lance Percival and Trevor Peacock.

April this year found Terry in A Fair Cop, yet another Sunday Night Play presentation for BBC television. Written by Christopher Bond it was directed by Darcy Conyers.

Cast

Gareth Adams...Fireman

Charles Cameron...Hilary

Leo Franklyn...Sgt Blunt

Basil Lord...Creaser Croker

Peter Mercier...Joe

Sheila Mercier...Millie

Larry Noble...Smiler Perkins

Brian Rix...P.C Percy Hobson

Andrew Sachs...reporter

Terry...P.C Gunboat Clitheroe

Carole Shelley...Betty

I often enjoy reading other reviews and comments about films and here are a few for Terry's next film appearance in Double Bunk. "I have to admit I love early British comedy from the 1950s and 1960s and for the life of me couldn't remember ever seeing this particular gem!" Offered a reviwere known as Didds via Amazon.co.uk "So sitting comfortably with cup of tea in hand I sat down for a dose of nostalgia and all I can say is, I wasn't disappointed what a cracking film: British comedy at its best."

"It's not a side splittingly funny comedy by any means, but it does have plenty of chuckle moments, and I watched with a smile on my face throughout."Norman Cheesworth, amazon.co.uk comment.

The British film industry of the late 1950s/ early 1960s seemed an incestuous thing: seeing   actors moving from one project to the next and often crossing paths. And this was the case with C.M. Pennington-Richards' genteel nautical comedy Double Bunk. Writing in her autobiography, actress Liz Fraser said that Bunk was her favourite film to have appeared in; offering a decent script and proving a happy experience to make.

Shot across eight weeks at Twickenham studios and upon location on the river Thames, Richards, known as 'Penny', was remembered as being "nice and friendly and [who] did a really good job. He was tremendous fun and always encouraged [us] to have fun as well.[8]"

Released at the end of March, the cast and crew had enjoyed a filming schedule across the Indian summer of 1960. Terry and Liz had both been in The Night we got the Bird, previously. Coincidentally, Double Bunk features the voice of a certain June Whitfield in Take it from Here, a popular radio show at the time. More of her later.

Starring in their third film together, Ian Carmichael and Janette Scott received top billing but it is their co-stars Sid James and Ms. Fraser that sing the infectious song heard during the opening credits. Written by Stanley Black, Jack Fishman and Mike Pratt, the track, called Double Bunk, was released on the Decca record label in February 1961. Terry would make a number of comedy singles during his career, with the classic My Brother, composed by Mitch Murray and arranged by Johnnie Spence for the Parlophone label in 1962.

This made Terry stable mates with The Beatles! It immediately proved popular and would continue to be played on radio to this day. Other releases would follow including Juanita Banana in 1966, and a single in 1976 with June Whitfield titled Nicholas the Circus Clown. An album called Laugh in with Terry Scott and June Whitfield was produced in 1975 on the MFP label.

Returning to the film, the pleasant Mr Carmichael would see his I'm Alright Jack associates Terry, Liz Fraser, Dennis Price, Irene Handl and others from that Boulting Brothers classic also put in supporting appearances. With its screenplay also written by its director, in Double Bunk we find spunky young couple Jack (Carmichael) and Penny (Ms. Scott) initially living in separate rooms at a boarding house, struggling to raise enough funds to begin their married life together back when the average cost of a new home was a little over £2,500 and a pack of cigarettes was a little less than 25p. So instead, they decide to invest in a houseboat and this is where things do not go as planned for the newlyweds. Duped by Harper (Reginald Beckwith), the man who sold them the 'Jasmine Gay', leaks immediately spring forth onboard whilst their greedy new landlord (the cad, Dennis Price) demands money for berthing fees and lots of other things too.

Jack, a vehicle repairman, sells his sports car to friend and colleague Sid (Sidney James) to raise funds for the wedding and in return gets remunerated and given a 'bubble' car in part exchange. Sid offers to help him fix up the boat, suggesting that they take her for a run on the river, as a sort of honeymoon trip. Only this being a screen Sid, it is nothing more than a rouse to get buxom young girlfriend Sandra (Fraser) onboard. Every man that sets eyes on stripper Liz seems to fall for her, but personally, I thought Ms. Scott has much the greater sex appeal in Double Bunk.

Both Jack and Sid are novice sailors and immediately cause all kinds of chaos for little boats and others using the waterways. One of their victims is angler Reverend Thomas (Miles Malleson), battered by the violent wash produced by the speeding boat. Naunton Wayne, so perfect in Nothing Barred, here plays a Thames officer chastising the new captains but he doesn't get to do much in the film apart from get flustered by the shapely delights presented by Fraser.

Terry has the briefest of roles as a lascivious river police officer who along with a colleague, observing from near London Bridge as the speedy boat passes by, makes a comment about bikini-clad Liz.

Confused by a combination of sudden fog and their compass being adversely affected by Sandra's portable radio, the shipmates end up lost in France. They are out of fuel and stuck there when up pops Watson (Price) and chums in a modern, streamlined boat which the newlyweds had mistakenly assumed was the one for sale at the start of the film (it was moored in the next berth).

The aroused Mr Price swiftly offers to take Sandra back home but Sid is dumped off after being refused fuel, even though the former has a huge stockpile on board. Sid and Ian enact a night time raid and steal some whilst also freeing Liz from Watson's clutches (watch out for Carry On Sergeant actor Gerald Campion as one of his guests).

With the novice crew lost, they decide to wait for the experienced other to set off for home in the following morning, so as they can follow. Spotted by leading sailor O'Malley (a bullish Noel Purcell, later to be seen in Doctor in Clover), a bet is wagered between the boats to see who will arrive back the quickest.

O'Malley manages to get drunk whilst manning the wheel whilst the Jasmine Gay struggles.

Zooming down the Thames, havoc is wreaked by the wash created by Watson's streamlined boat and it looks like they will win. But finally, Sid/Ian/ Janette and Liz prove to be the winners, with the prize being a year's free mooring fees. They decide to sell-up with Willoughby Goddard and Carry On actress Marianne Stone prospective buyers.

Highbrow critics panned the film upon its release whilst the tabloids liked it. However, Double Bunk proves to be a pleasing little voyage that you will want to take. There are a few déjà vu moments: namely Carmichael driving another bubble car (see I'm All Right, Jack), Sid driving another hearse (see What a Whopper and Too Many Crooks) and obviously, seeing Terry in uniform again! It was distributed by British Lion Films in association with Bryanston Films.

Terry extended his association with the Brian Rix Company by appearing in the Ray Cooney/ Tony Hilton comedy play, One for the

Cast

Ian Carmichael...Jack
Janette Scott...Peggy
Sidney James...Sid
Liz Fraser...Sandra
Dennis Price...Watson
Reginald Beckwith...Harper
Irene Handl...Mrs. Harper
Noel Purcell...O'Malley
Naunton Wayne...Thames Officer
Bill Shine...Thames Officer 2
Michael Shepley...Granville-Carter
Toby Perkins...Pukka Type
Miles Malleson...Rev Thomas
Jacques Cey...French official

Hedger Wallace...1st river policeman
Terry...2nd river policeman
Desmond Roberts... Freighter captain
Peter Swanwick... Freighter pilot
Gerald Campion...Charley
John Harvey...Johnnie
Graham Stark...flower seller
Gladys Henson...Madame de Solla
Willoughby Goddard... prospective boat purchaser
Marianne Stone...his wife
Tom Gill...Customs officer
Jack Sharp...Delivery Man
The voices of Dick Bentley and June Whitfield

Pot, at the Whitehall Theatre, London, that August. Virtually all its cast had previously acted in A Fair Cop, supplemented by Hazel Douglas, Helen Jessop and Terry, the latter fulfilling the role of Jonathan Hardcastle. Rix was Hickory Wood in a show directed by former actor Henry Kendall (look out for him in a small role in Nothing Barred).

The play had originated as Dickory Dock and had been tried out at the Richmond theatre. Its plot was detailed as thus by josef-weinberger.com: "When a wealthy Northern mill owner offers £10,000 to the son of a former business associate provided he is the only living relative, Billy Hickory Wood arrives in anticipation to collect his money. It isn't long before a procession of Hickory Woods follow, all claiming to be the sole living relation and rightful beneficiaries, creating a seemingly endless string of mistaken identities and hilarious confusion." The theatre brochure states that "The entire action of the play is continuous and takes place one mad-summer's night at Jonathan Hardcastle's country house."

Pot began its run on 2 August, 1961 to great reviews and would eventually close on 4 July, 1964 after some 1,210 performances. Produced by Rix Theatrical Productions, the cast was as follows;

Leo Franklyn...Jugg

Helen Jessop...Cynthia Hardcastle

Sheila Mercier... Amy Hardcastle

Terry... Jonathan Hardcastle

Peter Mercier...Clifton Weaver

Larry Noble... Arnold

Basil Lord... Charlie

Brian Rix... Hickory Wood

Hazel Douglas... Winnie

Guests: Jeanne Cook, Robert Checksfield, Pearson Dodd, Stuart Sherwin, Gerald Dawson.

"Were you always more into comedy than drama?" quizzed Don Grigware in a recent internet interview with Mr Cooney on broadwayworld.com, "No, I wanted to be either Marlon Brando or James Dean at the time. But, the gentleman I was working for, Brian Rix, was very famous, and he's still our best friend...he was the manager and the producer of the play I was in at the Whitehall theatre, which was famous at the time. So I wrote the play for him. Having been in the One for the Pot with him I saw the kind of things that made that kind of play work. Tony Hilton who wrote [it] with me didn't like the pressure of writing. He just wanted to be an actor where you're told what to do and you move there. Tony went back to acting, so I started writing by myself."

Many years later, Terry would subsequently act in another stage farce written by Cooney and the author reflected, "Reading dear old One for the Pot today one realises how innocent and unsophisticated a piece it was – even for 1961."

Brian Rix was first associated with the Whitehall theatre in 1950, having developed a dual career as actor/manager. Known for its small stage area, the Whitehall is still there but is now a listed building due to its Art Deco accoutrements (sadly boxed up from current view). In recent years the building had been sub-divided and today is known as the Trafalgar Studios.

Returning to Mr Rix, a guest on Terry's This is your Life tribute, where he would retell the same anecdote, writing in his autobiography, he describes a gag that he and the cast perpetuated on Terry on his final night after appearing in One for the Pot for 18 months. "In the play Brian's character takes a peculiar drug which sends him off barking like a dog and Terry's character had to respond to seeing him peeing up a lamppost and finding the audience laughing...all the cast left on stage would turn around to follow Terry's gaze so it was a suitable time to get them all going. As he yelled his line about the lamp post, and as they all looked off left through the windows, there was a lamp post, there was a dog and it was lifting its leg. I had dressed my understudy Gerry Dawson, in a dog-skin, had a lamppost built and a phallic tube and soda siphon

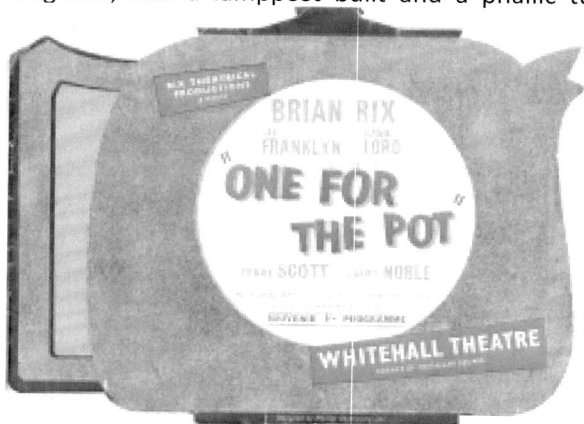

completed the necessary effect. The whole joke cost me about £5, but it cost a lot more...for the cast were quite incapable of another word and it was some time before we won the audience back...."

Producer Betty E. Box, wife of Carry On man Peter Rogers, was asked about her new film No, My Darling Daughter, made with Ralph Thomas, older brother to Gerald, the Carry On director, in a 1961 BBC interview, "It's a much more romantic comedy and it has much more story. As you know the Doctors don't have a great deal of plot, this one has. I think it has much more feminine charm in it."

Daughter starts of brilliantly with the silhouetted father and daughter team of Juliet Mills and Michael Redgrave singing the title song of the film. With its lyrics created by Herbert Kretzmer and David Lee, it's a catchy little number that will stay with you long after. As an aside, the incidental music heard in the film, composed by former EMI recording manager Norrie Paramor is both far too loud and intrusive and gets more so as the story progresses.

Cast as the school girl-aged daughter of leading Industrialist Sir Matthew (Redgrave, proving himself a dab hand at light comedy and looking very debonair), Juliet Mills as Tansy, was 20 by the time the film was released. Dressed in a St.Trinian's-type uniform, she looks far too grown-up for the part but is very pretty in this her film debut.

A doting Sir Matthew is clearly besotted with his daughter but upon seeing her poor school report, it is agreed that she should conclude her education at a Paris finishing school. The self-depreciating Tansy agrees but in a mix-up, his Private Secretary (Renee Houston) and junior management employee (a dashing Michael Craig) return her to boarding school, at St.Catherine's (a recognizable Pinewood studios location seen in a few Carry On films).

There is no female family presence in the lives of either Sir Matthew or his friend and colleague General Henry Barclay (a rasping Roger Lindsay, proving fabulous in his scenes alongside Redgrave). Therefore it is left to Henry's son, Thomas (Craig) to help with Tansy and the two youngsters spend most of their time in a state of mutual antagonism but have a discernible chemistry.

Renee Houston, later used so effectively as Kenneth Cope's mother in Carry On at your Convenience (1971), a film that Terry was due to be in, is also in And the Same to You (1960) as was Mr. Scott. Ms. Houston enjoyed a long show business career and here stifles her broad Scots accent. Joan Sims, an actress able to warm the heart whenever she makes an appearance on screen, adopts her own slight Scottish lilt for some reason in a part that mainly involves her laughing and gossiping as one of the pool of secretaries at Carr Industries. Known as the First Lady of the Carry On pictures, Joan would feature in an episode of Hugh and I and in the film A Pair of Briefs; both presented in 1962 and each involving Terry Scott.

Meanwhile, a doubting Thomas (Craig, resembling a young Bob Monkhouse) decides that he needs to question his life and what it is that he really wants from it. This also leads Sir Matthew to briefly do the same and both fathers worry about their children and prove effortlessly charming in their scenes together.

Cornelius, a young American lad, played by James Westmoreland but then billed as Rad Fulton, comes to Carr Industries after being given the task of relaying some business communications between his father's company in the States and Sir Matthew. But upon meeting Tansy, and feeling an instant attraction, they dash off together taking masses of photographs and doing the tourist thing all over London (a fun moment finds them at St Paul's Cathedral). The strapping lad forgets to pass on the letter and subsequently manages to lose it!

Compounded by the mix up and lack of response, Carr decides to fly to New York to personally sort out the deal after not hearing from them. Worried about his daughter's welfare, he insists that Tansy accompanies Henry (Livesey) on his annual fishing trip to Scotland, so as he can keep an eye on her. She refuses to go but Thomas threatens to tell Sir Matthew about her spending so much time with the young American. It makes no difference, as he secretly follows them there as the two seem inseparable and terribly keen on each other. Thomas finds this most irritating but doesn't yet acknowledge why.

Tansy decides that she wants to remain in London and not go to Paris, and her character is quite sweet, a bit of a klutz but pleasant enough. Upon realizing that her handsome friend will have to return to the States soon, she doesn't want this to happen. Sir Matthew's discovery, via some photographic slides, that Cornelius (Westmoreland) has been seeing his daughter, both in London and Scotland makes him furious. His actions necessitate that she be made a ward of court which means that in her absence, she is now regarded as being a runaway. Sir Matthew, with his Carr building housing eight floors of his various business concerns, sees this declaration make the front pages of many a newspaper and when Cornelius sees a copy, he realizes that she is in big trouble; indeed, as is he. Thomas independently goes up to Scotland to find Tansy, literally kidnapping her by plonking her in the back of his horse box to be driven back to London; Cornelius gets a bash on the head for his trouble.

Returning to confront Sir Matthew, who has no idea of what Thomas has done, he storms into the office only for Terry Scott to arrive, in full uniform, as police officer B214, who gets a little mixed up. Cornelius thinks it is him that will be taken off to the station but Terry, using a soft Yorkshire accent, is actually only there to issue a ticket to Thomas, after he parked in a prohibited area outside the building. He appears some 75 minutes into proceedings, and his second scene sees the two go outside, where the identity muddle is discovered, much to the delight and relief of the young man.

He and Tamsy agree to marry but only under duress from the adults and it will transpire that they do not want to do this after all. This leaves it for Thomas (Michael Craig), a little older than Tansy (Mills), with the actor in his early-30s here, to finally realize that he has feelings for her, which both father's had already encouraged. This all happens when he visits her whilst she is trying on wedding dresses. She then talks with Cornelius and they decide that their marriage is not now going to happen. Thomas and Tansy elope to Gretna Green, calling their respective father's whilst in transit, and they allow them to continue.

With its source material taken from the Harold Brooke/ Kay Bannerman play Handful of Tansy, it was left to Frank Harvey to furnish a screenplay for this lightly amusing feature which was released in British cinemas in August. Harvey does a pleasing job which is no surprise, as this is the man responsible for I'm All right, Jack (1959) and Heaven's Above (1963). Directed by Ralph Thomas, he had joined the Rank organization (the studio that would make No, My Darling Daughter!) at the end of World War II.

❸⓵❸ ❶❷❸❹ East st BRIGHTON 27010

Cast

Michael Redgrave... Sir Matthew Carr

Juliet Mills...Tansy Carr

Michael Craig...Thomas Barclay

Roger Livesey...General Henry Barclay

Renee Houston...Miss Yardley

Joan Sims...Typist   Peter Barkworth...Charles

David Lodge...Flanigan Terry...policeman

James Westmoreland (as Rad Fulton)... Cornelius

Court Benson...Allighnam

No unaccompanied children admitted after 7p.m

ALL PROGRAMMES MAY BE SUBJECT TO LATE CHANGE

Often in partnership with Box, Ralph would direct more than forty feature films, and was well into double figures by the time of working on this project quaintly defined by Howard Thompson on nytimes.com as "...a frisky and wholesomely appealing little comedy..." With many of the films originating from previously published books, three of his films provided exposure for Terry Scott: this one, A Pair of Briefs (1962) and Doctor in Clover (1966).

"I found Mary Had a Little... to be great fun from beginning to end. Recommended!" N Jeagle, imdb.com

Shot at Walton studios, Surrey in October 1960 and released in the following July, Mary had a Little... was directed by the American-born Edward Buzzell. A former actor/ writer, he had previously worked with the mighty Marx Brothers and Mary proved to be the last film that he directed. He was also co-composer of the title song which was sung by Dick James. Adapted by Peter Miller and James Kelley from the Arthur Herzog, Muriel Herman and L.Rosen play, its screenplay was furnished by Robert E.Kent and Jameson Brewer.

ⒶⒷⒸ①②③④

Cast
Agnès Laurent...Mary Kirk
Hazel Court...Laurel Clive
Jack Watling...Scott Raymond
John Bentley...Malcolm Nettel
Michael Ward...Estate Agent
Clifford Mollison...Watkins
John Maxim...Burley
Terry...police sergeant
Sidney Vivian...Grimmick
Patricia Marmont...Angie
Rose Alba...Duchess Noel
Howlett...Pottle
Trevor Reid...Dr Liversidge
Frances Bennett...Esther
John Cazabon...Fitchett
Charles Saynor...taxi driver
Mark Hardy...Hawkes
Michael Madden...Tigg
Vincent Harding...Carney
Tony Thawnton...Shakespeare

Terry comes into proceedings in the very last scenes, as a police sergeant having to make sense of the actions of the main protagonists standing before him. "Keep going, Sergeant," offers Scott (Jack Watling) ironically, "you're doing beautifully."

Watling plays a brassic theatre producer with a fiancée that wants to marry him (gorgeous horror queen Hazel Court).Overhearing psychiatrist and fellow club member Dr Malcolm Nettel (John Bentley) discussing the idea of nurturing the perfect baby; both physically and mentally via hypnosis. In desperation, Scott makes a wager with him that such a thing would never work but secretly planning to dupe his associate with the help of a certain French acting client Mary (Agnès Laurent).

Upon meeting, Dr Nettle and Mary have an instantaneous attraction but he believes that she is both pregnant and married, neither of which is true as Scott (Watling) talks her into tricking him. The very pretty Ms Laurent is quite charming but she sometimes delivers her dialogue without much understanding of what she is actually saying. Although, in one of the best moments, a bizarre dream sequence involving her being given advice and more, from Shakespeare (he is used as part of the con) it makes the film well-worth a watch. She is amusing in another moment towards the end when drunk and demanding that Scott impregnate her after she falls for the doctor but cannot find a way to tell him the truth. All the cast prove most watchable in this speedy black and white feature.

Terry's character attempts to decipher what exactly has gone on and his reaction to seeing Dr Nettel and Mary realise their feelings is a joy to behold. His response is the closing moment in the film.

Closing the year, Terry would appear in an episode of The Rag Trade, a popular comedy series co-written by Ronald Chesney and Ronald Wolfe, later of On the Buses fame. Broadcast on 8 December, this particular story was originally titled Golliwogs but later changed to Christmas Box. Peter Jones played Harold Fenner, with Reg Varney as Reg, Esma Cannon as Lily, Barbara Windsor as Gloria, Sheila Hancock as Carole, Ann Beach as Brenda, Colin Douglas as a policeman, Edward Caddick as a postman and Rita Smythe as Rita. Terry was cast as department store buyer Terence Nutley. The Rag Trade would enjoy a run across 5 series on the BBC originally, before re-emerging on ITV.

Reg works in the office at the Jones-owned clothing company whilst in the workshop next door, his all-female staff includes officious union rep Miriam Karling, sounding like a female Kenneth Williams, all nasal intonations and, kooky Sheila Hancock, little Babs Windsor and a dotty, scene-stealing Esma Canon in this black and white episode.

It's close to Christmas and the girls and Reg are looking to make a few quid by 'making' golliwog soft toys to sell on the side without the knowledge of their boss. Whilst he complains about the shoddy quality of the housecoats that his staff are producing, they need to get him out of the office before a buyer from the toy department of Baxters stores arrives. Reg is cajoled into dressing up as Father

Christmas in an attempt to surreptitiously sell their wares on the High Street and thus reach a wider marketplace for the gang.

Recorded live, with the cast sometimes stumbling lightly over the dialogue, the episode is very much in the farce department. A dozy PC comes looking for Reg after he is involved in an earlier scuffle but he has no idea that it was in fact Reg that he saw previously but totally misinforms them of the man he wants to speak with. In a fun script, Jones mistakenly thinks that the Santa outfit is a gift from the girls for him to wear to a charity fundraiser. Unfortunately for him, the copper enters the office and thinks that it is he that was causing the rumpus earlier on! Cue lots of fun as everyone denies knowing their boss and hence he is hauled away to the police station.

The gang has other things to contend with what with the imminent arrival of a certain Mr Nutley (Scott). Reg tells them that they have to treat their prospective buyer well and this will involve a look around the workshop before a drink or two to oil the wheels of selling the visitor three hundred of their soft toys at 22/6- a piece.

Arriving at the premises, it is none other than Terry Scott playing the moustachioed, dickie bow tie/ bowler hat wearer buyer. There is a funny exchange between him and Sheila Hancock after he presents her with his business card only for her to say its blank: "Allow me," offers the visitor, turning the card over and revealing his details printed there for her to read! It is a witty start and as he meets Reg and some of the others, they soon ply him with drink whilst also getting sloshed! The rowdiness increases and Reg vainly tries to get Terry to sign a cheque to pay for the order whilst their visitor takes a firm grip of both (Hancock) and Paddy (Karling) upon his lap and after dancing around the office together.

Unfortunately, the real boss returns whilst Terry is still present but the girls manage to guide him away and into the nearby ladies. Jones regales the Brylcreamed Reg and the others about his unfortunate experience at the cop shop and slowly begins to question the artefacts around him: whose bottle top glasses are these? The pipe? The over-sized bowler? He quizzes Reg but is not convinced by his declaration that they all belong to him as everything is too large for him and it all proves quite a laugh.

Meanwhile in the ladies, Terry has still not signed that darn cheque despite Paddy's best insistence: he needs his glasses from earlier which are still in the main office! She sets off to get them but the hilarious Esme Cannon, in a rouse to clean the Santa coat meant for her boss, enters the ladies and freaks out at the sight of a man therein and comes rushing out to the workshop. Meanwhile she drops the coat before fleeing. They try to convince the boss that this is all in her vivid imagination but the 2 men set off to confront the possible intruder. Entering therein, they are surprised to see that the room is empty but Paddy notices that the window is open.

Still drunk from the fun had earlier, Terry had climbed out onto the fire escape and down where he is confronted by the dozy copper of earlier, who thinks that because Terry is now wearing the Santa coat, that this is the man he called to arrest! Oh yes, a complete farce and all played out with much fun! Terry steps toward the copper and twirls him around before being pinched! Meanwhile Jones discovers the stash of gollies and gets to believe that they were intended for the local children's hospital!

The show would see many popular British TV stars make appearances, including a number of people that would work either directly with or in the same project as Terry elsewhere (the likes of Lynda Baron, Frank Thornton, Gwendolyn Watts, Dilys Laye and Vi Stevens etc).

Produced and directed by the esteemed Dennis Main-Wilson who moved into television after producing radio shows The Goons and Hancock's Half Hour, he would later work with Terry again, in 1964 on Scott On...Birds, as producer. Varney would also act in the 1966 cinema feature The Great St. Trinian's Train Robbery; as would Terry and both would work together again in 1963.

Terry was cast in television projects A Fair Cop, Flat Spin and A Clear Case (all Brian Rix projects) and Dial Rix: Balance Sheet, What a Drag and Round the Bend, the latter a 1962 television play that seems to mark Conyers final directed work.

"All the farce elements are there; prat falls, dressing up, mistaken motives, ham acting and totally unbelievable outcomes. Cars and scenery are great. If it seems dated now, that's part of the charm."

Vynor Hill, amazon.co.uk comment

The penultimate film to be directed by former actor Darcy Conyers, Nothing Barred was released in cinemas in October 1961. Conyers, was one of the writers of The Night we got the Bird, and he also performed producer duties on both films. This year he directed a trio of Brian Rix films: The Night we got the Bird, The Night we dropped a Clanger and Nothing Barred! Whilst this and the following year saw him at his most creative, directing eight TV episodes of Brian Rix Presents and Dial Rix.

Nothing Barred was written by John Chapman, remembered by his pal Ray Cooney as being "inventive, witty and methodical...[9]" London-born John was the nephew of "Mr Grimsdale!" actor Edward Chapman. An actor/ writer, he turned to television where his versatility made him a valuable commodity. With another Terry colleague, Dave Freeman, he would co-write Key for Two, a 1982 award-winning play. His light comedies often put the working class at the forefront and his professional association with Terry Scott would begin with TV series Hugh and I, after the two formulated the idea for the show with Hugh.

John had trained at R.A.D.A as an actor before focussing upon writing. Success soon followed in 1954 with his first play, Dry Rot proving a hit and running at the London Whitehall theatre for more than three years. He collaborated with Cooney and others and created more than two hundred comedy scripts for television, co-writing the precursor to Terry and June: Happy Ever After, with Eric Merriman. Eric, in the mid-1950s wrote all seventeen episodes of the Terry/ Bill Maynard BBC series Great Scott It's Maynard. With Chapman, he enjoyed early success as writer of Beyond Our Ken on radio. Born in Golders Green, where Terry would play in panto in 1962, Merriman produced the pilot script for Happy Ever After and more than thirty other episodes. In 1985 he would also furnish a couple of Terry and June, ones too (namely Mistaken Identity and Terry in Court). And prior to all these endeavours, he offered additional material for the Scott On series.

This was the third film release involving the Brian Rix team in 1961, and much simple pleasure can be taken from watching a troupe of actors putting in a fine collective stint across eighty three bustling minutes. Nothing Barred involves numerous cross purposes and coincidences and we begin at Whitebait Manor, a stately home in great financial difficulties. Naunton Wayne is Lord Whitebait, in another endearing role as a lovely chap taking it all in his stride. Ably supported by the devoted Spankworth (Charles Heslop), the two actors are so at ease together that it is a joy to watch them. Indeed, it s the latter who suggests that his lordship make a false insurance claim via a staged theft of a valuable painting belonging to the family. All this is discussed whilst bailiffs itemise household items in front of a small group of paying visitors and the two men.

The plan is to get habitual criminal Barger (Leo Franklin) to remove the art work in a fake break-in. However, this being a farce, friendly plumber Wilfred (Brian Rix putting in a funny turn) is mistaken for him whilst leaving Wormwood Scrubs prison, where he tends the plumbing system, Wilf thinks the two men are crackers but agrees to call at the house, as requested, thinking it just another plumbing job.

Meantime renowned cat burglar Barger returns home from his latest stretch in prison, only to discover a very young Bernard Cribbins has been taken in as a lodger by wife Elsie (Irene Handl, herself seen in a succession of Terry-related films). She learns of her husband's plans for a new robbery which just turns out to be Whitebait Manor.

In another case of people coming and going before a reveal, both Barger and Wilfred enter the house but in the mix-up, Barger gets arrested and returned to prison whilst the latter receives a £10 fine.

After falling for Whitebait's daughter (Ann Furbank), Wilf agrees to spring Barger from jail and visits him there whilst in disguise as possibly the least convincing looking woman in the world! Sid James in a couple of Carry On films springs to mind but in these films, this is all part of the fun. The incarcerated Mr Barger is sceptical but eventually agrees and plans are set for his escape during the weekly Sunday service at the prison church. Knowing precisely how the sanitation flow is structured, Wilf will not however be able to anticipate the eight convicts fleeing en masse on the day itself (one of them being Manuel from Fawlty Towers aka Andrew Sachs camping it up).

Three quarters of an hour in, the funniest moment in the film occurs with Wilf hollering down to the group through a manhole cover in an attempt to facilitate their escape; only for "P.C M83" to come along: it's Terry Scott. Wilf informs him that he has lost his budgie. The sceptical officer allows him to leave before removing the cover and whistling downwards, he receives a bird-like response but swiftly makes off; something his character in What a Whopper (1961) would have done!

Moments later, Terry again finds Wilf (Rix) in the middle of a different road once again talking down the drain cover, having now found Barger and the others via their collective singing; it meant that he could locate them in the underground sewage system. P.C Terry is bamboozled by this repeated action.

In his final scene, now spotting Rix venturing down a manhole cover opposite the Houses of Parliament, after a young woman falls down through the exposed cover and on top of him, P.C M83 wants to arrest him but Wilf sets off down the sewers with the officer just about managing to squeeze down the entrance point after him. Terry arrives, via a hatch, inside a ladies health club, as his quarry had done moments before. And like him, for no apparent reason, Terry disrobes and ends up with a large towel wrapped around him and a shower cap on top! He then somehow gets involved in a fitness dance class alongside a group of women in another amusing sequence (the Rix character had also done the same).

The gang eventually rendezvous with Wilf and Lord Whitebait but Barger doesn't want to get involved with their scheme. Whilst the law closes in, he and Wilf pinch a police car and to throw them off their scent, inform the radio controller that the assailants are disguised as clergymen. As the others get arrested, our duo return to Whitebait

❶❷❸ ❶❷❸❹ East st BRIGHTON 27010

Cast

Brian Rix...Wilfred Sapling

Leo Franklyn...Jim Barger

Naunton Wayne...Lord Whitebait

Charles Heslop...Spankworth

Ann Firbank...Lady Kate

John Slater...Lockitt

Vera Pearce...Lady Millicent

Arnold Bell...Governor

Alexander Gauge...Policeman

Jack Watling...Peter

Irene Handl...Elsie

Bernard Cribbins...Sneed

Wally Patch...newspaperman

Wilfred Lawson...Albert

Margaret Lacey...Gert

Terry...P.C Budgie

Henry Kendall...Parson

Larry Noble...Watchman

Dennis Shaw...Watchman/ convict

Andrews Sachs...Watchman/ convict

Lione Ngakame... Watchman/ convict

Keith Banks...1st Baliff

Frank Hawkins...2nd Baliff

Raymond Dyer...Cockney Dad

Jennifer Phipps...Cockney Mum

Oliver Freeman...Cockney Boy

Richard Kler...1st American

Reginald Hearne...2nd American

Ray Cooney...P.C at HQ

Tony Hilton...1st Waterboard man

Henry Longhurst...2nd Waterboard man

Janni Coomer...3rd Waterboard man

Gilbert Harrison...Clerk

Lorraine Clewes...Doris

No unaccompanied children admitted after 7pm
ALL PROGRAMMES MAY BE SUBJECT TO LATE CHANGE

Manor before being picked up and in these moments, Rix manages to lose his trousers in trademark farce style.

All safely ensconced in jail, Kate (Firbank) visits Wilf and they decided to marry. Family connections and so forth allow the groom and the others to attend the big day but all seize the opportunity to flee. Although, it has to be said that Wilf hesitates before being convinced by Barger to do so.

Another amusing scene comes at the close of the film, seeing Wilf, Whitebait and Spankworth pretending to be water sculptors, complete with Rix spurting water out of his mouth before being apprehended by Lockitt (the excellent John Slater from The Night we got the Bird).

Nothing Barred followed The Night we got the Bird later the same year having been an alternate title from The Night we sprang a Leak, to distance itself from the poor box office performance of the latter. The name change made little difference at the box office, with regrettably low returns recorded. The picture was another British Lion Films production with locations including Bushey studios in Hertfordshire and Shepperton studios, Surrey. With Barred, Terry would add another film role to a blossoming CV, released on DVD in 2014; he can be seen in the trailer.

"A typical Brian Rix farce full of light-hearted fun and confusion. Thoroughly enjoyed it great for a lazy afternoon." A. Shannock, amazon.co.uk comment

"A funny film with a good cast, this rather daft farce was fun to watch: worth watching." Musicals fan, amazon.co.uk comment

"Everything he touches...nearly comes off!"

That was the film poster strapline for Nearly a Nasty Accident. Jimmy Edwards, Kenneth Connor and Shirley Eaton received above-the-title billing, with an "also starring Ronnie Stevens, Richard Wattis, Jon Pertwee and Eric Barker" beneath it.

Directed by Don Chaffey and produced by Bertram Ostrer, the film was released by British Lion in association with Britannia Film Distributors through BLC. Chaffey would advance to direct cult classics on television and film including Jason and the Argonauts.

Terry and Peter Jones both had roles in Accident and appeared in the same scene, in this black and white comedy feature written by Jack Davies and Hugh Woodhouse and adapted from the David Carr/David Stringer play Touch Wood. Davies would also write the original screenplay for Father Came Too! (1964) and furnish an adapted script for Doctor in Clover (1966) both of which gave parts to Terry Scott.

Thankfully leading man Connor tones down the usual whiny/ gasping levels here and his performance was all the better for it. He played Wood, an enthusiastic but accident-prone tinkerer whose catchphrase provides the film's title. Eric Barker utilises an unidentifiable accent as an exasperated civil servant perturbed by the growing costs incurred by the latest catastrophe caused by little KC.

During the film, Wood manages to set off a missile, send an industrial-sized automatic dishwasher haywire, get himself carried along the tracks whilst altering a heating pipe under a train and the biggest calamity of all, opens the waterways which result in flooding part of Wales! It is here that Terry makes an appearance, as a previously unsuspecting goods driver whose truck gets washed away as a result of Connor's tinkering; much to the annoyance of new acquaintance Corporal Briggs; a gorgeous Shirley Eaton. Her character was on her way to the camp run by Jimmy Edwards where she has been assigned to become his new secretary.

Poor Terry, as Sam Stokes, adopting another man from-the-north accent, proves to be another victim of the bungling Wood, initially giving him and Corporal Briggs (Eaton) a lift whilst on his return journey as a driver for an electrical engineering firm. Coming on screen at around fifty four minutes in, he is resplendent in a peak cap, de rigueur for working class men and worn elsewhere by Sid James in a similar role in The 39 Steps (1959). He can barely keep his eyes open as he welcomes them into his cab, and soon enough, Wood takes the wheel to give the former a much-needed rest. But in a moment of distraction whilst looking at a map held by Briggs, they manage to drive off the main road and down along the Southern Union Canal private road (we see the sign onscreen). Connor thinks that it is a dry canal, green and overgrown but that summation proves to be wrong upon seeing the gushing water coming from behind the gates that he just opened, gasping, "You're quite right, these are canal gates and I've sort of let the plug out!" This all happens whilst Terry is snoozing in the truck below before awaking and being washed away whilst still inside. With no expensive special FXs budget seemingly available, in Terry's scene miniatures are used to represent the vehicle being washed away by the sudden outpouring of water and stock film footage being used to represent the violent flooding of fields.

In a light-hearted screenplay, we next see a traumatized Terry wrapped up in a blanket and back at the Army base in a funny scene with attendant doctor Peter Jones (whom Terry worked with in an episode of The Rag Trade), Edwards and others. "You'll never get Wales

Cast

Jimmy Edwards...Group Capt. Kingsley

Kenneth Connor...Wood

Shirley Eaton...Cpl. Jean Briggs

Eric Barker...Air Minister

Jon Pertwee...Gen. Birkinshaw

Ronnie Stevens...Flight Lt. Pocock

Richard Wattis...Wagstaffe

Joyce Carey...Lady Trowborough

Peter Jones...Flight Lt. Winters

Terry...Sam Stokes

Charlotte Mitchelll...Miss Chamberlain

Jack Watling...Flight Lt. Grogan

Joe Baker...Watkins

John Forrest...Fl. Lt Bunthorpe

Jack Douglas...Balmer

Cyril Chamberlain...Warr. Officer Breech

John Forrest...Flight Lt.

Vincent Ball...Sgt at Crybwyth

Harold Goodwin...mechanic

Ian Whittaker...Railway Transport officer

Emyrs Leyshon...Amb. driver

Fred Abbott...1st policeman

Robert Desmond...2nd p/man

Steven Scott...Kingsley's Orderly

Michael Lomax...driver

Keith Smith...Orderly

Frank Raymond...senior tech.

dry again, you know!" whines the driver, cared for by Dr Jones.

Another picture shot at Shepperton studios, Accident proved amiable fun and moved along swiftly, not outstaying its welcome and prospers by having a first rate cast. Jon Pertwee is aged to allow him to play a dotty old timer farmer, Richard Wattis, effortless in another bureaucratic role as Barker's deputy, Jimmy Edwards is bearable in a controlled performance, thankfully, resplendent with ridiculous handle-bar moustache accompanied by a booming voice and looking like he is having fun but knowingly going through the motions. He and Terry would act together again on a mid-1960s children's film.

That superb comedy bounder Terry-Thomas described the man thusly in his autobiography, "[he was] a splendid, exuberant person...a frightful egotist, nauseatingly erudite...[10]"

Returning to the film, Ms.Eaton is given little to do other than look lovely in uniform but it proves a delight to see her and Connor on screen together again and they would both feature in a number of other films, also. The same would be true for many cast members of Accident. Shirley can be seen in three of the early Carry Ons, including Sergeant, as was Terry, and in the TV comedy Great Scott, It's Maynard. Look out for Cyril Chamberlain, another RAF man, and victim of Connor's tinkering. He and Terry would both appear in 7 Carry Ons.

Broadcast on 12 November, on television, Brian Rix presented Flat Spin. This was his fourteenth, one hour TV project.

Cast

Ann Beach...Miss Chatham

Charles Cameron...Brig.

Sir Richard Kenway

John Chapman...Michael

Hubert Cross...man

Elspet Gray...Jane Kenway

Helen Jessop...Virginia

Larry Noble...Joe

Brian Rix...David Kenway

Andrew Sachs...Dino

Terry...Mr Drake

John Sharp...Sergeant

"If Boxing Day finds you a wee bit liverish after the Christmas festivities and even if it does not,' says Brian Rix, ' I can promise you that Will Any Gentleman? will prove the ideal tonic which can be taken in large doses by any gentleman or, for that matter, any member of the family." So at 8pm, across 90 minutes, Will any Gentleman? was broadcast on BBC television. Written by the 'father of modern day farce'[11] Vernon Sylvaine as a play originally, this had been released theatrically across cinemas back in 1953 with a very strong cast including comedic heavyweights Jon Pertwee, George Cole and Sid James. Sylvaine had established a working association with Rix and the Whitehall theatre which was further enhanced in 1963 when Terry acted in his Laughter from the Whitehall: Women Aren't Angels TV play. Wallace Douglas was the director.

Cast

Brian Rix...Henry Stirling

Jeanne Cook...dancer

Hazel Douglas...Beryl

Fabia Drake...Mrs Whittle

Leo Franklyn...Dr Smith

Helen Jessop...Honey

Jacqueline Jones...Angel

Basil Lord...Charley Stirling

Peter Mercier...Mendoza

Most of the cast were working together at the Whitehall, in One for the Pot, whilst Terry had escaped to Oxford, for the New Theatre's production of Babes in the Wood. Jeanne Cook was also in the Pot TV presentation; Hazel Douglas had a role in The Night We Got the Bird whilst Fabia Drake is in a few Terry-associated projects including What a Whopper! across her long career. Leo Franklyn, a well-established, London-born character actor, features in many Terry projects, in fact all that Terry was in; the gravel-voiced Leo was, too! Helen Jessop was also in Pot, the Dial Rix series and Laughter from the Whitehall TV productions. Jacqueline Jones could also be seen in Between the Balance sheets (1962) whilst Peter Mercier, brother-in-law of Brian Rix, was a long-term participant in many of the Rix film and television projects. His sister, Sheila Mercier is probably best-known as matriarchal Annie Sugden in Emmerdale Farm; she acted in almost all of her brother's various projects before being cast in the Yorkshire farm soap.

Larry Noble featured in The Night we Dropped a Clanger and many other Rix works as well as later on in an episode of Terry's Happy Ever After sitcom.

For pantomime that year, Terry took on the role of Miss Gooseberry Pimple, the new Governess in the aforementioned Babes. Written by od by Emile Littler presented at the aforementioned Oxford New Theatre from Boxing Day. Then falling on a Tuesday, the cast performed early matinees at 2.15pm (Monday/ Wednesday and Saturdays) and with a main performance at 7pm. It billed itself as "The Great Laughter Pantomime Babes in the Wood" and offered twelve scenes, several before the interval. Noticeable in its cast was Pat Kirkwood, a huge star of musical theatre before WWII. There is a colour illustration of Terry playing Miss Gooseberry created by Gilbert Sommerland and now held at the V&A museum, with an accompanying short note from Terry. What a sight he looked in a long, shoulder-length wig with curls! Terry would play again in Babes at the same theatre during for panto in 1973..

Cast

Vernon Drake...Sir Diddlum Dumpling, Sheriff of Nottingham

Dickie Henderson...Simple Simon

Terry...Miss Gooseberry Pimple, the new Governess

Maxine Shaw...Jack

Lynne Errington...Jill

Lauri Lupino Lane...Kind Heart, a Good Robber

George Truzzi…. Pie Face, a Bad Robber

Pat Kirkwood...Robin Hood

Margaret Macdonald...Maid Marion

Himself...Etcetera, a Rabbit

Anne Dalziel...Fairy Butterfly

Angela Handby...Principal Dancer

Eugene's Flying Ballet of Butterflyland, The Vera Legge Moonbeam Babes, The Sherwood Girls and The Normandy Singers.

Another busy year for Terry acting in a Sunday Night play shown on BBC 1 on 22 April 1962 and titled On a Clear Day; written by Christopher Bond, and once again directed by Darcy Conyers. Away from his acting, Terry had a hit record with novelty song My Brother. A joy to play again and again, it would forever be associated with him from this moment on. Using his little school boy character/ voice, the song would be included on endless children's compilation albums such as All Aboard! (EMI label, 1979) and is still being added.

Cast

Elizabeth Cummins...WPC Mary Blunt

Gerald Cross...clerk

Colin Douglas...DS Ormerod

Leo Franklyn...Police Sgt. Blunt

Judith Furse...WP Sgt. Bottle

Helen Jessop...WPC Lorna Peacock

Henry Kendall...Mr Justice Dryden

Basil Lord...'Fiddler' Cole

Sheila Mercier...Millie Blunt

Larry Noble...Mr Pringle

Brian Rix...PC Hobson

Terry Scott...PC 'Gunboat' Clitheroe

Carole Shelley...Betty Hobson

"Terry played a rather hopeless bachelor who dreams of aspiring wealth without having to work and is continually dreaming up ridiculous schemes to achieve it. As the gullible lodger, I was led by him into one adventure after another…"

Writing in his autobiography, Hugh Lloyd was referring to Hugh and I, a new sitcom which began on the BBC on 17 July 1962, with a total of six series running through to 1967. Producer David Croft in his autobiography recalls that co-stars Hugh and Terry had very opposing methods of learning their lines and were quite different in personalities. "I got on very well with Terry....he was a funny man and in my experience unselfish as a comic. He had a reputation for being difficult, but I found that he just wanted everything to be right and everyone to work their socks off to make the show good. Terry would work with enormous energy to achieve any object the plot required."

The diminutive Mr Croft, a writer/ producer and director hailed from a theatrical background; with both parents being actors. He signed up with Richard Stone, Terry's agent, just after the end of WWII and he would advance to become co-creator of TV gems Dad's Army, Are you Being Served? and Hi-De-Hi! But his role on Hugh and I was as producer only, although David did direct both the 1962 and 1963 Hugh and I segments included in the BBC special, Christmas Night with the Stars. He would also later produce the now-lost Hugh and I Spy series and the TV panto, Puss in Boots, in 1965, both of which starred Terry.

Incidental music in Hugh and I came from Wally Stott, the man who created the classic Hancock theme. John Chapman was the writer, with additional dialogue provided by comedy actor John Junkin (later to act alongside Terry in a funny episode of Terry and June and an actor on this show). In the first series, a collection of nine episodes were written, with the first, Fully Incomprehensible being shown on 17 July in a regular 8.45pm, Tuesday evening slot, with the rest of the series running on through to 11 September.

A new name in television had recognised Terry's obvious talent and suggested to him that he should be working on a television series. Terry was sceptical after having had a few false starts but when the name of Hugh Lloyd was mentioned, his ears pricked as the two had obviously already established a strong working relationship across summer shows and clubs. It would be Scott who suggested Chapman as writer and by the time of being Roy Plomley's guest on Desert Island Discs, Hugh and I had been running for four years and more than 60 episodes had been recorded. The presenter asked how much of the real Terry was like his TV alter ego, "Just a bit too much!" Laughed Scott in a programme that was subsequently broadcast in April 1966, "He's frightening the way he knows me. Course I must say, he blows me up a little. I'm not quite as bad, believe it or not, as

I sometimes appear [on screen]. Afterwards I think, I hope that, really and truly, I'm not that bad."

An official DVD release came in 2016 but containing only the surviving episodes across three discs, alas. Some had been lost or wiped whilst the remainder were recorded on monochrome film videotape or from a live transmission. The order of the episodes might also conflict with other listings as deciphering the exact chronology has proven tricky. But I have listed them in the best order that I could manage.

Hugh and Terry were getting on very well apart from Terry's petty mindedness being displayed at times with Hugh tending to ignore this rather than react. At the time of making the show, they lived a few miles apart; Terry in Wormley, nr Guildford and Hugh at Cobham. They also did club nights together whilst on the TV, at all kinds of venues across the country, including miners' clubs and colourful gigs in such places as Burnley and Greaseborough, near Rotherham amongst many others. Later, when they had become household names, the duo would take to advertising beer and be directed in a campaign which saw them working with Beatles film director Dick Lester. They would also attend a failed audition for Hollywood legend Otto Preminger who was casting a movie in the UK.

Episode one: *Fully Incomprehensible*

Hugh and Terry are joined by the cast regulars in this opening episode as we meet the folks who reside in Lobelia Avenue, Tooting, London.

Watch a couple of episodes of Hugh and I and the viewer forms the impression that Terry's pompous character, in his mid-30s and living at home with his mother, comes across as a bit of a Hancock clone. Fully Incomprehensible is a super start to the series and not only showcases the comedic talent of Terry Scott but also that of the dopey, accident-prone lodger, Hugh (Hugh Lloyd).

After reading about the handsome profits reaped by the insurance industry, Terry and Hugh visit a local company to gain an insight, with the idea being that they will start their own business from home. Here they meet Carry On actor Brian Oulton who almost persuades Terry to take out a policy before the boys run out of his office, shattering the glass in his door as a consequence. Clearly recorded live, Mr Oulton stumbles over his lines once or twice before returning at the close of the story.

Setting up Scott. Lloyd Insurance Co., the duo share a lovely bit of comedy when Terry attempts to fasten a sign outside the house, much to annoyance of neighbour Arthur Crispin (Wallas Eaton). Throughout the show these two would come into conflict, with Terry often pulling on his spectacles so as not to be hit!

Struggling to find any custom, Hugh and Terry call in at the Wormold's home and engage in a batty exchange with them but no sale. Patricia Hayes and Cyril Smith put in star turns, as Griselda and Harold, and often steal the scenes that they feature in throughout Hugh and I.

Mr Oulton tracks the boys down and demands compensation for his damaged door but ends up taking out a policy with Terry or at least he would have done if he had not been struck on the head by their sign on his way out!

Cast

Terry Scott...Terry

Hugh Lloyd...Hugh

Cyril Smith...Harold Wormold

Wallas Eaton...Arthur Crispin

Vi Stephens...Mrs Ada Scott

Patricia Hayes...Mrs Wormold

Also starring Norma Parnell.

Episode two: *A Brace of Pheasants*

Terry. "My friend and I, we want to buy some bangers."

Assistant. "Might I suggest the butcher's?"

A true highlight in the opening series, Hugh's desire to spend a holiday in Brighton is quashed by Terry using all their money to arrange a grouse shooting trip in Scotland. With additional dialogue supplied by John Junkin, also in a supporting role, this second episode finds the duo wishing that they had gone to London-by-the-sea come the story close.

Terry's penchant for hats is given an airing, whilst comedy partner Lloyd offers a series of facial gestures taken from the Stan Laurel school of bemusement. In a funny scene, both show their ignorance of the shooting culture upon visiting a rather posh equipment store in preparation for their coming trip. Anthony Sharp is a joy as the plumy sales assistant gradually unable to hide his contempt at their collective lack of knowledge.

Here they meet the portly Lord Popham (the "irrepressible" Fred Emney, as Hugh Lloyd remembered him) who will subsequently invite them to join himself and his wife on a shoot.

At Kings Cross train station, Terry arrives in full country attire; deer stalker, three-quarter pants and all, whilst Hugh lags behind, lumbered with transporting the bags. Years later, Nicholas Lyndhurst as Rodney in Only Fools and Horses would cover similar ground. Derek Guyler, remembered for his role in Please, Sir! features as a train worker and would return for future appearances in the show. But it is an over-excited Terry Scott that steals the scene once he and Hugh join a crowded compartment on board. Struggling for space, he still wants to chat and imposes himself on the others, getting them to hold his snacks for the trip, as Hugh looks on.

The duo join Lord and Lady Popham on an early shoot but manage to become embroiled in an army manoeuvres running concurrently.

Cast

Fred Emney...Lord Popham

Frank Williams...army officer

Deryck Guyler...ticket inspector

Judith Furse...Lady Sybil Popham

Anthony Sharp...shopkeeper

Also in the cast: Robert Raglan, John Junkin, Michael Stainton, Peggy Ann Clifford and Rosemary Neil Smith.

Episode three: *Here Comes the Bride*

Another cracking instalment finds both Terry and Hugh on crutches by the end of the episode. This is due to their shared interest in Norma (Jill Curzon), daughter of Mr and Mrs Crispin (Wallas Eaton and Mollie Sugden), and sustained after each of their attempts to do the latest dance fad the "twist."

A pedantic Terry is irritated at his tea being late due to Hugh chatting to Norma whilst meant to be tending to the garden. Seeing her in a swimsuit, both fall for her obvious delights but I have to say that her acting skills prove limited. Getting them to dance with her, Mr Crispin storms in and frog marches her home.

Constantly calling in to the Scott's, the Wormolds often do so as their television set frequently breaks down. But a cohesive conversation with them is rarely possible, as Harold (Smith) is hard-of-hearing and never gets the gist of what is being said.

Elsewhere, Terry secretly visits a marriage bureau run by Ms Willow, Irene Handl on top form, to set Hugh up with a wife. Unfortunately, the potty Gladys (Priscilla Morgan) is sent to meet him but there proves to be no spark between them, possibly due to Hugh having no idea why she is there.

Seemingly worried as to Norma's unsuitability for lodger friend Hugh, the latter decides that he and Ms Crispin will elope. But not telling her, he climbs into her bedroom at night and mistakes her for her mother Mollie Sugden (who likes the attention before she realises that it is not coming from her husband!)

Injured as a result of having been pushed off the ladder whilst making a hasty exit, Hugh is bed ridden and feeling blue that Norma has not come to visit him. When she does, the only problem being is that Terry is taking her out dancing as he fancied her all along.

Irene Handl exudes much warmth here in her single scene with Terry, they had worked on a number of projects together previously.

Cast

Cyril Smith... Harold Wormold
Wallas Eaton...Arthur Crispin
Vi Stephens...Mrs Ada Scott
Mollie Sugden...Mrs Crispin
Priscilla Morgan...Gladys
Patricia Hayes...Mrs Wormold
Jill Curzon...Norma
Irene Handl...Miss Willow

Episode four: *Royal Visit*

Now with writer John Chapman fittingly receiving a credit in the opening titles of the show, the super ensemble cast settled in nicely and sparked well off each other. Hugh Lloyd is often made to look the fool and this outing continues the trend when his character displays his naïve ignorance when placed in unfamiliar social settings. Frustrated at having to help clean the silverware on his Saturday off, in Royal Visit, that place is a posh menswear outfitters where he and Terry are dealt with by scoffing guest star Ronnie Stevens. That is until he sees a letter confirming an official visit is indeed being paid to Lobelia Avenue, to the Scott household, by a royal party. Councillor Jones (Frank Thornton) had previously called in to ask if they would like to facilitate the guests.

News soon spreads and the dreaded Crispin's call in, unsuccessfully pleading for Terry and his mum, Ada and Hugh to allow their Norma an opportunity to be presented, also.

All dressed up for the day of the visit, Terry and Hugh are kitted out in mourning suits (something that would be repeated in another episode and, much later, for Terry, in the 1972 film Bless this House).

Alongside his mother, looking a bizarre delight in a hat full of fake fruit, they anxiously await an arrival never comes.

Cast

Cyril Smith...Harold Wormold

Wallas Eaton...Arthur Crispin

Vi Stephens...Mrs Scott

Patricia Hayes...Mrs Wormold

Mollie Sugden...Mrs Crispin

Jill Curzon...Norma

Jerry Verno...Tompkins

Episode five: *A Fete worse than Death*

Vicar "Mr Lloyd, would you say that we were stampeded into things by Mr Scott?

Hugh "Yes".

A pompous Terry is on the church fundraising committee who agree to his idea of a history-through-the-ages pageant titled The Glory that is England. Written, directed and narrated by Terry, the cast attend a rehearsal where his exhaustive attempts at order soon collapse in an enjoyable episode dominated by Terry. Joan Hickson and Julian Orchard, both working with Terry elsewhere, were guest stars, with John Chapman script writer (with additional dialogue from John Junkin).

Cast

Joan Hickson...Miss Jenks

Julian Orchard...Mr Spriggs

Cyril Smith...Harold Wormold

Wallas Eaton...Arthur Crispin

Vi Stephens...Mrs Ada Scott

Patricia Hayes...Mrs Wormold

Mollie Sugden...Mrs Crispin

Jill Curzon...Norma

Also in the cast: George Betton, Betty Turner, Patsy Smart, Anna Gilcrist and Peggy Ann Clifford. Miss Gilcrist (Gilchrist) had been in What a Whopper! (1961).

Episode six: It's a Dog's Life

Attempting to do the Times crossword, Terry finds his patience tried by the irritations provided by both his mother and Hugh. Norma then calls in, with news of her father's whippet's latest litter and to see if they would like one of the puppies. Terry is adamant in the negative but the others like the idea.

Hugh takes things further by visiting the local dogs home and smuggling back a puppy, to be called Patricia, into his bedroom and away from Mr Scott. Not anticipating that the Wormolds have been invited around for tea, an amusing scene follows whereby Hugh pinches bits of food from the guests by stuffing it into his coat pocket. This confuses the permanently bemused Harold, dressed like an old-fashioned Neville Chamberlain, into thinking that he has eaten when really Hugh has pinched his liver and bacon for the dog. Hugh even involves Terry, nodding to indicate that Harold took his bacon rather than revealing his guilt!

Come evening time, Hugh frightens Terry and Mrs Scott by making all kinds of noise in his attempt to placate the dog. Patricia is eventually discovered and Terry makes Hugh return her before relenting and allowing him to take her back home with them. But that is not before Terry comes out with two extra dogs, too.

Cast

Cyril Smith...Harold Wormold

Wallas Eaton...Arthur Crispin

Vi Stephens...Mrs Ada Scott

Patricia Hayes...Mrs Wormold

Mollie Sugden...Mrs Crispin

Jill Curzon...Norma

Episode seven: *Putting on the Ritz*

Terry decides to commit himself to finding employment and decides upon working as an aid to a wealthy American whom he arranges to meet at the posh Carlton hotel. Dragging Hugh and his £14/10 wage packet along, the two manage to cause quite an upset at the hotel restaurant, with Hugh Lloyd particularly amusing here.

After much champagne and expensive nosh has been enjoyed, a huge bill arrives and the duo has to work in the kitchen to pay off the remainder of the astronomical charge. Fred Emney, as the dry-witted Lord Popham, returns in a rather oddly-written role.

Cast

Cyril Smith...Harold Wormold

Wallas Eaton...Arthur Crispin   Vi Stephens...Mrs Ada Scott

Patricia Hayes...Mrs Wormold   Jill Curzon...Norma

Fred Emney...Lord Popham

Jeremy Hawk...waiter

Also starring: Tom Chatto, Rex Garner, Charles Hill, James Forth, Laura Thurlow.

Episode eight: *Love thy Neighbour*

Shown on 4 September, this funny episode features an automobile theme; seeing Terry's neighbours, the Crispin's, buying a noisy/ fuel-filled car and causing problems by parking outside the Scott home. In the early hours, Terry and Hugh take evasive action by painting a line outside so as to deter the Crispin's from doing it again. Unfortunately they are seen by a policeman whilst doing this and ultimately fined £5 each (with Hugh paying for both of them, naturally). This being a comedy, Terry suggests to Hugh that he should buy a vehicle and after obtaining a wreck of a car and planning a trip with his mother and the dotty couple next door, they realise that neither of them can actually drive.

Cast

William Fox...Sir Ralph Springer

Cyril Smith...Harold Wormold

Wallas Eaton...Arthur Crispin

Vi Stephens...Mrs Ada Scott

Patricia Hayes...Mrs Wormold

Jill Curzon...Norma

Also starring: Arthur Hewlett and Roger Avon.

Episode nine: *Happy Birthday to You*

It is the morning of Hugh's birthday but his excitement is soon quashed upon discovering that no one seems to have remembered. As the day progresses, he begins to drop a hint or two.

Cast

Cyril Smith...Harold Wormold

Wallas Eaton...Arthur Crispin

Vi Stephens...Mrs Ada Scott   Patricia Hayes...Mrs Wormold

Mollie Sugden...Mrs Crispin   Jill Curzon...Norma

Also starring: William Fox, Arthur Howlett and Roger Avon.

Feedback proved positive when the surviving episodes were collected, "The opening episode is the weakest, but once past that Hugh and I reveals itself as a thoroughly decent sitcom that genuinely raises a laugh - either through John Chapman's dialogue or the pitch-perfect antics of the leads: a blustering, know-it-all Terry Scott and his put upon lodger Hugh Lloyd." Offers Ian Beard on amazon.co.uk, "There's good support too from Vi Stevens as Terry's mum, and two sets of neighbours: the permanently befuddled Patricia Hayes and Cyril Smith, (later Jack Haig), and the thinking-themselves-better Mollie Sugden and Wallas Eaton, plus their sex-pot daughter Jill Curzon."

Another purchaser, Anthony Howell, reflects, "[I] missed this when it was on TV so when I saw the DVD was available I wanted to watch it and I have not been disappointed at all." He adds, "The characters are very funny, Terry playing a slimy smart Alec who isn't as smart as he thinks he is, And Hugh being the dimwit who isn't a total pushover. Most of the episodes are good with some not so...but all very watchable." Whilst another fan, David Crabbe, also on the same site, writes, "I can just about recall this being on TV but more importantly I do seem to recall that everyone including any visitors to our home would sit around the old set and laugh hysterically throughout the entire show as I remember them doing likewise to Arthur Haynes. Amazingly they laughed a lot more and louder to these two and Haynes than I can ever recall them doing to good old Tony Hancock..."

Also on the small screen, Terry would be seen in the opening episode of a new BBC series of plays called Dial Rix back on 12 September. He would work on four of the nine episodes, all recorded live across fifty minutes, with the premise finding Brian Rix ringing up a relative at the start of each show and the story developing from there. Various issues of the day were lampooned. The first story, Between the Balance Sheets, written by John Chapman and directed by Darcy Conyers, was well-received but Rix was angry that his shows never seemed to be given a regular scheduling time. Sheets featured Terry as Mr Hemmingway and it also gave a role to Carole Shelley, seen the previous year in another Terry-associated project, No, My Darling Daughter! (1961)

Cast

Brian Rix...Basil Rix
Leo Franklyn...Uncle Luke
Elspet Gray...Pamela Rix   Patrick Cargill...Martell
Arthur Brough...englishman
Golda Casimir...Madame Martell
Robert Checksfield...chauffer   Linda Dixon...Miss Logan
Helen Jessop...Eloise   Jacqueline Jones...girl
Jeanette Landis...Simone   Peter Mercier...porter
Martin Miller...Mr Green   Terry...Mr Hemmingway
Carole Shelley...chambermaid   Stuart Sherwin...TV salesman

Then on 5 October, What a Drag, with its theme mocking cigarette advertising, became the second Dial Rix offering; again directed by Darcy Conyers from a John Chapman script.

Cast

Brian Rix...Bert Rix
John Chapman...Ted
Pearson Dodd...
Colin Douglas...TV producer
Leo Franklyn...Dr Blinker
Elspet Gray...Cynthia
Helen Jessop...Miss Nolan
John Le Mesurier...George
Andrew Sachs...Harry
Terry...Sydney Keen

Remaining in that month, Round the Bend became the third instalment in the series. This was directed by Darcy Conyers and co-written by Ray Cooney and Tony Hilton, and broadcast on 26 October.

Cooney began his theatrical career as a boy actor in 1946. He served his apprenticeship by playing in various repertory companies before graduating to Brian Rix's company at the Whitehall Theatre in 1956. With free time in between performances, many of the cast members took to writing and would advance to lengthy careers in this area. He co-wrote One for the Pot with Tony Hilton and many others, some with John Chapman.

As producer and director, he has been responsible for over thirty London productions. Advancing to 1983, Ray formed the Theatre of Comedy Company and he became its first Artistic Director. During Ray's tenure the company produced over twenty plays including having Terry in Run for Your Wife!

Tony Hilton had seen his television script for Round the Bend become a 1962 Brian Rix stable offering that facilitated a role for Terry Scott. Tony also created the film screenplay for The Night we got the Bird, and the theatre farce One for the Pot which was presented on BBC television back on 11 March with Terry in amongst its cast. Regrettably, in its condensed form, the play did not transfer well to television. The tricks and gags simply failing to come across as well as they had done so in front of a live theatre audience.

Cast

Brian Rix...Barrington Rix
Patrick Cargill...Bond
Hazel Douglas...Mrs Birkett
Leo Franklyn...Sam

Elspet Gray...u/known Rix

Terry...Maple

Another TV appearance came Terry's way in the form of the ITV pop music show Thank your Lucky Stars. With a running time of forty minutes, the show went out at 5:50pm on 15 December; he would feature in a busy line-up that also included subsequent panto co-stars Joyce Blair and Mark Wynter.

On Boxing Day, the fifth and final entry that year in the Dial Rix cannon arrived. Directed by Wallace Douglas and written by Christopher Bond, the farce No Plums in the Pudding delved into the area of the office Christmas party. Broadcast at 5pm, cast members Rix, Leo Franklyn, Basil Lord, Larry Noble, Peter Mercier, Hazel Douglas, Helen Jessop, Linda Dixon, Colin Douglas were all appearing at the Whitehall Theatre in One for the Pot. Also in the cast were Andrew Sachs, William Kendall, Elspet Gray, Gilbert Harrison, Hubert Cross, Peter Mercier, Joan Sanderson, John Chapman, Hugh McDermott and Patrick Cargill. Patrick was a plumy-voiced actor/ writer forever associated with the Father Dear Father TV series. He was in five Dial Rix episodes with Terry, between 1962-3.

Elspet Gray, a beautiful, RADA-trained actress acted in projects alongside Terry: No Plums in the Pudding and in a 1964 radio broadcast. She was married to Brian Rix, the lucky Mr Rix was a very hard worker and presented more than eighty television plays across his career, most of which would be recorded live. Some audio recordings were made and later, recordings on tape were facilitated only to be recycled by the BBC (due to high costs) and mostly now regarded as lost.

Cast

Brian Rix...Boy Rix   Patrick Cargill...Gunga Din

John Chapman...Teddy Gibbons

Colin Douglas...fat furniture man

Leo Franklyn...Jack

Elspet Gray...Penelope Rix

Helen Jessop...Norma

Larry Noble...Mr Jolliboy

Andrew Sachs...thin furniture man

Joan Sanderson...Mrs Hathaway

Terry...Toby Murgatroyd

Since first acting in the One for the Pot at the Whitehall back in 1961, Terry reprised his role for the BBC television broadcast of 11

March this year coming under the Sunday Night Play banner. The cast consisted of Robert Checksfield, Jeanne Cook, Hazel Douglas, Leo Franklyn. Helen Jessop, Basil Lord, Shelia Mercier, Larry Noble, Brian Rix and Terry as Jonathan Hardcastle.

Directed by Henry Kendall, another old hand in the Rix team, he was an actor/producer/ director whose career had started back in the 1920s, he also had an acting role in Nothing Barred (1961), with Terry also in that, too! Sadly, he died in June of that year.

Actor Nicholas Phipps, who has a part in the film, wrote the screenplay to A Pair of Briefs, which took its inspiration from the Harold Brooke and Kay Bannerman play How Say You? Ralph Thomas and Betty E.Box came straight from No, My Darling Daughter (1961) where the same playwrights saw their work adapted into a movie script.

The film opens with a somewhat gratuitous scene of the attractive Frances Pilbright (Mary Peach) preparing for his first day as a new barrister, whose comfortable life is immediately contrasted with that of Tony (Michael Craig); the former driving a sports car and living in a lovely house whilst the latter, a shared flat and riding a scooter to work! On their way to Chambers, their paths cross, literally, as they almost collide. Mr Craig is an actor who makes his acting look effortless, and once again he is ever-dependable and super cool; riding a scooter back in the days when you didn't need a helmet!

Tony (Craig) is constantly struggling with mundane cases offering little recompense, not helped by solicitor and house mate, Hubert (a smarmy John Stabding). Neither seems to be fans of female barristers and we overhear Tony saying as much when the newest member walks into Chambers: the sexy Ms.Peach. She's a young woman with far-reaching family connections (her uncle being Sir John (Ronald Culver) but it seems that even early on that the two will get together. All a bit predictable, as it is often the case in his films (think back to Daughter with Juliet Mills). Comic actor Graham Stark makes a brief appearance in the case preceding the one that Craig and Peach will contest and this allows us to visit a strip club run by Aussie Bill Kerr, where Amanda Barrie, Joan Sims and The Rag Trade actress Judy Carne all appear momentarily but memorably.

The always-dependable Brenda de Banzie plays 2 roles for the price of one here, initially a mink coat, chauffeur-driven lady driven to a posh hotel where she transforms into a dowdy character for plot reasons soon to become apparent. The plain Gladys (de Banzie) sets off to locate the spouse that deserted her, Sydney (a chipper Ron Moody) to prove that they were once married and he has breached her restriction of conjugal rights or something similar. He denies knowing her at all, whilst his brassy young partner Pearl (Liz Fraser) gives her short shift and so she decides upon a legal case.

Although Frances and Tony are from the same Chambers, each decides to represent opposing parties and that's when the drama starts. The exotically-titled Ms. de Banzie was also in Too Many Crooks (1959), a splendid comedy vehicle which offered a small role for Terry Scott. She made her name in theatre before stepping into films wherein she creates much warmth on screen.

Meanwhile, her absent screen hubby Moody would also be seen in Murder most Foul (1964), as can Terry, and he proves to be very funny in Briefs, as the shifty Sydney, sparking off a guffawing Liz Fraser. Comedy favourite Liz is not called upon much here but to look very sexy and have huge fun as someone who finds Sydney's witticisms absolutely hilarious (he often concludes a punch line with "...as the monkey said to the this/or that....").

On the day of the court hearing, Brenda asks a weary uniformed Terry Scott the way to Court 5, whilst Pearl (Fraser) is convinced by the others that she should not accompany her man in court and so she steps outside. Here she is met by dark suited, cap-wearing Mr Scott who mistakenly thinks that she is looking for a water fountain when she asks him where she could find a drink.

"A water fountain? I said a drink, not a wash!" She engages him in a bit of banter, flirting and then asking if he would like to accompany her. A billowing Terry says he cannot leave his post.

As the proceedings continue, outside we again see Terry as a sloshed Liz returns to the courts, skipping inside and soon causing a disturbance. She proves quite embarrassing in the film: gauche but great as a drunk! Ms Fraser is also in I'm All Right, Jack, The Night we got the Bird, The Night we dropped a Clanger and Double Bunk, whilst A Pair of Briefs concluded her acting association with Terry after featuring alongside him in these 5 films and an episode of early TV comedy series Great Scott, It's Maynard back in 1955.

Presided over by Judge James Robertson Justice, he of the booming voice and strong speaking voice, starred in 3 films which gave roles for a young Terry Scott: here, Father Came Too! and Doctor in Clover. Unfortunately, in Briefs he is not called upon for any humorous moments but only given lots of wordy dialogue and little else of interest, alas. The film is just a bit dull, the courtroom scenes are simply too wordy, the fault of scriptwriter Phipps, missing his usual moustache. Nicholas led quite an extraordinary life before entering show business and has an extensive list of writing credits.

Gladys (de Banzie) loses the case, despite the best efforts of her representative but she knowingly does not want to appeal. Outside the courts, Tony (Craig) sees her and Sydney talking before the latter burns their wedding certificate in front of her.

He follows her back to the staff entrance of a rather posh hotel, passing Anthony Sagar (an actor to be seen in Carry On Loving (1970) and a number of others in the series, back to Stores Sergeant in Carry On Sergeant (1958). Avoiding the attention of house detective Ronnie Stevens, Gladys tells him the truth and Tony returns to the chambers to tell Frances. The likeable, cheery Stevens would be in an episode of

Ⓐ Ⓑ Ⓒ ❶ ❷ ❸ ❹ East st BRIGHTON 27010

Cast

Michael Craig...Tony Stevens
Mary Peach...Frances Pilbright
Brenda de Banzie...Gladys Worthing
James Robertson Justice... Mr Justice Haddon
Ronald Culver...Sir John Pilbright
Liz Fraser...Gloria
Ron Moody...Sidney
Jameson Clark...George
Charles Heslop...Peebles
Bill Kerr...Victor
Nicholas Phipps...Sutcliffe
Joan Sims...Gale
John Stabding...Hubert
Amanda Barrie...exotic dancer
Judy Carne...exotic dancer 2
Barbara Ferris...Gloria
Myrtle Reed...barmaid
Terry...Officer at law courts
Graham Stark...witness

Ronnie Stevens...hotel under-manager
Cyril Chamberlain... policeman
Vivienne Martin...maid
Anthony Sagar...hotel meat porter
Michael Ward...dresser

No unaccompanied children admitted after 7p.m
ALL PROGRAMMES MAY BE SUBJECT TO LATE CHANGE

Terry and June from 1987 (The Family Way) and an older episode of Hugh and I. You will also see him as the TV host working with Norman Vaughan in Doctor in Clover (1966) and in Nearly a Nasty Accident (1961).

Back at chambers, the idealistic young woman fails to believe the news that her client does not want to appeal, until a letter is dropped off explaining her wises. Distraught, she is comforted by her colleague with a kiss!

However, after the shenanigans presented in his court earlier, Harry (Justice) wants to discipline the young barristers but they warn him that by doing so, it would be problematic. The former admires Tony's pluck at standing up to the billowing Judge and it somehow transpires that the young legal eagles are to be married. It is also revealed that JRJ knew exactly what Gladys was intending by finally removing any financial claim that he might have made upon discovering her new life.

The final scene is more amusing, seeing Sydney and Pearl at a petrol station with his former wife pulling up in her chauffeur-driven vehicle in a car crammed with four young boys.

"I don't know what to say!" blurts Sydney, upon seeing the glamorous Gladys. Deadpan, she replies, "Don't you Harry? Well, why don't you ask that monkey of yours!" This produces a huge guffaw from Pearl (Fraser).

Extras: Jameson Clark: who played a uniformed copper in The Bridal Path (1959), in a non-Terry scene, also features in this film. Bill Kerr: a perennial cheerful chap on screen, is briefly in Doctor in Clover (1966).

"There's a party going on there that I think you might like to join.."

This was part of the introduction to Christmas Night with the Stars, presented by popular actor Jack Warner on BBC 1 at 7:15pm on Christmas Day. It contained a shortened episode of Hugh and I, with a familial script by John Chapman and direction by David Croft. It was one of ten popular, light entertainment shows to be featured, including The Likely Lads. Running at less than double figures, this mini-episode found Terry and Hugh celebrating Christmas with family and friends at home, including Hancock regular Patricia Hayes, a comely Jill Curzon, Mollie Sugden, Charles Dyer, Jack Haig, Vi Stevens and Maurice Podbrey. The segment resurfaced in recent years and is detailed as: "A fondly remembered long running sitcom that ran...between 1962-68. Starring Hugh Lloyd and Terry Scott, both stars in their own right...the Scott character often has aspirations to wealth, devising grand schemes to make a fortune, whilst the slightly dozy Hugh works at the factory...and has nothing more than a regular income."

Terry will make three separate appearances on the show, in all. Also featured this year were June Whitfield, Russ Conway and Jill Curzon, each having a working association with Terry Scott at some point in their careers. The host was the bland Eamonn Andrews, whom Terry would meet again for his own This is Your Life tribute.

Streatham-born Ms Whitfield worked with so many comedy greats over the years: Hancock, Peter Sellers, Frankie Howard, Arthur Askey, Ronnie Barker, Peter Butterworth, Harry H Corbett, Eric Sykes et al!

Meanwhile, Terry was appearing in 'Babes in the Wood' at the Hippodrome, Golders Green, London. In a smashing cast, he was joined by Norman Caley, Hugh Lloyd (as Simple Simon), Terry (playing Miss Gooseberry Pimple), Charlie Naughton, Angela Puddy, Celia Cross, George Truzzi, Lauri Lupino Lane, John Gower, Margaret Heath, Mary Murphy and Elizabeth Hearn. Terry would return to this theatre some years later, utilising it as a rehearsal venue for another panto. Sadly, the Golders Green theatre (below) no longer presents shows of any kind.

1963 would prove to be an equally hectic twelve months, back in June Terry and Hugh played the Spa Royal Hall, Bridlington; after a recent early season of variety at Scarborough, in May. Here, headliner Russ Conway, the piano man, had a nervous breakdown. Agent Richard Stone offered

to put Terry on at short notice to replace him but he wasn't needed when Conway managed to soldier on.

Following the recent first series run of Hugh and I, from Tuesday 21 May, a batch of twelve new episodes made up the second series of this amusing BBC sitcom. Commencing with Lost Property, a further eleven continued through to 2 December, in an 8pm slot.

Episode one: *Lost Property*

Hugh. "You must think I'm daft?"

Terry. "I do. But what's that got to do with it."

This hugely enjoyable opening episode was broadcast on 21 May and asked 'What would you do with a case full of money?' Contributing writer John Junkin puts in a cameo appearance as a bus conductor perturbed by the behaviour of a day dreaming Hugh. Forming the wrong impression, he puts him off the bus after hastily gathering together Hugh's coat and possessions.

Arriving home much later, Hugh discovers that an attaché case has been inadvertently put in alongside his things and he gasps upon seeing what is inside it: £1,000 in bank notes. Terry wants to utilise the cash but eventually gets the idea to place an advertisement in the local paper to enable the owner, a certain "C.E.W", whose initials are inscribed on the bag, to collect it from the Scott residency. This proves a problem, as first neighbours Cecil and Griselda think that it his (seeing as his full name is Cecil Ernest Wormold) and then Crispin (Wallas Easton) thinks it might belong to his wife, Ethel Carmen aka Mollie Sugden!

Dismissing both, a chancer (Geoffrey Hibbert) calls and spies the case stuffed behind a cushion on the sofa before the others notice that he has done so. Terry almost gives it to him before the man's true identity s revealed and he flees. Concerned, Hugh demands that they take it to the police station. Of course, once there, Terry is happy to leave his details in case of a reward being offered but is furious with Hugh upon realising that he has left it on the bus.

Cast

Wallas Eaton...Arthur Crispin

Vi Stephens...Mrs Ada Scott

Patricia Hayes...Grizelda Wormold

Jill Curzon...Norma Crispin

Mollie Sugden...Mrs Crispin

Jack Haig...Cecil Wormold

Geoffrey Hibbert...Mr Blake

John Junkin...Bus Conductor

Dave Carey...Desk Sgt

Joan Emney...Second bus passenger

Vlasta Hardy...First bus passenger

Episode two: *Trad Fad Lloyd*

"It must be jelly, 'cos jam don't shake like that."

This has to be held to be one of the very funniest episodes of Hugh and I. Finding the know-all Terry clashing with the hip, jazz-loving Hugh in a smashing story that also gives much screen time to the sexy Norma (Jill Curzon). Both lads fancy her and it isn't surprising when you see her: all busty curves, slightly vacuous and far too young for either of them! Hugh Lloyd is in top form, visiting a record shop and seeing Norma dancing to a record in one of the listening booths (where you could hear a record played back to see if you might want to purchase it). She tells him that she is the singer in the Tooting Trad Types who are in need of a rehearsal space for an upcoming competition with a £200 prize. He offers the Scott living room not realising that Terry and his mother will be returning home after having tea at the Wormold's.

Terry is not a fan until being told about the prize money and he suggests that they need a manager and he knows just the man: him! Norma's dad usurps Terry, leaving him to set up his own band, the Lobelia Trio, consisting of his mother and the Griswold's. Conducted by Mr Scott, chaos reigns as they play the wrong music, get heckled by Crispin and in the confusion, Cecil (Jack Haig) plays God save the Queen instead of a Rachmaninov piece. Great fun.

Cast

90

Wallas Eaton...Arthur Crispin

Vi Stephens...Mrs Ada Scott

Patricia Hayes...Grizelda Wormold

Jill Curzon...Mrs Crispin

Mollie Sugden...Carmen Crispin

Jack Haig...Cecil Wormold

Also starring: Peter Reeves, Tom Gill, Jerry Verno, Anna Gilcrist, James McManus and Freddy Randall.

Episode three: *Wedding Bells*

Sitcoms always have certain character types and Hugh and I has its fair share of eccentrics. A cheeky Aunt Mavis (Margery Withers)imposes on Ada and Terry by arranging her daughter's wedding reception to take place at the Scott's without asking them in advance. A £50 cheque helps sweeten things but Ada wishes that she had been asked first. The money appeals to tight-wad Terry and so they agree.

Sheila Steafel as Ivy put's in a fabulously funny showing and Brian Tyler is fun as her intended, the rather wet, Syd. This episode also introduces Cecil, Jack Haig, as Mrs Wormold's brother-in-law. But his O.T.T performance proves embarrassing viewing before settling down in subsequent story lines; sad to see that Jack Haig had to be brought in to fill a character replacement.

Julian Orchard pops up as the worried organist at the local church where the wedding is due to take place. Ivy and her mother Mavis arrive at the Scott's and come the big day, the adenoidal bride-to-be has doubts. Seeing Hugh in his top hat and tails rekindles her interest in him before Syd turns up and says that the wedding is off as he has contracted measles from his original best man.

Cast

Wallas Eaton...Arthur Crispin

Vi Stephens...Mrs Ada Scott

Patricia Hayes...Grizelda Wormold

Jill Curzon...Mrs Crispin

Mollie Sugden...Carmen Crispin

Jack Haig...Cecil Wormold

Julian Orchard...Mr Spriggs

Also starring: Brian Tyler.

Episode four: *April in Paris*

Hugh's plans for a few days away camping prove a flop and upon his swift return Terry persuades him to take a flight to Paris with him. Checking-in proves an ordeal before advancing onboard where Terry has to explain the function of many things including seat belts, sick bags, boiled sweets to help ease air pressure (the latter of which proves alien to both of them). After arriving in Paris, attempting to book a room proves difficult as neither of them speak more than a sprinkiling of French. Misunderstandings abound with hoteliers Jacques Cey and Sonia Windsor (both in past episodes) and the boys end up trapped in a lift.

When they are eventually released, the two little Englanders decide to head back to the airport. Frank Williams, seen in episodes of Hugh and I and The Gnomes of Dulwich, features as a plane passenger who inadvertently pinches Hugh's food!

Cast

Vi Stephens...Mrs Ada Scott

Also starring: Ian Wallace, Ken Roberts, John G.Heller, Robin Hunter, Peter Whitbread, Jen Browne, Beth Harris, Sarah Brackett.

Episode 5: *Prison Visitor*

Terry. "I want you to regard 33 Lobelia Avenue, Tooting, as your haven and rest."

Another smashing entry finds a pious Terry trying his hand as a prison visitor but immediately irks hard man inmate "32439" (Kenneth J.Warren), enjoying himself).

After the uncomfortable visit, Terry and his dopey mother are shocked upon discovering that he has escaped and come to their home with a gun. Roughed up and threatened, Hugh also joins the trio, reluctantly after failing to understand Terry's signals a moment earlier that there was a problem. Daft neighbours Cecil (Jack Haig) and Grizelda (Patricia Hayes) turn up unannounced, wanting to watch the end of Z Cars on their TV after their own breaks down. Inviting themselves in, neither seems to have a clue as to what they have walked into.

Hugh then fails in his attempt to seek help from a confused Mrs Crispin (a glowing Mollie Sugden) and in his innocent vagueness, always a contrived plot device in comedy-land, she feels insulted and so sends her furious husband round to confront him. The fugitive cannot quite believe the continuous disruptions in a fun episode which ends with Hugh and Terry both being taken away by the police!

Following the sad death of Cyril Smith in March 1963, his character, the hard-of-hearing Harold, was replaced by brother-in-law Cecil.

Cast

Jack Haig...Cecil

Kenneth J.Warren...Prisoner #32439

Also starring: George Betton and Frank Sieman.

Episode six: *The 19th Hole*

A misguided snob, Terry attempts to improve Hugh's social interaction by getting him involved with the bowls club. But when sexy Norma calls around to invite him to the cinema, Hugh eagerly accepts and goes off with her instead. An annoyed Terry is agitated still further upon discovering that the Crispins are the newest members and so he decides to turn his attention to golf. The transparent animosity between Crispin (Wallas Eaton) and Scott is never far waya and it always provides the viewer with a chuckle or two.

Taking Lloyd along with him, Terry and Hugh are soon shown to be out of their depth at a rather posh golf club frequented by a plumy-voiced Pat Coombs (going aginst type) and the ubiquitous Peggy Ann Clifford. It is whilst there that they see Lord Popham (Fred Emney), a man that never rememebers having met them previously but who invites them to play a round. Hugh proves hopeless whilst Terry manages a fluke by hitting a hole-in-one.

Back at the clubhouse, where drinks are not cheap, Terry is obliged to buy a round, such is the custom upon achieving such a feat.

Cast

Wallas Eaton...Arthur Crispin

Vi Stephens...Mrs Ada Scott

Patricia Hayes...Grizelda Wormold

Jill Curzon...Norma Crispin

Mollie Sugden...Mrs Crispin

Jack Haig...Cecil Wormold

Fred Emney...General Lord Cecil Popham

Also starring: Charles Hill, Fred McNaughton, Dennis Ramsden, Ian Gray and Jeremy Hawk.

Episode seven: *A Turn for the Nurse*

Nurse. "Are you feeling all right?"

Terry. "Oh yes."

Nurse. "I thought you were looking a little odd."

Hugh. "Oh that's quite usual."

When Mrs Scott is bed-bound with a bad back, the usually pampered Terry has to take care of the house. But having no idea as to where anything is stored, let alone any domestic capabilities, he enlists Hugh. Ever the sly operator, Terry also manipulates Mrs Wormold (Patricia Hayes) to help.

A young Derek Nimmo is the doctor making a house call but in a delightful mix-up, he ends up treating Cecil instead. Mrs Crispin also mucks in and a third lady, from the WRVS, arrives with more food for the boys but ultimately, they miss out as everyone quarrels.

When an attractive District Nurse (Jean Harvey) arrives, both Hugh and Terry vie for her attention and they even ignore the pretty Norma when she calls in. Mrs Scott makes a swift recovery and so Terry feigns discomfort in his finger from a splinter suffered earlier so as to get the nurse to return. It works, but only in the new guise of the ample Peggy Ann Clifford, a supporting player in many episodes of Hugh and I. Jean Harvey would return in series five.

Cast

Vi Stephens...Mrs Ada Scott

Patricia Hayes...Grizelda Wormold

Jill Curzon...Norma Crispin

Mollie Sugden...Mrs Crispin

Jack Haig...Cecil Wormold

Jean Harvey...Nurse Kay

Ellis Powell...WVS Lady

Episode eight: *Where there's a Will*

What is it about the sudden arrival of a distant relative that sitcom writer's are so enamoured with? In this episode, Terry's Auntie Maud unexpectedly returns to the UK after making a life for herself in Australia. Quite the character, wealthy, elderly Maud (Enid Lorimer) is fussed over by her fawning nephew when aware of her money.

There is a smashing visit to a fun fair which ends with Terry being stretchered away after experiencing the roller coaster ride with her and Hugh in a show that looks both contemporary and old-fashioned. There is the use of the split screen and modern graphic titles but contrast this with Terry seen rushing about preparing a bedroom for his aunt accompanied by music, in a sequence out of a silent movie. Exhausted, when Hugh annoys him after Maud relocates to the neighbours, a manic Terry tips a bowl of water meant for his aching feet, all over Hugh's head. Watch his gasping response! Ms Lorimer would return in series four in a different role.

Cast

Wallas Eaton...Arthur Crispin

Vi Stephens...Mrs Ada Scott

Patricia Hayes...Grizelda Wormold

Jill Curzon...Norma Crispin   Mollie Sugden...Mrs Crispin

Jack Haig...Cecil Wormold   Enid Lorimer...Auntie Maud

Episode nine: *A Sink of Iniquity*

Terry. "What you gonna do with all those extra muscles, anyhow?"

Asks Terry to friend and lodger Hugh, engaged in a health kick in another enjoyable storyline involving some plumbing problems and various accidents/ wrongdoings caused as a result.

Still vying for the appreciation of Norma (Jill Curzon), both men offer to help her with an electrical issue at home. Checking the fuse box, Terry accidentally puts his foot through the kitchen sink and is obliged to pay for an expensive replacement.

Shelling out £17/ 10, this is where their problems really begin; as the sink unit is too large to get through the door. Norma suggests that they try via the back way but in doing so, Terry develops a 'stitch'. Only in the wonderful world of the sitcom, could a nearby removal gang pick up the item, thinking that it is meant for them. In vain, Terry and Hugh run after the vehicle as it speeds off.

Reporting the unusual loss at their local police station proves difficult; as a very confused and highly amusing Sgt Deryck Guyler manages to misunderstand the aforementioned events. He proves a delight here and the actor had already featured in episode two of the first series, as a railway ticket man.

Events prove taxing for both Terry and Hugh in this story and are perpetuated by the latter when he accidentally fuses the electricity along the whole street: he also damages the water pipes at the Crispin's too!

Cast

Deryck Guyler...Sgt

Also starring: Darryl Richards, Dorothy Darke and Jerry Verno.

Episode ten: *Holding the Baby*

Hugh and Terry try their hands at childcare after a baby belonging to a friend of the Crispin's next door is left withthem. Rather than Ada (Vi Stephens) staying at home whilst everybody else goes on a beano to Brighton they volunteer to help: how hard could it be?

Stuck with the infant all day, the boys decide to visit their local baby clinic for help. There they see Whopper! actress Molly Weir but even with support they still manage to take the wrong baby home! Rushing back, they eventually locate their little one after Terry hits the fire alarm to bring the mothers outside to take their prams away.

Cast

Wallas Eaton...Arthur Crispin

Vi Stephens...Mrs Ada Scott

Jill Curzon...Norma Crispin

Mollie Sugden...Mrs Crispin

Margaret Courtenay...Clinic advisor

Also starring: Elizabeth Benson and Anna Gillcrist.

Episode eleven: *The Root of all Evil*

In a nice play on words, poor Hugh is troubled by a nagging toothache in this the twentieth episode (including both series).

Not even the sight of a comely Norma in skimpy tennis attire is able to turn his commitment to play bowls with Terry. In Root Terry's boisterous character proves a little irritating; seeing

him pulling and tugging at Hugh, he could easily turn into a bully. Discoveringh Hugh's discomfort, Terry becomes all paternal but in truth, it is only because he wants to play tennis with Ms. Crispin.

Eventually visitingthe dentist, a very reluctant Hugh is not comforted by a gloating Terry, elated that he hasn't got the problem. After treatment, Hugh returns and feels fine only for Terry to have a problem after munching on a stick of rock given to him by a young lad in the waiting room. A delighted Hugh watches as Terry is literally picked-up by the dentist and carried into the treatment room.

Cast

Wallas Eaton...Arthur Crispin

Vi Stephens...Mrs Ada Scott

Patricia Hayes...Grizelda Wormold

Jill Curzon...Norma Crispin

Mollie Sugden...Mrs Crispin

Jack Haig...Cecil Wormold

Also starring: John G.Heller, Maria Lennard, Sheila Bernette, Philip Needs, Jerry Verno, Barnaby Gilbraith and Betty Miller.

Episode twelve: *A Place in the Sun*

In a barmy episode which concludes the second series, a playfully convoluted plot takes Hugh and the Scott family on holiday to a cottage by the sea instead of the usual Brighton boarding house liked by Hugh.

Upon their arrival, the Tooting trio are shocked at discovering that the place is a real dump, with only a single bedroom, Terry and Hugh have to sleep on camp beds. And they haveto contend with an uninvited guest, the first of many, whiffy tramp Fred Emney. Who should be in the nearby caravan but the Crispins and they are not the only ones, as they and many others traipse into the coattage to utilise the limited water supply.

Terry, Hugh and mum decide not to stay and look everywhere for a decent hotel before finally stumbling into one with vacancies. Here they meet a rather eccentric lady, about to sound the gong to acknowledge that the dining room is open. After she does, the place fills up quickly and we discover the batty Wormold's amongst them, the Crispins and Fred Emney, now employed as the cook!

Broadcast on 6 August, it would be followed by a short Christmas special on Wednesday evening, 25 December within which Terry, Hugh, Vi Stephens, Patricia Hayes and Jack Haig would feature as part of the traditional Christmas Night with the Stars show on BBC1.

Cast

Wallas Eaton...Arthur Crispin

Vi Stephens...Mrs Ada Scott

Patricia Hayes...Grizelda Wormold

Jill Curzon...Norma Crispin

Mollie Sugden...Mrs Crispin

Jack Haig...Cecil Wormold

Also starring: Rose Hill, John Lesley, Terry Fearis, Mary Jordan.

With variety shows proving less successful than before, Hugh and Terry are in seaside resort Weston-super-Mare for an extended summer season at the Knightstone Pavilion for their show Let's Make a Night of It. It has been noted elsewhere that Terry played the nearby Playhouse theatre during his career (his name is mentioned on their website under the 'history' section). They did well at Weston and frequently smashed box office records according to Hugh Lloyd.

As was common on BBC radio, the summer seasons at places like Weston, Great Yarmouth and Torquay would be showcased in broadcasts from all of the venues. Indeed, Terry and Hugh made three appearances on the radio; in a programme titled Holiday Music Hall which went out in July, a Seaside Night show was aired in August, and a Holiday Highlights programme was presented that September.

The Knightstone Pavilion and Opera House opened in 1902 and could accommodate 2,000 spectators. It proved a major draw for both locals and holidaymakers and consequently, drew many acts there: Max Miller, Morecambe and Wise, Adam Faith, Norman Wisdom, Frankie Howerd and many others appeared back when variety shows were the norm. Tastes changed and the Pavilion needed to adapt to compete; hence by the time that Terry went there, extended summer seasons were implemented.

The duo would often appear at public events and they continued to do so whilst at Wetson, judging a beauty contest at the Art Deco-inspired Tropicana open air swimming pool.

The prize on offer for the winner was a decent £50 which was presented to a young holiday maker from Reading. The local newspaper commented, "And when the judges, Terry Scott and Hugh Lloyd, handed her the cheque, she gave each of them a big hug. "This is wonderful', she said, 'I am really thrilled -I never expected to win'."

Another appearance saw them amuse the children at a fair at Weston town hall in aid of the Children's Society in September 1963. They would return to the resort in the following year.

Their spell in Weston was to prove significant in not only proving enjoyable for patrons but equally on a professional basis, Duncan Wood, then Head of Comedy at the BBC, came and watched them and ticked many boxes for fitting the duo into a new comedy format that grew into Hugh and I.

If you go looking for the Knightstone Pavilion today, you will indeed find the building but not looking quite as it once was: it is now refurbished and encompasses a lavish housing complex and café.

There was a really bad winter in 1963, and so television viewers would have had their heating on in anaticipation of watching the BBC TV panto Dick Whittington starring Terry Scott, Hugh Lloyd and Reg Varney in an adaptation co-written by John Law and Harry Carlisle. Peter Whitmore directed this hour-and-half production broadcast on 25th December at 5.45pm.

Also in the extensive cast were Norman Mitchell, Patricia Lambert, Yvonne Marsh, Gerry Lee, Barbara von der Heyde, David Davenport, Alec Bregonzi and Ken Parry.

Mitchell would find a role in the film version of Bless This House (1972) and was also in The Great St Trinians Train Robbery (1966) and he made a number of Carry On appearances. Former ballet dancer David Davenport would also later be seen in Carry On Henry (1971). Alec Bregonzi, coincidentally, like Terry, would discover that his scenes would be cut from the final print of Carry On at your Convenience (1971).

Terry then returned to the small screen just after 8pm in another Christmas Night with the Stars. He and Hugh Lloyd featured in a shortened edition of Hugh and I again alongside other popular BBC shows of the time. Russ Conway again featured in the show. David Croft and John Chapman again provided the director and script roles.

Radio Times billed "A Christmas misadventure involving Brian Rix and Terry Scott..." in a half-hour feature that also included Patricia Hayes, Wallas Eaton (who was also in twelve episodes of Hugh and I) and David Graham in a festive radio offering called Yule be Surprised. It was written by John Cleese and Eddie Maguire.

Consisting of thirteen episodes, the third series of Hugh and I is broadcast from 4 January through to 15 May 1964, with a festive special on Christmas Day. The show moved to a prime time, 9.20pm Saturday evening slot initially, before switching to Fridays at 8pm.

Episode one: *New Year Resolutions*

In an attempt to be kinder, Terry decides to be nicer to Hugh, not something that comes naturally to him.

Cast

Vi Stephens...Mrs Ada Scott

Patricia Hayes...Griselda Wormold

Jack Haig...Cecil Wormold

Also starring: Harry Brunning, Robert Raglan and Jacqui Wallis.

Episode two: *Pen Friends*

Arranging to pick up their friend from the railway station, Hugh and Terry manage to miss them.

Cast

Vi Stephens...Mrs Ada Scott

Also starring: Rex Garner, Margo Croan, Dave Carey, Jerrry Verno, Barney Gilbraith and Charles Hill.

Episode three: *Coal Comfort*

Returning after a break of repeats, episode three sees Terry succumb to the power of advertising and here in the case of the coal board's "Buy a bigger Bunker" campaign.

Coal was shown on Saturday 22February.

Cast

Vi Stephens...Mrs Ada Scott

Mollie Sugden...Mrs Crispin

Cardew Robinson, the Fakhir in Carry On Up the Khyber (1968) is in this. With Jacquie Wallis, Clifford Mollison, Rose Hill, Walter Sparrow.

Episode four: *Emergency Ward*

Some sources list this episode as having been broadcast as episode 4 on the 7 March 1964. In fact, it appears likely to have been repeated on this date. However, as there is a large gap in between this and the next episode (22nd Feb), some uncertainty remains.

Terry and Hugh battle for medical assistance via the NHS in this topical story line. This episode no longer exists in the archives.

Also starring: Geoffrey Hibbert, Marjorie Rhodes, Roger Avon, Dorinda Stevens, Frances Guthrie, Leoni Forbes, Katy Greenwood, Felix Bowness, Pamela Hewes and John Lesley.

Episode five: *Wheel of Fortune*

Lord Popham (Fred Emney) surfaces again after a chance meeting with the boys takes them to a gaming club and the lure of the roulette wheel.

Cast

Fred Emney...Lord Popham

Vi Stephens...Mrs Ada Scott

Patricia Hayes...Griselda Wormold

Also starring: Dennis Ramsden, Maurice Podbrey, Dave Carey, Harold Berens, Arnold Diamond, Sheila Falconer, Const Luttrell, David Chapman.

Episode six: *Central Cheating*

Like the five previous episodes of series three, this is another now deemed lost from the archives. The Scott household goes crazy by installing more than twenty radiators and two boilers...

By now the show was utilising a number of the same actors to fill the supporting roles: Barney Gilbraith, Charles Hill, Clifford Mollison, Derek Nimmo, Glen Melvyn, Ken Laird, Fred MacNaughton, James McManus.

Cast

Vi Stephens...Mrs Ada Scott

Episode seven: *Escort Duty*

This is an amusing little episode which finds Terry once more attempting to find employment and dragging along the gormless-looking Hugh to visit an agency's office that had been advertising for escorts. Terry gets the wrong impression prior to actually speaking to the manager but is soon interested upon being paid £50 plus expenses to take two Italian visitors out for an evening.

Visiting them at their posh hotel, mamma vets them prior to introducing her attractive daughters; Maria and Sofia. Before doing so, the boys grossly exaggerate their social status. Terry hopes to attend a boxing match whilst Hugh balks at the idea. However, in a mix-up, Hugh attends the fight and Terry is quite literally bored to sleep at the opera!

Also with April Ostrich, Vicki Woolf, Aidan Turner, Sonia Windsor, Paul Chapman, Peter Whitbread, Ronnie Brandon, Bill Maxam.

Episode eight: *Door to Door*

The show switched to Friday nights at 9pm. Making a living as confectionary salesmen proves difficult for the lads; especially when the Army is perturbed at them for attempting to sell 'Brigadier' biscuits.

Cast

Vi Stephens...Mrs Ada Scott

Mollie Sugden...Mrs Crispin

Also starring: Jacquie Wallis, Clifford Mollison, Kenneth Laird, Robert Dorning, John Harvey, Philip Anthony, Jacqueline Jones, John F.Landry, Laura Thurlow, Tony Lambden, William Raynor, Sheila Bernette and Freddy Powell.

Episode nine: *The Girl in the Poster*

Hugh falls for a beautiful girl featured in an advertising campaign in what has since become another lost episode.

Cast

Vi Stephens...Mrs Ada Scott

Patricia Hayes...Griselda Wormold

Mollie Sugden...Mrs Crispin   Jack Haig...Cecil

Also starring: Jacquie Wallis, Clifford Mollison, Joan Newell, Frank Williams, Christine Eastley, Julie Ross, Jean Marlowe and Tony Poole.

Episode ten: *A Fat chance of Slimming*

Often rather plump and having his weight mentioned in most of his sitcoms by the cruel writers, here Terry's character seeks to lose weight by joining a slimming clinic.

Cast

Vi Stevens...Mrs Scott

Also starring: Jacquie Wallis, Fred Emney, Damaris Hatyman, Edwin Apps, P.Ann Clifford, Sidonie Bond, Walter Swash, Peter Thompson.

Episode eleven: *The Day of Reckoning*

Following an argument with Terry about a rise in his rent, Hugh decides to find alternate lodgings.

Cast

Vi Stevens...Mrs Ada Scott and also starring Rose Hill.

Episode twelve: *In the Doghouse*

Patricia the dog is expelled from the house by Terry, after he thinks it could be her that is causing him an allergic reaction. In reality, the spaniel was a member of the Scott family.

Cast

Vi Stephens...Mrs Ada Scott

Also starring: Jacquie Wallis and Clifford Mollison.

Episode thirteen: *A Chain Reaction*

Along with episode eight through to twelve, this final entry in series three is another lost gem. The storyline consists of the local council planning to replace Lobelia Avenue with a controvesial new main road. It aired 15 May 1964.

Cast

Vi Stephens...Mrs Scott

Mollie Sugden...Mrs Crispin

Also starring: Jacquie Wallis, Clifford Mollison, Fred Emney, Aidan Turner, Judith Furse, John Chapman and Cameron Hall.

A short episode was featured in Christmas Night with the Stars, 7:15 pm, BBC 1. Vi Stephens, Jill Curzon, Mollie Sugden and Jack Haig joined Hugh and Terry for this insert.

"Agatha Christie's delight: extraordinary lady detective finds herself hot on the heels of homicide..." Murder Most Foul film trailer

Released theatrically in March 1964, Terry appeared in this black and white M-G-M film in another police man role. He featured in the trailer for the film as over the titles we see and hear the cry of a silhouetted woman whilst a uniformed Terry pulls up his bicycle upon hearing her scream! A character as strong-willed as the mighty Miss Marple, exquisitely played across four films by Dame Margaret Rutherford, with a face as expressive as the mug belonging to Mr Sid James, could quite easily irritate. But Agatha Christie's creation, always one step ahead of the police officers investigating any given crime, is played perfectly here by the actress. Margaret was the sort of female equivalent of Alastair Sim, and the charming Ms Rutherford is also in the Terry-associated film I'm All Right Jack (1959). She was awarded an Oscar for Best Supporting Actress, for her performance in The VIPS (1963).

The film opens at night, with footsteps moving towards a building and revealing the identity of a chubby police officer in an ill-fitting uniform: one Terry Scott. Walking towards the deserted Hangman's Rest public house, he taps the window and is given a pint of bitter, oblivious to the murderous shenanigans occurring in a house nearby. A silhouette struggles and a female form is left hanged as the officer finishes his drink, hands the glass back into an unseen person inside before paying up and jumping onto his peddle bike. A moment later he sees the body and P.C Wells (Scott) rushes inside only to discover a man attempting to alter the rope and with £100 in bank notes scattered in front of him, set off by a single rose in the middle. Filmed on location in the village of Sarratt, Hertfordshire, Terry has the first two minutes of the film, complete without dialogue before he utters the single line, "What's all this 'ere?"

As the opening credits play out, we see him again in a court room sequence which thankfully has no dialogue either, only the jaunty music score accompaniment by Ron Goodwin (he would work on all four Marple films). "That woman's made a mockery of my one and only murder!" Bemoans Terry in his umpteenth courtroom scene, as the murder case goes before a jury. The result is a mistrial as the jury could not agree a verdict, well, eleven of them could but one: a certain Miss Marple does not agree to a guilty verdict being recorded, much to the irritation of Inspector Craddock, a character that appears in all the films (played by Charles Tingwell) .

Written by David Pursall and Jack Seddon, the premise being taken from the Christie novel Mrs McGinty's Dead, originally published in

1952, with its protagonist being Hercule Poirot but the film producers tinkered with this and placed Miss Marple (Rutherford) as its focus in their films. The author was said not to have been a fan of the idea but cinemagoers seemed to like it as Murder most Foul was the third of 4 Miss Marple films made in the 1960s, these being: Murder she Said (1961); Murder at the Gallop (1963); Murder most Foul (1964) and Murder Ahoy concluded the series in 1964, with them all directed by George Pollock. He had directed And the Same to you, the 1960 comedy that gave Terry a role. Its screenplay writers would later provide the script for Carry On England (1976) a non-Terry entry in the series and be involved in the What a Carry On TV series.

Early into the story, Miss Marple goes to the home of the victim, Mrs McGinty, where the sister of the 'victim', a comely Meg Jenkins, is tidying the property. And so begins Marple's investigation, as she roots around her belongings to look for possible clues. Her visit being keenly noted by P.C Wells (Terry), who informs Craddock, who in turn pays her the first of many visits! The amateur sleuth thinks that the deceased was a possible blackmailer of an actor in the Cosgood Players and so she decides to infiltrate the company at the Palace theatre (where they are next due to perform). The actual venue utilised belongs to the Watford Palace theatre, clearly known to the Watford-born Terry. Miss Marple goes along and auditions for Cosgood (Ron Moody from A Pair of Two Briefs, here in a very different role) but fails to create the right impression until she discloses her independent financial means and he adds her to the cast/ company. About to leave, one of the actors drops dead in front of everyone, before Inspector Craddock makes an appearance with a 'tacheless Windsor Davies in tow.

The plot thickens as another cast member dies as Miss Marple joins the company at their lodgings and so becomes embroiled in the mystery in this black and white world. To reveal the murder would be wrong, so let us just say that the guilty party soon sets their sights on eliminating dear Marple on the calamitous opening night.

Do look out for Terry in the DVD trailer for the film. Also of note in the cast is a young-looking James Bolam. Dennis Price of Double Bunk and I'm All Right Jack has a very small role, too.

"Murder Most Foul is probably the best of the four," declares agathachristiereader.wordpress.com. "The film looks and feels so vibrant in all its monochromatic glory, and the cinematography is astounding (check out the shadows in the scene where Marple auditions). The theatre troupe are wonderfully realized – props to the casting director on this front. Rutherford effortlessly portrays a worldly vibe, and feels much more at home in the everyday world than Poirot."

The Watford Palace theatre which was used in some scenes in the film is still there today, located on Clarendon road near the High street, this lovely Grade II listed venue shows live events and films.

Along with comedy partner Hugh Lloyd, Terry made an appearance back down in Weston-super-Mare at the Winter Gardens on 1 August. The duo formed part of the "Sunday at Three" concert team.

A year seeing many projects, Terry also featured in a radio broadcast of One Man's Meat a programme which initially aired on BBC radio on 26 July at 2.30pm. It starred farceur legend Brian Rix, Terry and Elspet Gray, and the Radio Times listing states that Scott was then currently appearing in Let's make a Night of It at South Parade Pier, Southsea. Only a two minute excerpt exists.

Looking at interior photos from the period, the theatre there had a lovely horse-shoe design which curved on each end towards the stage and seats below. Southsea, which has Portsmouth as its neighbour, had a number of public entertainment venues back in the 1960s and many artistes with a Terry Scott association or not played there, including Bob Monkhouse, Billy Cotton, Frankie Howerd, Dickie Henderson and Tommy Steele. The Pavilion theatre was located through an amusement arcade and past the auditorium was a deck where steamer trips could be taken.

Terry's agent was on holiday across the Solent on the Isle of Wight and took him out on a dinghy on a rather windy day. Failing to move himself across the boat when told to do so, the sailors were capsized, "...not, I may say, more than 50 yards from the shore." Chuckles Richard Stone recounting the insignificant mishap in his autobiography, "But Terry's publicity agent, Margot Lovell, was also on holiday on the island. Never one to miss an opportunity, she phoned the press. One tabloid the next day carried a headline, 'Terry Scott in Solent Drama!'"

Once labelling itself 'The centre of entertainment', South Parade Pier is today a listed building. It dates back to 1879 and was struck by three separate fires which caused extensive damage to its structure. Rebuilt by 1908, a 1,200-seater theatre was added post-1904.

Utilised in WWII, by the 1950s, a local youngster by the name of Peter Sellers would try his luck on the stage there. Following a change of ownership in 1967, a second fire destroyed much of the theatre and in 1974 it again suffered, only this time when Ken Russell was directing a scene from his musical Tommy (1971) in the building. Closed entirely to the public by 2012, its future is still in the balance.

Only in the 1960s could a music show be based on the premise of coming from an ice skating stadium and be presented by David Jacobs! But that was the case for this short-lived show which was broadcast between July - September and ran across nine programmes; Terry participating in number six, broadcast on 11 August, with Lulu and the Luvvers also performing.

Defined by Barry Took as being "...a tongue-in-cheek parody of the somewhat portentous documentaries of the day,[12] Scott On... begins this year, with only a single programme, which was filmed before a live studio audience, and known as Show of the Week: Scott On...Its usual run time was 45 minutes but some episodes would over-run. Titled Scott on Birds, you could see it at 9:45pm, BBC 2, Saturday 19 December. This one-off delved into the female form, seeing Terry reunited with Dennis Main-Wilson, the two had worked together back in 1961 when Scott featured in an episode of The Rag Trade.

Supposedly written with Roy Kinnear in mind, and also said to be a sketch show to showcase for Kenneth Williams, he did not follow the

Cast

Margaret Rutherford...Miss Jane Marple

Ron Moody...Driffold Cosgood

Charles 'Bud' Tingwell...Insp Craddock

Andrew Cruikshank...Justice Crosby

Megs Jenkins...Gladys Thomas

Ralph Michael...Ralph Summers

James Bolam...Bill   Stringer Davis...Jim

Francesca Annis...Sheila

Pauline Jameson...Maureen

Annette Kerr...Dorothy

Alison Seebohm...Eva

Windsor Davies...Sgt Brick

Neil Stacey...Arthur

Stella Tanner...Florrie

Dennis Price...Harris

Terry...PC Wells

Lucy Griffiths...Miss Rusty

project through and so Terry stepped in as a very late replacement. Birds was meant to be a one off special but the series ran for thirty one episodes between 1964-1974.

An extensive writing team across its five series consisted of then-police officer Dave Freeman, Marty Feldman, Barry Took, Bryan Blackman, Dick Vosburgh, Eric Davidson, Eric Merriman, John Kane and Humphrey Ventnor.

Terry appeared in all twenty four episodes, whilst June Whitfield was in twenty two, with Carry On co-star Peter Butterworth, Colin Jeavons and future co-star Frank Thornton all featuring in three. Jacqueline Clarke, Stuart Sherwin and Dilys Watling played in two episodes whilst an extensive list of others made single appearances; most notably Lynda Baron, Pat Coombs and Jill Curzon who all had extend working connections with Terry. Ms Clark would again work with him in a couple of episodes of Scott On as well as play in a stage farce alongside him many years after. Mr Sherwin would work with Terry Scott across five different projects between 1961-1979 after first co-starring together in the Brian Rix piece Will any Gentleman?

Father Came Too! was a somewhat sedate little picture which would offer Terry a very brief cameo role this year. Directed by Peter Graham Scott from an original screenplay by Jack Davies with Henry Blyth. Scott, no relation, was well-regarded in the film industry and was known for engaging his actors with their scenes. His extensive CV encompassed duties as producer, director and more. He went on to enjoy great success on the small screen with The Onedin Line and Children of the Stones.

Stanley Baxter and Sally Smith are newly- weds, who away on honeymoon discover that their planned purchase of a property has fallen through. To save money, Juliet suggests that they stay with her father, the titled Sir Beverley, as portrayed by a blustering James Roberts Justice, at his palatial drum. He agrees but only as a stopgap.

There is some fun to be had in watching the new son-in-law lock horns with his dominant father-in-law whilst Sally gets caught in the middle. Sir Beverley (Justice) wants his daughter to remain living with him but Dexter (Baxter), would prefer that he and his new wife live in their own home. Not surprising when he soon labels him cheekily as a "miserable, sanctimonious old buzzard."

Dexter, a travel agent by profession, stumbles upon a local estate agents run by aspiring thespian Roddy (a hard-working Leslie Phillips), who learning of the formers relation and status in the acting profession as something of a national treasure, sets about ingratiating himself.

Phillips is on good form here and provides much of the energy. Sally casually tells her new hubby to take her father's money so that they can purchase a property but Dexter steadfastly refuses. Father Came Too is a rather dated affair, with Juliet Munro's character a stay-at-home wife and not seeming to do much at all.

When a lovely property in Pilsbury called Rose Cottage, comes up for sale, the newlyweds want it but the only problem being is that the house is being sold via auction. Things are confounded by the interests of an older couple equally set upon buying.

Advancing to the day of the auction, being conducted by Roddy (Phillips), a person prone to flowery soliloquies, he describes the property as being "a Tudor paradise surrounded by health-giving fresh air…" Whilst on the way, the couples clash once again and local traffic warden Arthur Mullard is not amused. Although not enjoying a scene with Terry in this film, the two would advance to share screen time in the far out comedy Gonks go Beat (1965). Luckily the Munro's put in the winning bid and subsequently are able to move in to the cottage to begin married life.

Of course, things do not run smoothly and immediate their idyllic lives are abruptly upset by the arrival of laconic farmer Peter Woodthorpe and his herd of dairy cows running wild over their front lawn! Unbeknownst to them, the farmer takes up the public right of way which runs right through the property grounds. Daddy brings in a young designer to remodel the cottage but gets short shift by the new Lord of this particular manor who employs his own local builder.

A predictable yet affable chaos soon ensues with the arrival of Ronnie Barker and his team made up of a youthful Kenneth Cope, Phillip Locke and Timothy Bateson. Liverpool-born Cope would have noticeable roles in two Carry Ons with a Terry connection: At your Convenience (1971) and Matron (1972). The many problems at the cottage make the investment into becoming a money pit for the cash-strapped Dexter. Meanwhile father and daughter go shopping for a bathroom suite and are dealt with by Terry's future pantomime co-star, the fabulous Mr Julian Orchard.

The plot gets a little silly as slapstick ensues following Sir Beverley's moving in to assist with the renovations. Roddy (Phillips) continues to ingratiate himself with Sir Beverley and helps or rather, hinders things by helping them decorate. Cue plenty of pratfalls involving standing on wallpaper, falling through the roof, brushes in faces and so forth. Dexter loses his job and the couple ask Sir Matthew to leave feeling that he truly has overstayed his welcome. He begrudgingly goes, being driven away in his expensive car by Lang (Sydney Bromley) but not before his daughter joins him!

Left alone in the finished property, complete with all mod cons in a gadget-strewn kitchen, Dexter makes use of the facilities but such a high demand on electricity sets the fuse box alight. Earlier the meddling Sir Matthew had insisted upon a higher wattage being installed despite the protestations of Josh (Barker).

With no telephone yet connected, Dexter rushes out onto the road desperately flagging down a passing 'ton-up' motorcyclist (a young Nicky Henson) to take him to the fire station. He does so but on the way, a traffic policeman stops them and refuses to believe Dexter's story about the cottage being on fire. With no time to wait, he rushes off and finally arrives at the fire station. Unfortunately it is deserted, except for the large old fashioned engine (think something that would look fitting in an old Norman Wisdom or Will Hay feature) as all the volunteer staff are at the local village pageant. Only a chirpy Cardew Robinson, an old actor friend of Hugh Lloyd, is present and he seems in no hurry.

Alas when they do go, the path of the antiquated vehicle is blocked by the ongoing events in the village where a "history through the ages" theme is being presented. Many people are milling around whilst others, including Peter Jones and Fred Emney, are dressed up as characters such as Francis Drake, Charles II and Mary Queen of Scots. It is on the latter float that we find Terry standing as the masked executioner, dressed head-to-toe in black and complete with axe. Organiser of the day, the chipper Roddy inspects the floats and offers encouragement to all; coming to this one, he jokes "...don't lose your head!" Terry mouthes "no" before chaos ensues as the proceedings get rather silly, whilst missing firemen Ronnie Barker and Co join the engine.

A rousing soundtrack speeds up the action and in Terry's other appearance, still at the pageant, his float is jolted by another vehicle leading to him inadvertently beheading the poor Mary, to the shriek of a woman in the crowd. "What's going on?" asks Hugh Lloyd, revealing his head from beneath the chest of the tragic figure that he had been portraying. Norrie Paramor was the film's conductor and music writer.

Sadly, by the time that they get to the cottage, it has been destroyed by the fire and they leave a desolate Dexter. Juliet (Smith) and her father soon arrive, unaware of events, and the couple reunite. An always chirpy Mr Chipperfield drives up and brings them the good news that a new motorway is being planned; running straight through the property and that they will not only get their money back but make a handsome profit. Also, he offers them another home nearby which is available immediately. The young couple walk off happy only for Sir Matthew to woo the estate agent's sexy assistant Lana (a lovely Barbara Roscoe) by taking her off in his luxury car.

Made by Independent Artists Studios in Beaconsfield, London, Father Came Too! Is not especially funny but does provide a few chuckles along the way.

ⒶⒷⒸ ❶❷❸❹ East st BRIGHTON 27010

Cast
James Robertson Justice...Sir Beverley Grant
Leslie Phillips...Roddy
Stanley Baxter...Dexter
Sally Smith...Juliet
Eric Barker...Mr Gallagher
Kenneth Cope...Ron
Ronnie Barker...Josh
Phillip Locke...Stan
Timothy Bateson...Wally
Terry...Executioner
Hugh LLoyd...Mary Queen of Scots
Fred Emney...Sir Francis Drake
Peter Jones...Charles II
Cardew Robinson...fireman
Peter Woodthrope...farmer
James Villiers...Benzil
John Bluthal...Robert the Bruce
Julian Orchard...salesman
Nicky Henson...motorcyclist
Arthur Mullard...Traffic warden
Michael Ward...man at auction
Vanda Hudson...Nell Gwynne
Geoffrey Dunn...Mr Trumper
Sydney Bromley...Lang
Clifford Earl...motorbike policeman
Barbara Roscoe...Lana
Anita Sharp-Bolster...Mrs Trumper

No unaccompanied children admitted after 7p.m
ALL PROGRAMMES MAY BE SUBJECT TO LATE CHANGE

Curiously, Terry Scott is listed in the opening credit alongside the talented Eric Barker, Kenneth Cope, Hugh Lloyd, Fred Emery and Peter Jones after following the headline cast of Messers Robertson-Justice and Baxter alongside Sally Smith; kudos to Terry's agent for getting him such a prominence in the cast listing.

Extras: Timothy Bateson: features in a 1981 episode of Terry and June titled In Sickness and in Health.

Eric Barker: enjoyable as Stanley Baxter's agitated bank manager in Father Came Too! has quite a professional connection with Terry. Both can be seen in Blue Murder at St Trinians (1957), Nearly a Nasty Accident (1961), Doctor in Clover and The Great St Trinians Train Robbery (both released in 1966).

James Villiers and John Bluthal: both glimpsed in the film also have roles in Carry On films which included Terry, namely Carry On Sergeant (1958) and Carry On Henry (1971). John also appears in the 1968 film made for the Children's Film Foundation, A Ghost of a Chance, which Terry stars in.

Christmas Day on BBC1 at 7.15pm saw Terry a part of "a specially recorded programme featuring your favourite light entertainment artists". Introduced by Jack Warner, remembered today for his seminal role in Dixon of Doc Green, alongside Hugh Lloyd, Terry appeared in a shortened episode of Hugh and I. John Chapman provided the script and David Croft directed the full cast. The show was in good company, as it sat next to The Likely Lads and Dick Emery.

The latest series of Hugh and I, a bigger batch of fourteen episodes, was broadcast from 3 January 1965 onwards.

Episode one: *Mum's Suitor*

Future Dad's Army star John Laurie was a guest star.

Episode two: *The Old Folks Home*

Cast

Vi Stevens...Ada Scott

Patricia Hayes...Griselda Wormold   Jack Haig...Cecil Wormold

Also starring: Robert Raglan, Rose Hill, Peggyann Clifford, Moya O'Sullivan, George Betton and Kathleen St. John.

Episode three: *Terry Mason*

Cast

Vi Stevens...Ada Scott

Patricia Hayes...Griselda Wormold

Jill Curzon...Norma

Jack Haig...Cecil Wormold

Also starring: Dave Carey, Patsy Smart, Frank Thornton, Charles Cameron, Kevin Brennan, Molly Weir, Sidney Vivian, Carol Austin and Alan Baulch.

Episode four: *The Critics*

Cast

Vi Stevens...Ada Scott

Jill Curzon...Norma Crispin

Also starring: Charles Dyer, Robert Dorning, Laura Thurlow, Kathleen St. John, Blake Butler, Patrick Tull, Josephine Pritchard and Anne Sharp.

Episode five: *The White Man's Grave*

Cast

Vi Stevens...Ada Scott

Jill Curzon...Norma

Also starring: Charles Dyer, Robert Dorning, Laura Thurlow, Kathleen St. John, Blake Butler, Patrick Tull, Jo Pritchard, Anne Sharp.

Episode six: *On the Ball*

Cast

Vi Stevens...Ada Scott

Jill Curzon...Norma

Mollie Sugden...Carmen Ethel Crispin

Also starring: Charles Dyer, Fred Emney and Ian Trigger.

Episode seven: *Going, Going, Gone!*

Pat Coombs and Jacques Cey appear in this episode; both Terry working associates during his career.

Cast

Vi Stevens...Ada Scott

Jill Curzon...Norma

Mollie Sugden...Carmen Ethel Crispin

Also starring: Felix Bowness, Peggy Ann Clifford, Claire Gordon, Pat Coombs, John G. Heller, Hannah Norbert, Derek Royle, Amy Dalby, Enid Lorimer, Jacques Cey and Lee Fox.

Episode eight: *No Business, like Snow business*

Cast

Vi Stevens...Ada Scott

Patricia Hayes...Griselda Wormold

Jill Curzon...Norma

Also starring: Charles Dyer

Episode nine: *A Bird in the Nest*
Cast
Vi Stevens...Ada Scott
Patricia Hayes...Griselda Wormold
Jill Curzon...Norma
Mollie Sugden...Carmen Ethel Crispin
Jack Haig...Cecil Wormold
Also starring: Charles Dyer, Amy Dalby, James Ottaway, Nan Munro, Michael Bird and Harold Bennett.

Episode ten: *The Choir*
This story found roles for Carry On actors Charles Hawtrey and Peter Gilmore, whilst also finding a part for Terry's old pal Stuart Sherwin.
Also starring: Charles Cameron, John Cater, Wally Patch, Peter Reeves, Beatrix Mackey.

Episode eleven: *Horses for Courses*
Cast

Vi Stevens...Ada Scott
Patricia Hayes...Griselda Wormold
Jill Curzon...Norma
Jack Haig...Cecil Wormold
With Arthur English, Arnold Ridley, Barrie Gosney, Jeffrey Gardiner.

Episode twelve: The Suit
Aired on Sunday 11 April, at 7:25pm, on BBC 1.
Cast
Vi Stevens...Ada Scott
Patricia Hayes...Griselda Wormold
Jill Curzon...Norma
Jack Haig...Cecil Wormold
Also starring: Katy Greenwood, Alan Baulch, Claire Gordon and Betty Cooper.

Episode thirteen: *Bun Fight*
Broadcast on Sunday 11 April.
Cast
Vi Stevens...Ada Scott
Patricia Hayes...Griselda Wormold
Jill Curzon...Norma
Jack Haig...Cecil Wormold

Also: Katy Greenwood, Alan Baulch, Claire Gordon, Betty Cooper.

Broadcast from Manchester, The Eamonn Andrews Show was a late night chat show which gave Terry the first of his two appearances, on 31 October, which he would follow up with another in 1967, two years before the series ended.

Remaining on the TV, Terry acts in Brian Rix Presents: The Brides of March. Co-directed by Wallace Douglas and Rix, the former worked on many of the TV productions presented under the Rix banner. John Chapman provided the script as he would do so for Hugh and I.

Cast

Diana Appleby...Vena

Sally Douglas...Oleena

Leo Franklyn...Arthur

Peter Gray...Haroun

Ann Hamilton...Sally

Monique Lewis...Rakeesha

Sheila Mercier...Mrs. Spencer

Nan Munro...Mrs. Scudamore

Dennis Ramsden... Policeman

Brian Rix...Tony

Derek Royle...van driver

Jacki Salt...Sassar

Terry...Ken Scdamore

Jerry Stovin...Jack Krasner

Suzanne Vasey...Maloo

Thanks to Richard Stone, Terry and his comedy partner Hugh Lloyd played shows at the Winter Gardens, Margate, in another, twice-nightly production of Let's Make a Night of It.

Billed as the stars of "Hugh and I", they again played in Let's Make a Night Of It and were joined by radio impersonator Clifford

WINTER GARDENS

General Manager and Licensee : J. D. GREEN, F.I.M.E.

Nightly at 6.30 & 8.45

RICHARD STONE presents

TERRY SCOTT HUGH LLOYD

B.B.C.TV.

"HUGH & I"

in

'Let's Make A Night Of It'

with

CLIFFORD STANTON

JOSE STEWART ★ KEN & ANNA ALEXIS

LOBELIA AVENUE LOVELIES

JACKIE BROWN and HIS QUINTETTE

JOE McBRIDE ★ TERRY FEARIS

Reserved 9/-, 7/6, 6/- ; unreserved 3/6

Stanton, Jose Stewart, Ken and Anna Alexis, the Lobeliia Lovelies, Jackie Brown and His Quintette, musician Joe McBridge and Terry Fearis. Locals or holidaymakers could gain admission to either the 6.30 pm or 8.45pm shows for unreserved (3/6) or reserved seats 9/-, 7/6 and 6/-.

Still in 1965, Terry played Mother Goose in a BBC television, Christmas Day presentation filmed at the Golders Green Hippodrome, London. The cast included past working associate Norman Vaughan as Mother Goose's son, Jon Pertwee as the Squire, Joanna Rigby as Prince Colin, Anna Dawson as the Squire's daughter, Lauri Lupino Lane, Kay Lyell, Susan Denny, Bernadette Milnes, The Lynton Boys and a young David Jason as King Goose. Directed by Travers Thorneloe and with Eric Rogers as musical director, it went out just before Doctor Who.

Vaughan had previously been in six episodes of Scott Free in 1957 and was also in a 1956 episode of Great Scott, It's Maynard. Vaughan proved very effective in engaging the children in the audience but like Terry, he could be dogmatic/ dictatorial around other actors and so it was down to producer David Croft to steer rehearsals away from their power struggle! Vaughan would also tour in A Bedfull of Foreigners, a theatre farce originally written for Terry. Whilst Lauri Lupino Lane who would also enjoy a role in Carry On Loving (1970) came from a family line with a strong panto tradition.

Mother Goose was adapted by John Law, a writer most known for creating the "class" sketch for The Frost Report (with Messrs Corbett and Barker and John Cleese) and a screenplay for the colourful James Bond flick Casino Royale.

"Top line comedians Kenneth Connor and Terry Scott star in this story of two rival islands, Beatland and Balladisle, whose young inhabitants are constantly staging a war of music."
Thanet Times article.

Gonks go Beat is a curious piece of 1960s nonsense ultimately presents itself as showcase for its various musical acts including Lulu and the Luvvers, Nashville Teens, Graham Bond and Cream drummer Ginger Baker. There are some groovy songs, cheesy ballads mixed in but with its best moment coming in the exhilarating 'drum battle' moment featuring Baker and a half-dozen others in a piece arranged by the "stylish and charismatic[13]" Mike Leander.

Nearly a nasty Accident star Kenneth Connor was top billed here, offering up another irritating, direct-to-camera performance. Although I did have a soft spot for him, as a child, especially in Carry On Sergeant (1958) where he is fun with Dora Bryan. Receiving equal second billing with Frank Thornton in the opening credits, where we hear Lulu belting out the infectious Choc Ice track, who knows what Terry's agent must have said to get him involved in a project labelled "a Technicolor extravaganza" by an anonymous regional newspaper.

It is not without its glorious moments, there is a lovely cameo from Jerry Desmonde, making the script sound like Shakespeare in a brief moment with Connor. And Reginald Beckwith, an actor seen in Terry-related film projects Double Bunk and The Night we got the Bird (both 1961) also proves amusing in a blink-and-miss-it cameo.

Just over half-hour into proceedings, Terry makes his entrance as 'Chief Justice – The Prime Minister' of Balladisle, a place where "music hath charm, let's keep it that way." Perspiring under a full wig and gown, he presides over a beach front court and proves quite amusing in a film wherein all the established comedy actors ham it up relentlessly, whilst the young cast seem to, through no fault of their own, be playing in another film entirely. Although watch any Marx Brothers feature and that also the case.

Steve (Iain Gregory) one of the youngsters from the nearby Beatland, where "If you're with it, you're in" is brought before his court. Terry wants his island to win the annual Golden Guitar contest soon to be staged at the Echo Chamber presided over by Mr A&R (Thornton, another of those actors that seems to have acted with everyone, here has lots of wacky dialogue to spout in a movie reminiscent of The Monkees TV show mixed with the Banana Splits). Steve is kept under the supervision of drum master Arthur Mullard, delivering his lines as though English is not his first language. However, he and Terry are amusing in their brief moments together, assisting the billowing Prime Minister, with neither required to put in a subtle performance.

Just before the hour mark, mistaken news is brought to Terry by his drum master (Mullard) relating that the PM's daughter, Helen (Barbara Brown) being kidnapped and taken to Beatland. A flustered Terry immediately declares war, unaware that she and Steve have runaway together after falling in love. "That's a bit strong, innit?" queries Mullard.

"Well of course it's strong. God blimey!" rasps the PM as they grapple each other's uniform lapels in one of the funniest exchanges in the film.

We next see Terry in full battle uniform, resembling Mussolini in his elaborate attire, he checks his young 'soldiers' in anticipation of the upcoming battle. Only they carry musical instruments instead of rifles!

He gets to give a rousing speech which snakes between channelling Sir Winston Churchill and William Shakespeare!

The battle commences, including Terry in the melee, before Helen explains the truth to him. Furious, he refuses to allow her to perform.

Mr A&R resides over the said competition, with Lulu and The Nashville Teens both playing, and Terry in attendance alongside his opposing number. Unable to distinguish a winner, A&R, a sort of benevolent Wizard of Oz figure, decrees that the islands will be united and known henceforth as Musicland: a place where all forms of music is to be welcomed. The story closes with Terry and the others on stage dancing but before we say goodbye, Mr A&R holds up the glistening prize in what is meant to be an awe-inspiring moment but just seems a bit cult-like.

Directed by Robert Hartford-Davis, also given credit for the story, Robert spent many years working in the industry and as writer/director he made the star-studded film The Sandwich Man (1966). Gonks, "The craziest musical adventure ever on planet earth!" according to its subsequent DVD cover, would seem to be the only accredited screenplay written by Jimmy Watson. Peter Newbrook, who co-created the story, spent many years in the film industry and

developed a working relationship with David Lean. Peter also served as Director of Photography on Gonks. Graeme Clar, writing on the excellent spinning wheel website, commented, "As there are few surprises, you might as well enjoy the music, which includes a group driven about an empty airfield miming and a prison-based duelling drummers sequence, both of which are surprisingly entertaining. And for cheap laughs, Lulu gets rated a "Miss" at the contest finale. But mainly

ⒶⒷⒸ ①②③④

this is as dated and goofy as Gonks themselves, which also make an appearance." The budget must have been tight, as the film relies upon its studio-bound sets located at Shepperton, with its island scenes proving as realistic looking as the fauna in Carry On up the Jungle. But there is a great sequence involving a band playing an instrumental as they drive along in cars, which did manage to escape the confines of the studio; often cited as the first pop video promo.

A short run of two episodes made up the first series of Scott On this year and utilising an ensemble cast. Scott On Money: broadcast Saturday 15 May. Scott On Food: broadcast 5 June.

By 27 December and Terry is back on the TV appearing in a large cast for Women Aren't Angel's, a Vernon Sylvaine farce directed by Wallace Douglas under the 'Laughter from the Whitehall' banner.

Sheila Mercier...Elizabeth

Larry Noble...Special Constable

Dennis Ramsden...Major Gaunt

Brian Rix...Wilmer Popday

Terry...Alfred Bandle

Maxwell Shaw...Pierre

Leonard Whitting...Albert

In January 1966, series five of Hugh and I arrived on BBC 1. The episode titled Goodbye Dolly finds Terry falling for a 23-year-old Margaret Nolan, later to memorably appear in a number of the Carry On pictures including with the Terry in Henry. She played the Dolly of the title; daughter of his neighbour who seems to respond to his interest favourably. A photo of the twosome was included in the Radio Times and there is also another lovely shot of them in the Getty archives. Ms Nolan, a former glamour model known as Vicki Kennedy, proved dextrous in pursuing an acting career at the time and would often contact producers detailing them of her availability.

Episode one: *Night Life*

The latest series started its run on 3 January and continued until the end of March.

Also starring: Dave Carey, Barry Linehan, John Cater, Gillian Wray.

Episode two: *Pot Luck*

Cast

Mollie Sugden...Carmen Ethel Crispin

Also starring: Marjorie Rhodes, Betty Cooper, Mo Dwyer, Emma Drew, Stephanie Heesom and Jean Harvey.

Episode three: *It Never Rains*

Also starring: George Moon, Dilys Watling, Bill Pertwee, Peter Butterworth and Doris Hare.

Episode four: *Goodbye Dolly*

The aforementioned and much under-rated Margaret Nolan co-stars in this episode as Dolly, the object of affection...

Also starring: Felix Bowness, Jeffrey Gardiner, Carmen Silvera, John Inman, James Donnelly and Sydney Dobson.

Episode five: *The Gas Man Cometh*

Cast

Mollie Sugden...Carmen Ethel Crispin

Future TV and theatre co-star of Terry's; Deryck Guyler, is in this.

Also starring: Wendy Richard, James Perry and Kenneth Thornett.

Episode six: *Ministering Angel*

Cast

Vi Stevens...Ada Scott

Also starring: Geoffrey Hibbert, Peggy Marshall, Anna Wing, Angela Lovell and Rosemary Martin.

Episode seven: *With a Pinch of Salt*

A large guest cast: James McManus, Sheila Bernette, Charles Cameron, Arthur English, Pat Coombs, Harold Bennett, Stuart Sherwin, Arnold Ridley, Gillian Wray, Bill Pertwee, Leslie Dwyer, Michael Finlayson, Peter Vernon, Ann Tirard, Norman Atkyns, Hedger Wallace, Edward Rhodes, Tom Mennard and Frankie Holmes.

Episode eight: *Costume Piece*

Cast

Mollie Sugden...Carmen Ethel Crispin

Jack Haig...Cecil Wormold

Writer/ actor John Junkin, a dialogue contributor to the show, found himself in amongst the cast for this episode. Also starring: Charles Cameron, Barry Linehan, Wendy Richard, Tony Sympson, Lynn Clemence, Fred Hugh and Peter Hughes.

Episode nine: *It's in the Stars*

Gretchen Franklin, remembered for her role as Ethel in Eastenders, makes an appearance here; she would also feature in a Terry and June storyline some years later.

Cast

Patricia Hayes...Griselda Wormold

Jack Haig...Cecil Wormold

Also starring: Felix Bowness, Alan Baulch, John Inman, Victor Platt, Robin Hunter, Jay Denyer and Bridget Bryce.

Episode ten: *Huntin', Shootin' and Fishin'*

Guest star Moyra Fraser would work with Terry in the touring play called Sign here Please!

Also starring: Fred Emney, Aidan Turner, Wendy Richard, Jeremy Hawk and Rowena Cooper.

Episode eleven: *Tooting Footlights*

Cast

Mollie Sugden...Carmen Ethel Crispin

Jack Haig...Cecil Wormold

Recognisable Terry colleagues Julian Orchard and Wendy Richard co-star. Also with James Ottaway, Arthur Hewlett, Wanda Ventham.

Episode twelve: *The Christening*

Cast

Mollie Sugden...Carmen Ethel Crispin

Jack Haig...Cecil Wormold

Also starring: Felix Bowness, Anna Wing, Tony Sympson, Sydney Bromley and Audrey Noble.

Episode 13: The Jackpot

Monday 28 March marked this final episode in the series. Lodger Hugh would win £5k on the premium bonds in the 1966 series, and from there they embarked on world cruises and comedy adventures.

Cast

Vi Stevens...Ada Scott

Mollie Sugden...Carmen Ethel Crispin

Jack Haig...Cecil Wormold

Also starring (amongst others): Rex Garner & Blake Butler.

"They're only a bunch of school kids!"

Frankie Howerd

The Great St Trinian's Train Robbery was the penultimate entry in the series (The Wildcats of St Trinian's would follow in 1980 but with major cast changes) was released in cinemas across the country in March and unlike its predecessors, it was filmed in colour. It gave Terry a 'guest star' role in what is nothing more than a cameo.

Headline stars are Frankie Howerd and Dora Bryan, the former incognito as male hairdresser 'Alphonse of Monte Carlo' (similar to Terry in Doctor in Clover), with Ms Bryan being the latest self-serving headmistress employed at St Trinian's. Clearly inspired by the actual Great Train Robbery of a few years earlier, Howerd and his gang   pull-off a daring £25m robbery of a Royal Mail loco, stashing the mailbags of cash in a disued house, ready for collection when the scene quietens. Unbeknownst to them, the property has been purchased as the new home of St Trinian's.

Robbery was again written by Launder and Gilliat, with an added credit for Leslie Gilliat, Frank's brother (also given a Producer nod and one of the story originators, too). With the film "presented and directed by Frank Launder and Sidney Gilliat" a duo that made more than 40 films together. Howerd is always a good watch, as he basically plays the same character and here he is the best thing in a plodding feature which only livens up in its final chase scenes.

With a new Labour government, represented by Raymond Huntley, the arriving face of the Minister of Schools, where Richard Wattis has remained, alongside Carry On man Peter Gilmore and the super Culpepper Brown, once again played by Eric Barker.

The tightly-organised gang, led by Howerd but controlled by a voice-only Stratford Johns, includes familiar faces Reg Varney, Arthur Mullard, Norman Mitchell, Cyril Chamberlain and others who return to the house to retrieve their ill-gotten gains. However, they are confronted and driven off by Amber (Bryan), her female staff (including a scrumptious Margaret Nolan) and the girls. This is where the "kids" quote is made by Alfred (Howerd) who fails to realise that these youngsters are no ordinary children; they are St Trinian's girls!

In a subsequent plot rouse, Alfred is ordered to enrol his precocious daughters at St Trinian's so as they can help get the stashed cash out. But when one of the younger girls there discovers some of the money, she is observed by Harry (George Cole).

At 101 minutes into proceedings, he calls the police to lay claim to the reward money offered for finding the cash. Sgt Terry takes the call, documents its contents but is unconvinced at its authenticity, as many others have staked a claim and will continue to do so.

As the proceedings intensify, both Harry and insurance investigator Noakes (Colin Gordon) are in danger after being identified by the head of the gang. The team infiltrate a parent's day event at the school, disguised as caterers, with Harry and the girls later deciding to confront them. This comes after the funniest bit in the film which involves Frankie Howerd unintentionally participating in a Morris dancing troupe performing at the school (as amusing as it sounds).

A few minutes later, Amber also contacts the police where Officer Terry says that he will make a note of her details. Ms Bryan proves a little irritating in her gauche performance but she improves especially when repeatedly voicing her reward claim or when manipulating her equally crooked beau, Sir Horace (Raymond Huntley).

Terry makes his final appearance on screen, still at the station, when receiving a call from Noakes who tells him that the stolen loot has just been removed from the school in the caterers/ crooks van. Sgt Scott nonchalantly accepts this information before fully absorbing it and then blathering the important details back to his own self! And that is the last we see of him The Great St Trinian's Train Robbery.

In the best section of the film, the gang use an old steam loco loco to move the many money bags but are dogged by Harry and his girls. They dislodge the carriage with all the cash inside before they then become pursued by the crooks. If only the whole of the film was enjoyable as these moments.

Broadcast on Monday 11 April, Terry was the guest on Desert Island Discs. Sadly less than ten minutes remains of the radio recording in what proved to be an interesting chat between him and presenter Roy Plomley. However, the list of favourites chosen by Terry was documented and is as follows:

Sleeping Beauty by Tchaikovsky, Mike Nichols and Elaine May Improvisations to Music (Rachmaninov's Piano Concerto No 2), Sir Hamilton Harty: A John Field Suite No 1 (Polka), Peggy Lee with I Go to Sleep, Bach's Toccata and Fugue in D Minor, Zero Mostel and Maria Karnilova: Do You Love Me? Mozart's Der Hölle Rache (from The Magic Flute) and Hector Berlioz with Symphonie Fantastique.

Two weeks later, Terry played the records on the popular Housewives Choice, "It was five hours work for each days programme but it was worth it," acknowledged the actor, who also received many letters praising his guest appearance.

For those too young to remember it, Housewives Choice was a daily request show broadcast by the BBC with different weekly presenters.

Terry and Hugh advanced to fulfil a summer season at the Wellington Pier Pavilion, Great Yarmouth as part of a production presented by the 'impresario of pleasure,' Bernard Delfont. Brother to Lew and Leslie Grade, this hugely experienced personality had previously presented Morecambe and Wise at the same venue back in 1964 so by the time they followed with their Showtime '66, they were in very good company.

The duo fulfilled charity appearances, opening the nearby Old People's Welfare Committee fete at Beaconsfield recreation ground and signing autographs for charity for sixpence.

Terry and Hugh both loved football, with the former a Watford supporter and the latter, a Chester City nut. Back in the day, the lads also played in a football match locally, with the duo in the same line-up as Donald Peers and the Dallas Boys (both appearing in the stage show alongside them). Fellow summer season actors Dickie Henderson, Frank Ifield, Gerry and the Pacemakers and Ted Rogers also featured. Rogers, later of 3-2-1 game show fame, would present a BBC radio show featuring Terry and Hugh and many of the artistes doing a summer season at Great Yarmouth, which aired at the end of the first week of September. Terry would much-later guest on a festive edition of 3-2-1 in 1979. On Terry's show, Doreen Hermitage, Gill and

Freddy and George Truzzie also featured at the Pavilion theatre too.

The pier complex was a lovely-looking structure, with a tower on either side of a curved roof entrance which by the 1960s was a prosperous and thriving resort heavily reliant upon tourism. Yarmouth, a working dock at the start of the decade, as a resort found itself competing against the new novelty of affordable foreign flights. Only a decade earlier the seaside town was described in a tourist film as being "the East coast playground of Britain..." Originally 70ft in length, the Wellington pier was struck by a schooner shortly after opening in 1853. Reduced to 50 ft, the site suffered subsequent fire damage and both its ballroom and Pavilion were destroyed in 1954. Only the latter would be rebuilt and reopened in 1958. However, today, the theatre is no longer

Cast

Frankie Howerd...Alfred/ Alphonse

Dora Bryan...Amber

Reg Varney...Gilbert the Wheel

Raymond Huntley...Sir Horace

Richard Wattis...Manton Bassett

Portland Mason...Georgina

Terry...Police Sgt

Eric Barker...Culpepper Brown

Godfrey Win...Truelove

Colin Gordon...Noakes

Arthur Mullard...Big Jim

Norman Mitchell...Willy the Jelly

Cyril Chamberlain...Maxie

Leon Thau...Chips

Maureen Crombie...Marcia

Barbara Cooper...Mabel

Elspeth Duxbury...Veronica

Carole Ann Ford...Albertine

Margaret Nolan...Susie

Jean St.Claire...drunk

Lisa Lee...Miss Brenner

Peter Gilmore...Butlers

Michael Ripper...Eric, the liftman

George Benson...Gore-Blackwood

Meredith Edwards...Chairman

Jeremy Child...Monty

Aubrey Morris...Hutch

William Kendall...Parker

Edwina Cowell...Dr Judd

Philip Buchel/ Betty Buchel...tango dancers

Sally Geeson...un-credited schoolgirl

Sally-Jane Spencer....schoolgirl

Susan Jones...Lavinia

functioning as such and the complete structure has since been rebuilt (asbestos was removed at one point). It is now a bowling venue/casino, with slots amusements filling the rebuilt space in 2008.

Back when Terry played there, Yarmouth had a number of attractions, including the Wellington Pavilion, Brittania pier, Windmill theatre, Royal Aquarium and Regal/ ABC cinema/ theatre.

Saturday 7 May found Terry making his final appearance as a guest on the pop music show Thank your Lucky Stars which would conclude its five year run this year. It was hosted by actor/ singer Jim Dale.

November this year and Hugh and I returns to BBC1 with a slight change in premise now seeing the duo having moved out of their Tooting flat. The new series was given a Tuesday night slot and to promote it, the lads featured on the cover of Radio Times.

Premise of the show had to change due to the death of Terry's screen mother Vi Stephens in March of this year. Back in the television land of the mid-1960s, two single men could not to be seen to be sharing a flat and so it was contrived for Hugh to win on the Premium Bonds leading the duo to head off on a world cruise, as previously mentioned. Just as in some of the Carry On films, the cast of Hugh and I anticipated filming in exotic foreign locales but familiar UK locations Great Yarmouth and Hertfordshire were utilised!

And on to the sixth and final series of Hugh and I. Tuesday 29 November marked the broadcast of the opening episode and series six ran through to Tuesday 17 January 1967 with eight new episodes.

Episode one: *Troubled Waters*

A large cast is utilised for this series opener, most noticeably Pat Coombs and Patsy Smart; both of whom had been in earlier episodes.

Also starring: Robert Raglan, Glenn Melvyn, Charles Cameron, Harold Bennett, Reg Dixon, Brian Peck, Geoffrey H. Wallace, John Parker, Brian Hewitt-Jones, Mercia Mansfield and Tony Handy.

Episode two: *Morocco Bound*

Usual writer John Chapman is replaced for this single episode, with a script provided by Ronnie Taylor, who would advance to later writing the David Jason series A Sharp Intake of Breath.

Also starring: Frank Williams, Clive Morton, Geoffrey Sumner, Avril Elgar and Olwen Brookes.

Episode three: *Beau Jesters*

Also starring: Maurice Podbrey, Harold Berens, Aidan Turner, John G. Heller, Jay Denyer, Carl Duering, Eva Wishaw, Robert Gillespie, Howell Evans, Jan Leeming, Bernard Martin and Butch Hudson.

Episode four: *Arabian Knights*

Future Terry and June co-star Diana King made a guest appearance here and Norman Bird would work with Terry and June on a subsequent episode of Happy Ever After. With Peter Thompson, Derek Francis, Norman Bird, Guy Deghy, Jimmy Thompson, Sheree Winton, Michael Peake, Edwin Brown, Tim Buckland.

Episode five: *Hold That Tiger*

Shown on 27 December with the remaining episodes three episodes broadcast in January 1967.

Also starring: Georgina Cookson, William Kendall, Ronnie Corbett and Percy Edwards.

A great honour was afforded Terry as he played in Cinderella at the luxurious London Palladium. Headlined by pop star Cliff Richard and The Shadows, Terry and comedy partner Hugh Lloyd played Cinders' Ugly sisters, Teresa and Eunice, with Cliff starring as Buttons, The Shads as Broker's men and Pippa Steel as Cinders. Also in the cast were future and present Carry On squad members Jack Douglas, as Baron Hardup and Peter Gilmore, as the prince. Avril Yarrow, Bill Tasker and Patricia Merrin joined Tudor Davies as Dandini, and the speciality act was a baby elephant called 'The Adorable Tanya': Terry was not a fan, as he had been pushed down a stairs by her!

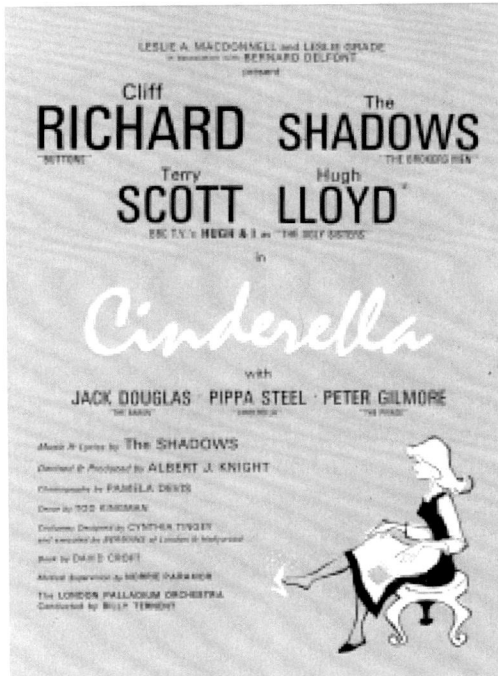

Across his career, Peter Gilmore acted in many Carry Ons and also had roles in films that Terry also participated, namely Carry On Henry (1971), Carry On Up the Khyber (1968), The Great St Trinians Train Robbery (1966) and in a film released this year, Doctor in Clover.

Billed as "The Magnificent Pantomime", British Pathe news covered Cinderella's stay at the Palladium, which commenced on 10

December with two shows daily, at 2:45pm and 7:30pm. With the music and lyrics by The Shadows, along with Cliff they had made an immediate return to the Palladium after appearing there last year.

Its book created by David Croft, Terry and Hugh sang the third number in Act I, Where can my man be? This year's production would prove memorable for producing the infectious Cliff hit record In the Country. The show was still on by 31 December.

The Palladium first presented pantomime back in 1914, on a strictly matinees-only basis and Aladdin was initially offered there in 1922 and returned from that year forth. The 1956 Aladdin saw a break in tradition with Norman Wisdom cast in the role of Principal boy, launching an era that was to last for fifteen years.

The role of "boy" was filled by stars such as Cliff, Frank Ifield, Frankie Vaughan and Tommy Steele but it was not until Cilla Black played the role in 1970 that tradition was restored.

The Palladium became a mecca for all variety performers and is a Frank Matcham design which opened in 1910. It soon became known for staging Royal Variety Performances by Bernard Delfont. Later Lord Delfont, he had an association with Terry that went back to the mid-1960s at Great Yarmouth and in 1980 Terry and future TV wife June Whitfield would be presented to the Queen Mother. Back when he was teamed with Hugh, they did perform for the Queen at the Royal Household Christmas Party at Windsor Castle c.1966, whilst enjoying success with their Hugh and I sitcom.

"Betty Box and Ralph Thomas now prescribes their latest, hilarious remedy guaranteed to cure the blues & all depression: Dr in Clover."

That was the claim made in a film trailer this year which found audiences seeing Terry in a brief but amusing moment in Doctor in Clover. He comes into things as a rather exasperated hairdresser visited by a despairing Leslie Phillips in need of a change of image.

The screenplay was written by Jack Davies, in this the penultimate feature in the popular medical series of seven films mainly taken at source from the Richard Gordon novels.

With its wards full of recognisable faces such as Dandy Nicholls, Danny Green, Harry Fowler, Alfie Bass and Noel Purcell, Doctor in Clover easily passes away an hour and half of your time. In a more major role is an amusing Arthur Haynes (we never discover what is actually ailing him but he gets a lot of witty dialogue and his moments with a deliciously vampish Fenella Fielding are most amusing. Visitors appearing briefly also catch the eye; namely Hancock regular Bill Kerr and Peter Gilmore.

On the staff side, we briefly glimpse a young Wendy Richard, and Joan Sims gets a large role as the new matron initially coming into conflict with Sir Lancelot (a returning James Robertson Justice) but subsequently falling for him in a case of mistaken identity!

Leslie Phillips steps back into his white coat as a slightly mature doctor refreshing his medical knowledge after a time spent in jail. His interaction with Justice proves most rewarding and the two actors make the proceedings roll along amusingly. A number of the cast had previously appeared in the 1962 film A Pair of Briefs (as had Terry).

In Clover, much fun is had with Dr Gaston (Phillips) falling for the charms of a younger French physiotherapist as portrayed by Elizabeth Ercy, who gives him much to think about. It is via his failure to woo her that in despair, Leslie's character pays a visit to "Robert of Tight Street" aka a slightly aloof Terry Scott, looking marvellous in a pale blue, button-downed top and swept back hair. The doctor is seeking to rejuvenate himself in the hope that it might do the trick and so pays a visit to swinging Carnaby Street, the neighbouring location of a fashionable hairdresser recommended by a trendy boutique assistant; a young Nicky Henson. All very matter-of-fact Robert (Terry) has the gall to recommend that the trade mark Leslie Phillips moustache is removed, "...it's right out now, you know." With a glint

in his eye, Terry looks at his client in the mirror before adding, "It's awfully tired (his hair). Would you consider wearing a piece?" The 'tache is removed and what a change in appearance: as if Samson has lost all his strength. But no, Leslie now feels that he is 'with it' but he still doesn't get the girl in a film in which he also chases comely nurse Shirley Ann Field.

Doctor in Clover has some fun moments, including whenever Joan Sims makes herself known as pernickety jobsworth Matron Sweet but it does seem quite dated and has a bit of sexism in it, too. Terry associates Eric Barker and Norman Vaughan, the latter a TV co-star across episodes of Scott Free and last year's Mother Goose, features as the commentator for the TV crew recording an operation at the hospital.

So what did fans think of the film? J.A Bradford, on Amazon.co.uk said, "...very different in tone, comedy style, and look from the early 1960's entries. Music composed for this entry seemed to be subconsciously trying to take the style and storyline of the production very much into the swinging era. It probably worked, but I'm still not sure! As with Doctor in Trouble, Leslie Phillips is the reason for watching this film, and I wasn't disappointed! Seeing him enter the

Carnaby Street hair-dressers and asking the stylist, (played by Terry Scott as you've never seen him before,) to make his character look more 'With it' and the resultant scene that follows is priceless!"

Film4.com offered, "Although Doctor in Clover lacks the wit of the earlier films, replacing it with iffy slapstick (a food cart bumps Gaston, he slips on spilled food, clutches at a fire extinguisher, then it ejaculates white foam over all and sundry) and bawdier 1960s sex-comedy, there's still enjoyable material here...for the most part Doctor In Clover involves wards, sexism from a more innocent age and cavalcade of hit and miss old-school gags. It's easy-going, but dated."

ⒶⒷⒸ ❶❷❸❹ East st BRIGHTON 27010

Cast
Leslie Phillips...Dr Gaston Grimsdyke
James Robertson Justice...Sir Lancelot
Shirley Anne Field...Nurse Bancroft
John Fraser...Dr Miles Grimsdyke
Joan Sims...Matron Sweet
Arthur Haynes...Tarquin
Fenella Fielding...Tatiana
Jeremy Lloyd...Lambert
Noel Pucell...O'Malley
Robert Hutton...Rock Stewart
Eric Barker...Prof Halfbeck
Terry...Robert the hairdresser
Norman Vaughan...TV man
Elizabeth Ercy...Jeannine
Alfie Bass...Fleming
Jean Bendetti...Man in French film
With Susan Farmer, Harry Fowler, Peter Gilmore, NIcky Henson, Robin Hunter, Barry Justice, Bill Kerr, Justine Lloyd, Bill Kerr, Roddy Maude-Roxby, Lionel Murton, Dandy Nichols, Anthony Sharp, Ronnie Stevens.

No unaccompanied children admitted after 7pm
ALL PROGRAMMES MAY BE SUBJECT TO LATE CHANGE

BBC comedy series Hugh and I concludes its run in January 1967 with its final three episodes broadcast from 10 January onwards.

Episode six: *Chinese Crackers*

This is another on a long list of lost or deleted episodes. A copy of this one is said to be held in an American archive. David Jason, known and loved for his role as Del Boy in Only Fools and Horses, features. He had already worked with Terry Scott and they would, much later, lend their voices to the Danger Mouse animated series. John Le Mesurier can also be seen; he and Terry had previously played Magistrate and policeman, respectively, in the 1959 film comedy Too Many Crooks.

Also starring: Cecil Cheng, Kristopher Kum, Robert Lee, Geoffrey Lumsden, Peter Reeves, Lucille Soong and Tommy Yapp.

Episode seven: *A Touch of the Rising Sun*

Also starring: Edwin Brown, Stella Tanner, Pik Sen Lim, Peter Elliott, Julie Allan, Barbara Yu Ling, Julie Martin, Alec Bregonzi, Evelyn Lund

Episode eight: *Adios, Amigo*

This final ever episode of Hugh and I was broadcast on 17 January. **129**

Also starring: Felix Bowness, Vicki Woolf, Paul Stassino, Vic Wise, Bruno Barnabe, Murray Kash, David Lander, Keith Ashley, Mike Earl.

On 5 February Terry and Hugh made a television appearance on the Eamonn Andrews Show with the Rolling Stones and Bobby's Girl singer Sarah Maughan. Hugh recounts in his book that Terry was intending to confront Mick Jagger about the band trashing his Palladium dressing room whilst he was appearing in the evenings in Cinderella. One day it had been rumoured to have been used by the group when they worked on another show at the same venue, something quite common back then. The skinny singer got in first by saying how much the band had enjoyed the panto and Hugh and Terry's performances. This threw Terry and he never did mention the complaint. The show was recorded live before a studio audience and incorporated chat and music across 45 minutes. Ms Maughan would co-start with Scott in a 1985 pantomime.

Hugh and Terry also featured on Five to Ten, a religious programme for BBC radio. The London Palladium Show saw Terry return to this esteemed theatre for an early evening television presentation made on 12 March. His old radio team mate Bob Monkhouse hosted.

Commencing on Monday, 12 June, a new farce called I Want to See Musov! (later re-titled Sign Here please!) arrives at the Grand theatre, Leeds, "The international laugh success" was originally written by

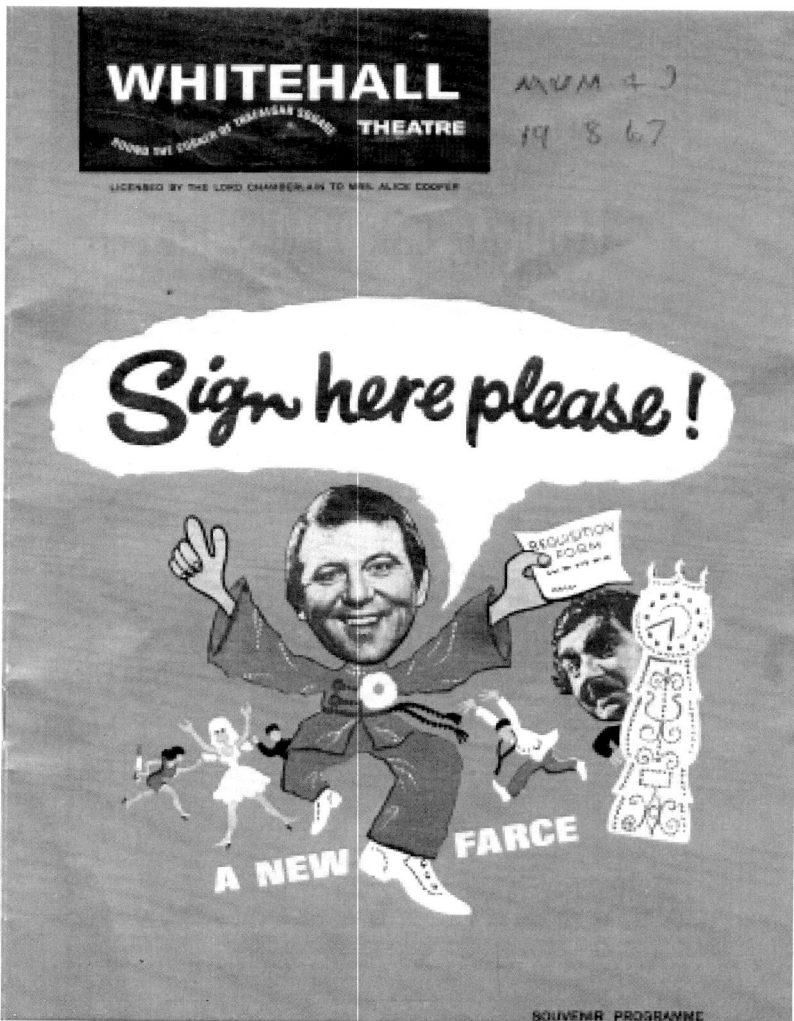

Valentin Kataev, adapted by Marc-Gilbert Sauvajon, with an English version provided by a recent Terry work colleague and fellow soccer nut, Marty Feldman.

Performances started at the usual 7.30pm, whilst on Saturday, there were two shows: 5pm and 8pm. Whilst performing in the play, Terry also managed to squeeze in the BBC 1 early evening show Dee Time, hosted by popular dj/ presenter Simon Dee. He was joined by The Dalys, Mike Newman, Bernard Herrmann and the Northern Dance Orchestra, The Turtles and Teddy Wilson.

July saw Terry appearing alongside host Billy Cotton, The Cotton Singers, The Gang Show, The John Tiller Girls, Leslie Crowther, Lulu and singer/ writer Kathie Kay in The Wakey, Wakey Tavern TV show.

On 16 August, he made the news after collapsing at the Whitehall theatre where he was playing in a run of Sign here Please! the new title for the aforementioned Kataev play. Terry was joined in the cast by Peter Bayliss, Ambrosine Phillpotts, Moyra Fraser, Derek Royle, Terence Bayler, Diane Appleby, Jacqueline Ellis, Edward Palmer, Anne Woodward, Paul Gillard and Arthur Howard. Directed by Anthony Howard, Terry knew the Whitehall well, after a stint down in Bournemouth, too. A flyer promoting the play offered, "Perfect entertainment for the whole family." Hilary Spurling, then theatre critic for The Spectator, described it"...a production...which is considerably smoother and more detailed than we are used to..."

BBC1 presented another pantomime, with Terry, Hugh Lloyd and unfunny Liverpool comic Jimmy Tarbuck starring alongside each other in a show that was shown Xmas Day.

Come the new year, Terry was cast in a solitary episode of the popular BBC comedy series The Very Merry Widow, which would stretch to thirteen episodes across three series, all virtually since-lost. Written by Alan Melville, he acted in a single story from the opening series called Treble chance would be a fine thing. Broadcast on 15 January 1968, star of the half-hour show was film actress Moira Lister with Terry camping it up something rotten as Godfrey Scott, another dickie bow tie lover. The series title references Jacqui Villiers (Ms Lister), the main character, and her liking of a drink.

Below: Terry in I Want to See Musov aka Sign here please!

Although not appearing in this specific episode, Terry's future theatre co-star Donald Hewlett co-starred and Diana King, later in Terry and June, also features.

Coming swiftly after the final series of Hugh and I had been shown, a half dozen episodes of Hugh And I Spy, all now deemed lost, were broadcast between 22 January - 26 February. Once more written by John Chapman, David Croft acted as both producer and director across the whole project.

Regrettably, the sequel to the popular Hugh and I series, Hugh and I Spy, is another casualty of being lost or wiped by the BBC archives. A set of six episodes was made and screened by the channel through January and February. The series continued with the Terry/ Hugh partnership, only this time giving it an espionage twist and closing on a cliff hanger.

Episode one: *Yellow Peril*

Terry and Hugh featured in a script by John Chapman and John Junkin, co-starring Lucilee Soong as Miss Lee in the first of the half-hour episodes which went out on Monday 22 January. Ms.Soong, in recent years, has worked in America. Old work associates Julian Orchard and Diana King feature, too.

The amiable John Junkin, a very popular comedy TV face in the 1970s, would make an un-credited appearance in Doctor in Clover (1966) after initially working with Terry in the second episode of Hugh and I in 1962. It would not be the last time that they worked together professionally, as John would also play a police sergeant in a 1980 Terry and June episode. Along with Terry Nation, John had also contributed ideas for the And the Same to You (1960) screenplay.

Also starring: Rex Garner, Aidan Turner, John Parker, Cecil Cheng, Stephanie Gathercole, Annabel Leventon, James Beck, Queenie Watts, Mark Neath, Andy Ho, Doel Luscombe, Peter Brookes, Richard Woo, Dickie Martyn and Cindy Oswin.

Episode two: *The Heights Of Madness*

Also starring: Rex Garner, Fred Emney, Charles Cameron, Nan Munro, Harold Bennett, Cecil Cheng, Annabel Leventon, Richard Woo, J. G. Devlin, John Ringham, Gay Cameron, Jonathan Holt, Therese McMurray and Carolae Donaghue.

Episode three: *Checkpoint Charlies*

Whitehall associate Andrew Sachs has a role in this one. It also featured Norman Mitchell, Robert Gillespie, Robert Lee, Cecil Cheng, Stephanie Gathercole, Richard Woo, John Hewer.

Toni Palmer, Ernst Ullman, Carl Jaffé and Tony Von Barton.

Episode four: *Holy Smoke*

Also starring: Rex Garner, Fred Emney, Victor Platt, Robert Lee, Lucille Soong, Cecil Cheng, Stephanie Gathercole, Richard Woo, Nan Braunton, Franz Van Norde, Nicolette Pendrell, Edward Sinclair and Ken Haward.

Episode five: *Five in a Bed*

Also starring: Rex Garner, Fred Emney, Jacques Cey, Carmen Silvera, Kristopher Kum, Steph Gathercole, Annabel Leventon, John Ringham, Derek Sydney, Brian Tully, Godfrey Kenton, Nev Barber.

Episode six: *Tea or Coffin*

This final episode was later discovered on an internet auction site and has since been preserved after a screening at the British Film Institute in 2013. Tea or Coffin featured series regulars Fred Emney and Rex Garner as well as Dino Shafeek, later working with Terry in panto at the Bristol Hippodrome.

Also starring: Derek Sydney, Robert Gillespie, Jasmina Hamzavi, Francisca Tu, David Toguri, Roger Carey, Julie Mendez, Rafiq Anwar, **133** Paul Anil and John Louis Mansi.

A radio special broadcast was headlined by singer Dickie Henderson who "introduces some of the stars who are shining on the South Coast this summer". These included the cast of The Winter Gardens, Bournemouth Star Time '68: Frank Ifield, Michael Bentine, Terry and Hugh Lloyd, Semprini, the New Faces, The Eric Delaney Band and Ivor Emmanuel as well as others playing in Weymouth. Terry, Hugh and the cast began their run in Bournemouth from Tuesday 6 August and continued through to 28 September; working hard in two daily shows (7.20pm and 9.40pm). Proceedings commenced with the Eric Delaney Band and The Rita King Dancers with the headline act, Frank Ifield. Terry and Hugh performed next on the bill prior to a bit of dancing and then eccentric comedy man Michael Bentine. Following the interval and after a brief glance through the one shilling programme, Terry and Hugh returned for a number called "It makes a change" after a bit from Eric Delaney. Mr Ifield finished off the show with his set. Ifield recorded number one hits in the early 1960s and is probably most easily remembered for the song I Remember You. Produced by Bill Roberton, Jack Douglas' brother, he had worked with Sid James and Hancock.

There is always something extra special about a Carry On period film and Carry On up the Khyber is such a film. Set in India, 1895, Talbot Rothwell provided the screenplay in what was only Terry's second time of working with the comedy film makers. Again playing a man in uniform, here he is Sgt Major MacNutt of the 3rd Foot and Mouth regiment, whose motto is "Always ready for Action," but to the locals, they are known as "Devils in skirts."

Protecting the Khyber Pass, the so-called 'gateway to India', the British soldiers are all clad in kilts and officially prohibited from wearing underwear (although MacNutt and Widdle, Charles Hawtrey, rather let the side down).

Terry looks very smart in his uniform, medals pinned to his chest, white pith helmet or boat-shaped other, sash, gloves, stick and belt holstering his pistol, he proves perfect casting as a bellowing, blustering army man in the sixteenth film in the Carry On series.

There are some lovely comedy moments between him and Hawtrey, the latter a troublesome recruit marched off in synch with Terry, with accompanying music, to be chastised by Captain Keene (Roy Castle). Angela Douglas plays Princess Jelhi, daughter of the Khasi of Kalabar (Kenneth Williams) who falls for the stiff-upper-lipped Keene whilst her father plots to rid his country of the British invaders.

Sid James is Sir Sidney Ruff-Diamond, Governor of India, more pre-occupied with taking 'tiffin' than his other duties. Whilst his wife, played by the fabulous Joan Sims, becomes besotted with the Khasi, almost betraying her husband by taking a photograph of the Brit soldiers revealing whether or not they are wearing prohibited underwear. This discovery is used by the Khasi and Bungdit Din (Bernie Bresslaw) to dispel the myth of invincibility that many rebels hold them.

Keene, Sgt Terry, Hawtrey and the weak-willed missionary Belcher (a hilarious Peter Butterworth) infiltrate the rebels with the intention of recovering the incriminating picture. Crudely adopting fake beards and native dress, the foursome burst into the Khasi's palace, where big Bernie mistakes them for tribal leaders and offers them the shapely delights available from a very busty Alexandra Dane, Valerie Leon and others. Kissing and cuddling, Widdle (Hawtrey) causes mayhem until a furious Din (Bernie) enters to rectify his error.

A deadline for execution is set but Jehli and Joan Sims set about rescuing the boys by disguising them as women! The men do look a sight dressed in fetching saris and veils but the plan appears to be foiled when Bernie assumed that they are the dance troupe sent to entertain the Khasi. Widdle accidentally blows their cover by inadvertently revealing his underwear but in the resultant confusion, they manage to escape. Regrettably, in their haste, Joan drops the photo and the Khasi orders an immediate attack upon the Khyber Pass outpost.

Arriving there, the six find all the soldiers dead apart from Ginger (Peter Gilmore). He and Terry had appeared together in panto at the London Palladium in 1966. The rebels storm towards the pass, where Keene (Castle) initially volunteers to man the defence and allow the others an escape route. MacNulty (Scott) suggests that he should do this and orders Widdle to also remain, whilst the others flee. Unbeknownst to the two remaining, all the weapons have been sabotaged, leaving them defenceless. Manning a machine gun, Terry commences cranking it up to start firing at the oncoming enemy only for the device to play music via a gramophone record in a superb visual gag; a nearby cannon has also been 'corked' and ends up firing backwards when they try to utilise it.

Meanwhile, Sir Sidney partakes in continuous 'tiffin' with the many wives of the Khasi, until his private secretary (Julian Holloway) tries to warn him of his wife's return. Pleading for her husband's forgiveness at her foolishness with the Khasi, Lady Rough-Diamond (Sims) becomes incensed by "the filthy old governor" upon discovering what he has been engaging in i.e. illicit affairs.

135

Below: Terry (top row, immediate right) imortalised as a Carry On gang member from Khyber, illustration courtesy of stevelilart.co.uk

Keene is pleased to see that Whittle and MacNulty have made it back to the embassy building (in actuality, the manor house at Pinewood studios), with Sgt Terry taking immediate charge of the men. A chance to surrender is rebuffed by Sir Sidney who decrees that the evening's formal dinner will commence as they ignore the onslaught of an impending invasion.

In what has since become regarded as a classic Carry On moment, the guests continue to dine whilst gunfire and explosions abound. A small band plays on and only Belcher (Butterworth) reacts to the mayhem; jumping and looking terrified as the building rumbles and the guests are caked in mortar dust. The sequence took three days to film and the "Oh dear, I seem to be a little plastered!" ad lib from Joan Sims was kept in the final cut.

Terry comes in and informs Sir Sidney of the battle outside, returning there to react to Johnnie Briggs' "bullet in the sporran" line. Sidney steps outside and orders the men to retreat and to then raise their kilts to reveal to the enemy that underwear is no longer worn. This sends them scurrying away, all observed by him, Terry, Keene (Castle) and Major Shorthouse (Holloway).

As the group returns inside, it is left to Terry's off screen friend Peter Butterworth to deliver the final line, "Of course, they're all raving mad, you know!"

Khyber is held as the best in the series and actress Joan Sims felt it was, too. UK cinemagoers in 1968 acquiesced, making it the most popular film of the year. The Carry On film makers never went very far when shooting their pictures; Camber Sands or around the Pinewood studios area, Windsor or Brighton being the furthest. But for Khyber, much of the cast and crew decamped to Mount Snowden, north Wales, for one week's cold location shooting during May 1968.

Director Gerald Thomas and an erudite Kenneth Williams were briefly interviewed by a local television crew and some charming, soundless footage of Terry larking about with a bespectacled Roy Castle survives.

Tommy Cooper from And the Same to You (1960), a film within which Terry Scott also appeared in, was originally going to play the Fakhir role but having proved unavailable it went to Cardew Robinson, who had worked with Terry previously.

Scott returned to the popular series after a ten year break, since appearing in the first offering Carry On Sergeant (1958). Involved with that film, he was overheard by producer Peter Rogers

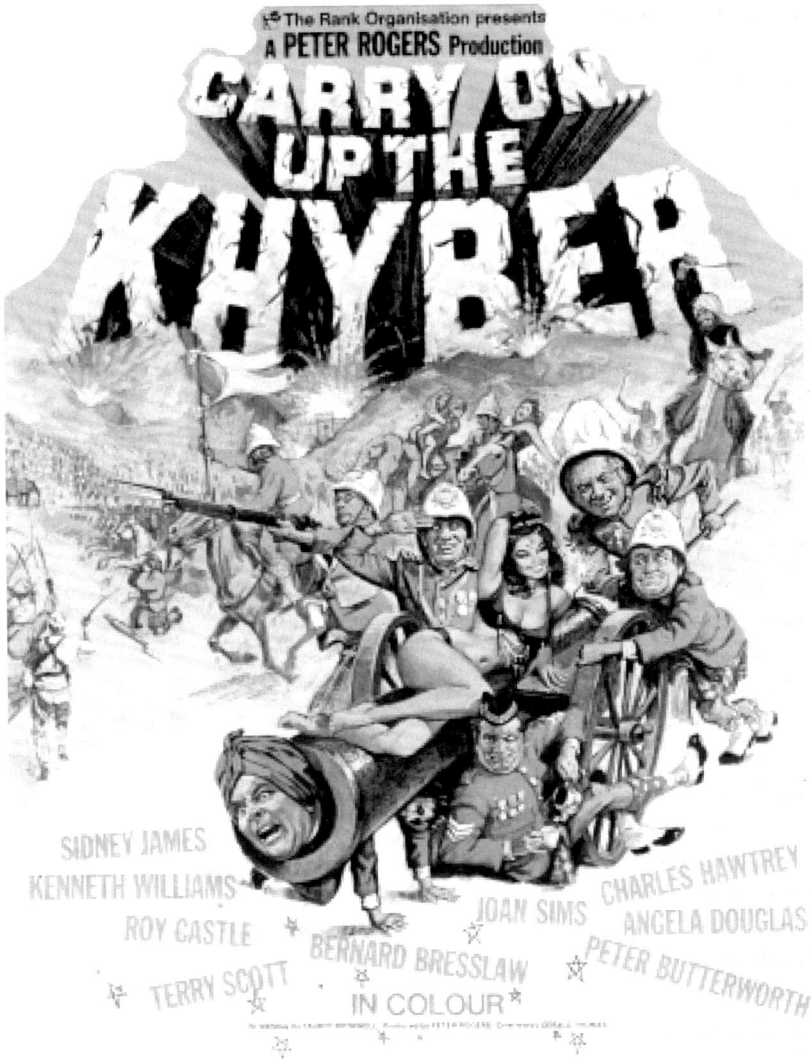

The Rank Organisation presents

A PETER ROGERS Production

CARRY ON UP THE KHYBER

SIDNEY JAMES
KENNETH WILLIAMS
ROY CASTLE
TERRY SCOTT
BERNARD BRESSLAW
JOAN SIMS
CHARLES HAWTREY
ANGELA DOUGLAS
PETER BUTTERWORTH
IN COLOUR

wondering to himself just what he was doing in such a small role back when his theatre work was proving successful. He would not appear in the next one but would return swiftly enough, for a memorable role in Carry On Camping (1969).

After a three year hiatus, Scott On... returns to BBC television on Sunday 29 September at 7:25pm, where Terry was joined by his future 'wife', the brilliant June Whitfield, in the episode Scott On Marriage. Remembering the time that she first worked with him, June felt a little in awe of his established name in the business but

GALES OF LAUGHTER—
AS THE WINDS BLOW UP THE KHYBER
AND THE KILTS OF THE 'CARRY ON'ARMY!

The Rank Organisation Presents

A PETER ROGERS
PRODUCTION

CARRY ON
UP THE KHYBER

in COLOUR

SIDNEY JAMES
KENNETH WILLIAMS
CHARLES HAWTREY
ROY CASTLE
JOAN SIMS
ANGELA DOUGLAS
TERRY SCOTT

Screenplay by
TALBOT ROTHWELL
Produced by
PETER ROGERS

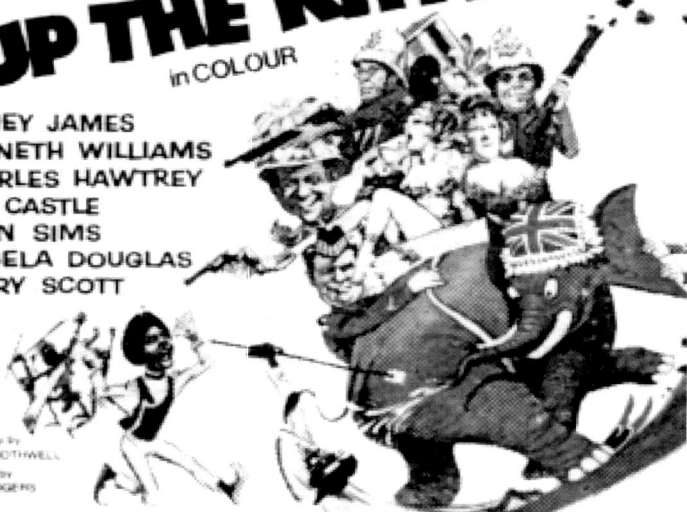

she clearly left an impression upon him that would see them working together, on and off, for the rest of his career.

Written by Leicester-born creative Bryan Blackburn, he had worked with many light comedians and here uses a mixture of chat and sketches, interspersed with dancers moving to the love and marriage song, each wearing bridal wear and top hats/suits!

Marriage was only the third Scott On since its inception back in 1964. Terry is featured talking directly to the camera and introducing/ acting in sketches that relate to a chosen topic. Recorded in front of a live, studio audience, Scott On shows a dynamic Terry, quite different from the one we would see later on in the TV sitcoms.

Terry and June team up together for the very first time as a posh hippie couple being interviewed by a perplexed Peter Butterworth working very hard in dealing the randy couple spread out on top of a plastic, inflatable sofa and its comedy value (and very funny they are too, especially Butterworth's attempts at chatting with them).

Also in the cast: Carmel Cryan, Pearl Hackney, Leslie Meadows, Elizabeth Edmiston, Bella Emberg and others. Ms Hackney would act in 2 episodes of Happy Ever After and in 1976, in an edition of TV hit Whodunnit? when Terry was on the panel.

For the pantomime season, Terry played Martha (the Nurse) with Hugh and Dickie Henderson at the Wimbledon theatre for their production of The Adventures of Robin Hood. With music and lyrics from The Shadows, it was produced by Bill Roberton with its book written by David Croft. Peter Gilmore played Robin in amongst a large cast: David Hartley, John Gower, Garry and Cheryl Burfield, Melanie Munro, Arthur Parry, John Turtle, Ronald Sinclair, Alan Schneider, Richard Smith, Mary Hewing, Ron Richards, Rita King Dancers, Kirby's Flying Ballet, Bel Canto Singers and Pierre Picton's Crazy Car.

"Two grown-up men carrying on like hooligans, in front of innocent little children?"

Based upon an original story by Ed Harper, A Ghost of a Chance was developed into a script by the experienced juvenile writer Patricia Lathom and directed by Jan Darnley-Smith for the Children's Film Foundation (CFF)/ Fanfare Films Ltd. With its brisk running time of 50 minutes, A Ghost of a Chance is not to be confused with the equally smashing, 1970s TV series The Ghosts of Motley Hall.

Shot on location in Buckinghamshire, the film employed a superlative cast of comedy actors, namely Terry, Ronnie Barker, Bernard Cribbins, Patricia Hayes, Jimmy Edwards, Graham Stark and some lesser-known but recognisable faces. Ms. Hayes had worked with Terry Scott in the early-1960s on Hugh and I, and many of the others also have a working association with him, which I will detail in a moment.

Plot wise, a trio of youngsters make use of a derelict mansion house as their play area, with the hope of it eventually becoming a youth centre (aided by their friendly dotty librarian, Hayes). The building was once the home of the Hermitage family and the children soon discover that Sir Jocelyn (Edwards) still resides there, alongside the worrisome Thomas (Stark), the latter having a penchant for removing his head although unlike Worzel Gummidge, he only has the one to utilize! Stark is in fine form as the dour spirit forever linked to big Jimmy Edwards' character. Jimmy had worked alongside Terry in Nearly a Nasty Accident (1961) whilst Stark had small roles in the Terry-related films Double Bunk (1961) and A Pair of Briefs (1962).

Terry plays Wells, a manager of a redevelopment team working for Mr Prendergast (Ronnie Barker in a bowler hat, a recognisable i.d of

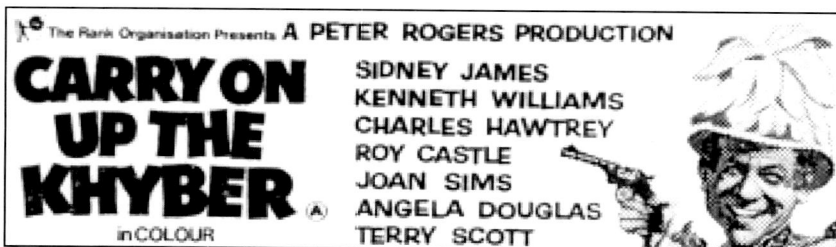

a wrongdoer in CFF movies) and assisted by the dozy Ron (Cribbins), "I'll do the thinking, you get the stuff!" Both Terry and Bernard are known for their distinctive voices and who can forget the latter as the voice of Tufty or The Wombles? And like his co-star, Cribbins also made comedy records, his most famous being Right Said Fred. It really is great to see these performers together and the introductory quote is taken from Miss Woolie discovering the two men wrestling on the floor after being disturbed by the ghosts/ children.

Ronnie Barker and Terry appear at the old house and are overheard by the kids detailing their plans to demolish the property the following day. But first, Prendergast (Barker) wants to salvage the wooden panelling in the hall as he recognises the place as a "goldmine". Bernie and Terry subsequently return to do this task unaware of the children and resident ghost's plans to sabotage their every move. This they do by removing tools, locking/ unlocking doors, spooking them and resulting in poor Terry's face being covered in soot and then given a soaking during some lovely slapstick moments. In fact, Terry very much plays the Ollie role to Mr. Cribbins' Stan.

Ghost is a quintessential 1960s piece, complete with heavy use of loud, incidental music and would have been shown at the Saturday morning cinemas clubs where admittance was under a shilling.

With little time to spare if they are to save the building, Ms Hayes, the children and ghosts (invisible when outdoors), speed off to locate the absent mayor, who is unaware of the impending demolition. As the bulldozers arrive, the ghosts set about interfering with the machinery and there is a marvellous sequence seeing Barker, Terry and Bernie being chased around by the out-of-control dozers. It proves a treat to see Scott and Barker reunited on screen some four years since they shared moments together in Father Came Too!

If you are wondering what happens in the end, they manage to bring the mayor to the property in time to halt the destruction.

Hurrah!

Cast

Stephen Brown...Mike
Mark Ward...John
Cheryl Vidgen...Jane
Jimmy Edwards...Sir Jocelyn
Graham Stark...Thomas Dogood
Patricia Hayes...Miss Woolie
Bernard Cribbins...Ron
Terry...Wells
Ronnie Barker...Prendergast
John Bluthal...Assistant Mayor
Roy Evans...Driver
Jerod Wells...Demolition man
Norman Pitt... Demolition man

Carry On Camping (1969) is probably the most repeated picture in the series to be shown on television. Leading man Sid James said that he went to see it in a Blackpool cinema whilst there for the summer season. There, he was amazed to hear the delighted audience enjoying the film (what a pleasure it must have been to have experienced seeing a Carry On with an audience).

For Terry, he was playing the clubs with Hugh Lloyd before filming commitments on Camping.

Shot during winter 1968, if you look closely, you will see the actor's breath during the plunging temperatures (the story is supposed to be set in summertime!) Camping was the seventeenth in the series and followed on from the excellent Carry On up the Khyber (1968) which Terry also had a role in. An 'A' certificate, it was released theatrically at the end of May this year.

Story wise, we find an ageing Sid and big Bernie (Bresslaw) keen to get their buttoned-up girl friend's Joan (Joan Sims) and Anthea (Dilys Laye) under canvas, at a nudist camp site; something that they neglect to mention when being seen off by Joan's mum, Mrs Fussey (an ever-excellent Amelia Bayntun). She and Terry would soon share an amusing scene as patient and doctor in Carry On Matron (1972).

Meanwhile city gent Peter Potter (Terry) dreams of enjoying a luxurious holiday abroad, as glimpsed in the glossy brochures that he brings home. Greeted by Harriet (Betty Marsden), his deliciously annoying wife, seen checking through their camping equipment, persuading her looks a tricky task. Not listening to a word he has to say, poor Peter fails to get his way and another bothersome outdoor trip is arranged for the couple.

Setting the tone for their break, the middle-aged Potters commence their adventure on a tandem, dressed in matching khakis! Terry's pouting is a joy to behold as it seems that he has been the victim of many a mishap on previous trips and Harriet, complete with her idiosyncratic laugh, all air out and then gulped back in again, gleefully recalls them, much to his obvious dismay.

Elsewhere, the pupils and staff of Chaste Place girl's boarding school, the latter represented by a stuffy Doctor Soaper (Kenneth Williams) and buoyant Miss Haggard (Hattie Jacques) are also making their way to the so-called 'Paradise' camp. Barbara Windsor is the main figure, no pun intended, amongst the pupils, all looking far too old for their parts.

Having to cycle to the camp site, the Potters stop for a picnic in a field where they are not the only occupants. With their breath frozen, chatting Terry and Betty realise that there is a bull about to attack and with his red handkerchief tucked into his top, you can guess the result. In a clever bit of editing, director Gerald Thomas shows his actor being shot over a hedgerow and onto the muddy ground but we never actually see the creature.

On another blustery day of location filming, the couple pitch their tent and Terry goes off to a local farmhouse, familiar to him from the previous year, to get some milk. The farmer, a billowing Derek Francis, thinks that Terry is the one responsible for getting his daughter pregnant and pursues him with a shotgun, "Bullseye!" He manages to shoot Terry up the bum.

Nearby, Sid and Co arrive at the camp and the boys are dismayed to discover that it is not a nudist site after all. Not only that, the proprietor, a greedy Mr Fiddler (Peter Butterworth in his best Carry On role) takes pound note after pound note off them for various charges.

Glimpsed in silhouette form in their cramp tent, in a truly iconic Carry On sequence, Charles Hawtrey watches and listens to Harriet plucking buckshot out from her husband's behind. Soaked from having lost his own tent, Charlie calls in on them and is invited to stay the night. Revealing their sexless marriage, Terry manages to ignite the seat of his trousers when he touches the naked flame coming from a large gas canister inside their canvas home. He dashes outside and plonks his bum into a bucket of water! In a superb piece of choreographed comedy involving all three actors attempting to undress for bed, Terry manages to put his arm into Charlie's jacket and he, in turn, sticks his leg into Terry's pyjama bottoms.

Setting off very early in the morning, so as to lose Charlie, the Potters ride off and eventually arrive at Fiddler's site. Potter's disappointment is palpable upon being informed that past visitors such as them, are welcomed back on site.

In the meantime, the sexually-frustrated Bernie and Sid look more than delighted to see the school party's arrival, especially when spotting a busty Babs amongst them. This will make Joan and Anthea jealous when the boys chat with her and a girlfriend later.

Unfortunately for the Potters, Charlie finds them again and spends another night with them. Peter, disturbed by the snoring of both Harriet and their guest, awakens early and stepping outside, gasps as Kenneth and the girls begin their stretching exercises on the muddy 'grass' opposite. Joined by Harriet, still not listening to him, she cooks them breakfast. There is a photograph of the actors taken during rehearsal, where both are wrapped up against the elements but come the actual scene, they were obliged to remove. The production crew sprayed the trees and grass to make it appear like summer, too!

Keen to remove his unwanted company, Terry goes off alone one morning and gets quite sloshed. It is then that he accepts a pretty young woman's proposal for a bit of, excuse me: 'nookie'. Of all the main characters, he is the only one to be participating in these off-screen moments (apart from Babs and her friends engaging in a bit of snogging with some locals). However, Hattie's character does pursue Kenneth after thinking that he is interested in her. Returning to the camp site, an invigorated Peter (Terry) removes Charles from their tent and ladles a huge vat of mushy peas slosh over his head for good measure. He also directs Harriet inside where the two rekindle their romantic relationship. (It works, as we hear her surprised response).

Babs and her pals are excited to discover a rave up in the next field where many hippie-types gather as a band plays.

A PETER ROGERS PRODUCTION

IN COLOUR

CARRY ON CAMPING

SIDNEY JAMES · KENNETH WILLIAMS · CHARLES HAWTREY
JOAN SIMS · TERRY SCOTT · HATTIE JACQUES
BARBARA WINDSOR · BERNARD BRESSLAW · PETER BUTTERWORTH

A PETER ROGERS Production

CARRY ON CAMPING

in COLOUR

SIDNEY JAMES · KENNETH WILLIAMS · CHARLES HAWTREY · JOAN SIMS · TERRY SCOTT
HATTIE JACQUES · BARBARA WINDSOR · BERNARD BRESSLAW · PETER BUTTERWORTH

SCREENPLAY BY TALBOT ROTHWELL   PRODUCED BY PETER ROGERS   DIRECTED BY GERALD THOMAS

Disturbing the likes of Sid and the others, they set about breaking it up. Only Babs, Charlie and the girls all go off with the departing revellers; the opposite of what Sid had intended. Hattie and Kenneth chase after them on the Potters tandem. With the new and positively assertive Peter unperturbed, it looks like his and Harriet's relationship will be different now since he has exerted some chutzpah.

Sid/Joan and Bernie/ little Anthea head off to separate tents, with Joan looking directly at the camera and making their intentions clear to the audience. The only hurdle being that her mother has just arrived on site. Anthea (Ms Laye) saves the day by letting loose a ram which chases off the unwanted guest!

On television, the second full series of Scott On is shown. Directed by Peter Whitmore, he and Terry would begin developing the idea of extending the domestic comedy sketch featuring Terry and June Whitfield into a full series. This would but not happen for a few years.Scott On, whose format was termed 'documentary comedies' gets six episodes shown between 21 September - 2 November.

Scott On Habits opens the series on Sunday 28 September for

another forty five minutes of observations. It was followed by Scott On Superstition; Scott On The Seven Deadly Sins; Scott On Leisure; Scott On The Body and finally, Scott On Christmas.

A real departure from the norm, The Gnomes of Dulwich began on Monday 12 May, 8:50pm, on BBC Two. Writing on the Independent website in 2008, Anthony Hayward offered, "...[It was] a slightly surreal and less successful sitcom...about three life-sized gnomes in one garden – Big (Terry Scott), Small (Hugh Lloyd) and Old (John Clive) lined up against plastic impostors in the next."

What a Carry On!
Select the FUNNIEST SCENES Contest:

SIDNEY JAMES · KENNETH WILLIAMS
CHARLES HAWTREY · JOAN SIMS · TERRY SCOTT
HATTIE JACQUES · BARBARA WINDSOR
BERNARD BRESSLAW · PETER BUTTERWORTH
star in
"CARRY ON CAMPING"

Presenting the first of six, half-hour episodes of this curious little comedy from the mind of Dad's Army co-creator Jimmy Perry, the unusual premise of the show found Terry and Hugh Lloyd as the aforementioned stone gnomes living in the front garden of 25 Telegraph Road, Dulwich. Resplendent in their long beards, rosy red cheeks and elongated hats, each episode filled the same slot and the series would run concurrently until 16 June.

We have to thank Jimmy's wife for persuading her husband to develop his initial idea for a short sketch intended for Morecambe and Wise, into a series. Presented by the new BBC 2 channel, oversized sets were constructed to make the actors appear tiny. The show left an indelible mark upon Terry Scott. "Whenever I pass a garden decorated with gnomes and Mr Bunn, our baker, has some, I start wondering of they've had a good night. I've even had an impulse to trespass and start moving the gnomes about!"

THE RANK ORGANISATION presents A PETER ROGERS PRODUCTION

CARRY ON CAMPING IN COLOUR

SIDNEY JAMES · KENNETH WILLIAMS · CHARLES HAWTREY
JOAN SIMS · TERRY SCOTT · HATTIE JACQUES

It seems that Perry, then flying high after two series of Dad's Army under his and David Croft's shared belt, was pleased to have gotten Scott and Lloyd to star in the project despite their initial concerns. Joined by Clive Dunn, this trio of British-made, stone gnomes soon come into conflict with so-called 'Empire' plastic gnomes nearby. The title for the show was a play on the-then Prime Minister, Harold Wilson, commenting about Swiss bankers as the 'gnomes of Zurich'.

Cast members found their costumes both hot and hefty to wear whilst taking an age to be made-up in their distinct make-up (termed "gnomification" by the actors). However, the effect was striking and Terry and the others soon found themselves able to get into character next to the oversized scenery. Radio Times included a photo of Terry and Hugh in a May edition of the listings magazine that could be purchased from your local newsagents for eightpence. Sadly, all the episodes are now deemed lost although there was a clip featuring the characters that featured on a compilation show.

Director Graeme Muir had an fulsome CV as both a producer/ director and here was supported by Producer Sydney Lotterby here and across many of the great BBC sitcoms including Some Mother's do 'Ave 'Em and Porridge, lots of which he also directed. The music for the show was supplied by the prodigious composer/ arranger Ronnie Hazelhurst. His catalogue, amongst other things, would include Happy Ever After and The Last of the Summer Wine.

Gnomes was of significance to the professional partnership of Scott and Lloyd as it marked its close. They would work together once more but not in any way like they had up to this point.

Hugh Lloyd, M.B.E, with his expressive comic face, was to be remembered in his 5 Aug 2008 Stage obituary, by Patrick Newley, as being described as resembling a melancholic mole by. He was 85.

Leon Thau, one of the gnomes, was an actor/writer that like Terry, had a role in Carry On up the Khyber (1968) and The Great St Trinian's Train Robbery (1966). Whilst for a generation of children, co-star John Clive will forever be loved for his work on the 1970s show Roberts Robots, whilst others may remember him for Carry On Abroad (1972).

Like Terry, but separately, he also performed on stage in The Mating Game.

Episode one

"...Big fishing with his rod, Old fast asleep holding his spade, and Small feeding his frog all day. But their serenity is not all it might seem at first glance. Even stone gnomes can have trouble, trouble with the neighbours-especially when they are different."

That was how bbc.co.uk defined the premise of the new show.

Cast

Terry Scott...Big
Hugh Lloyd...Small
John Clive...Old
Leon Thau...Plastic

Guest cast

Horace James...Gnome
Max Latimer...Gnome
Gillian Phelps...Gnome
Celia Robinson...Gnome
Michael Slater...Gnome
Lionel Wheeler...Gnome

Episode two

Small develops feelings for a female gnome and seeks advice from the Top Gnome, played by Dad's Army grouch John Laurie.

Cast

John Clive...Old
Leon Thau...Plastic

Cast

Sidney James...Sid Boggle
Charles Hawtrey...Charlie Muggins
Joan Sims...Joan Fussey
Kenneth Williams...Doctor Kenneth Soaper
Terry Scott...Peter Potter
Barbara Windsor...Babs
Hattie Jacques...Miss Haggard
Bernard Bresslaw...Bernie Lugg
Julian Holloway...Jim
Dilys Laye...Anthea Meeks
Peter Butterworth...Fiddler
Betty Marsden...Harriet Potter
Trisha Noble...Sally
Brian Oulton...Mr. Short
Derek Francis...Farmer
Elizabeth Knight...Jane
Sandra Caron...Fanny
Georgina Moon...Joy
Jennifer Pyle...Hilda
Jackie Poole...Betty
Sally Kemp...Girl with Cow
Amelia Bayntun...Mrs. Fussey
Patricia Franklin...Farmer's Daughter
Michael Nightingale...Man in Cinema
George Moon...Scrawny Man
Valerie Shute...Pat
Vivien Lloyd...Verna
Lesley Duff...Norma
Anna Karen...Boarding Girl
Valerie Leon...Miss Dobbin
Peter Cockburn...Commentator (voice/ uncredited)

Lyn Dalby...Rita

Anne De Vigier...Dolly

Guest Cast

John Laurie...Top Gnome

Roger Brierley...Gnome

Colin Bean...Gnome

Linda James...Gnome

Episode three

Creator Jimmy Perry was able to indulge his love of gnomes in this series and had the canny idea to feature characters that lived secretly away from the noisy "human beans" all around them. In this episode, the gnomes are taken by the fun had by their human neighbours but wonder if it looks more trouble than it seems.

A familiar face making a guest appearance was Jack Haig from Hugh and I, an actor that would subsequently pick up again with Terry in episodes of both Happy Ever After and Terry and June. Story wise, the gnomes come in to strife with their European neighbours.

Cast

John Clive...Old

Leon Thau...Plastic

Lyn Dalby...Rita

Anne De Vigier...Dolly

Guest cast

Roger Brierley...Gnome

Linda James...Gnome

Jack Haig...Gnome

Nicholas McAdle...Gnome

Mathew Robertson...Gnome

Shirley Stanwell...Gnome

Alan Haines...Gnome

Tony McLaren...Gnome

Episode four

Terry, Hugh Lloyd, John Clive, Leon Thau, Lynn Dalby and Anne De Vigier were joined by a guest rota of gnome actors.

Cast

John Clive...Old

Leon Thau...Plastic

Lyn Dalby...Rita

Anne De Vigier...Dolly

Guest cast

Roger Brierley...Gnome

Linda James...Gnome

Chris Gannon...Gnome

Colin Spaull...Gnome

James McManus...Gnome

Bernard Spear...Gnome

Episode five

Roy Kinnear guest starred as a replica 'Big' in this episode where he is introduced into the pond where the gnomes all live. However, he is an exact replica of Terry's Big, even coming from the same place. The question is, can the two co-exist?

Mr Kinnear, the much-missed comedy actor, would also act alongside Terry in Eric Sykes' Mr H is Late (1988).

Same principal cast joined by guests:

Roger Brierley...Gnome

Linda James...Gnome

Ronald Fletcher...Gnome

Episode six

The final one of the series was broadcast on Monday 16 June with Hugh and Terry being joined in the fun by a large list of guests, including creator Jimmy Perry. The gnomes find themselves having being sold off, leaving their familiar home for a new life at a very famous address: 10 Downing Street, London.

Guest cast

Colin Bean...Gnome

Jimmy Perry...Gnome

Nigel Hawthorne...Gnome

Barry Cryer...Gnome

Frank Williams...Gnome

Myfanwy Jenn...Gnome

Gilda Perry...Gnome

Derek Lanyon...Gnome

Marguerite Young...Gnome

Regarded as gamble of sorts by series producer Peter Rogers, moving the Carry On team to television proved to be a popular one, with Carry On Christmas becoming a huge ratings success this year.

Mr Rogers need not have worried as his cast brought a mass of small screen experience to a programme that only let's itself down by looking a bit cheap (wobbly sets etc). Made by Thames for ITV, it was shown on Christmas Eve in a 9:15 pm slot and watched by 18m+. This saw it top the festive TV 'Top 10' list.

With Sid James as Scrooge ably supported by Terry, Charles Hawtrey, Hattie Jacques, Barbara Windsor, Bernard Bresslaw and special guest star Frankie Howerd, Talbot Rothwell wrote the script which was directed by Ronnie Baxter. There are some silent on screen moments where loud incidental music is used before a full scene is played out.

Terry appears in the second scene, as a choir member that gets blown up by Sid's comedy bomb! Just as June Whitfield remembered Terry as always singing louder than everybody else, he does here.

Scrooge is to be visited by the spirit of Christmas past/ present and future (Charles Hawtrey/ Babs and Bernie Bresslaw, respectively). Whilst Terry plays "Doctor Frank n Stein", looking smart in a green velvet waistcoat, check trousers and frilly shirt. Visited by Count Dracula (a delightful Peter Butterworth) Terry is overwhelmed by the potion that he has concocted before reappearing in cheap werewolf gloves, hairy face and fangs.

Enter Frankie, now in slight disguise as a doctor to tend to her. Terry has to stifle a snigger when Howerd clearly fluffs his line before they carry on and finish a very enjoyable interaction.

Next we find Cinderella (Windsor) with ugly sisters Aggie (Butterworth) and Baggie (Terry). "Sharp as a Teddy Boy's tyre-slasher," quips Peter to his equally outrageously-dressed sibling. Terry favours a blond wig with a 'flapper' feel to his fashion sense, minus one eyelash. Camping it up wonderfully, the actors then speak in rhyme. Hawtrey enters as Buttons; then along with Ms Windsor, their 'flabber' is indeed 'gasted' at seeing Howerd enter as the "good fairy". Looking glorious in a silver dress and complimentary hair, he is absolutely brilliant in a scene where Charlie cannot stop grinning.

The final moment sees Sid as Scrooge changing his ways but giving the wrong impression to a woman in the street when he attempts to give her some money to have "a good time." Nearby Bobbie Bernie Bresslaw arrives and takes him away in a smashing close to the show.

Panto commitments concluded another strenuous year for Terry as he based himself in Newcastle, at the sumptuous Theatre Royal, in

Cinderella. Directed by the vastly experienced Freddie Carpenter, Scott was cast as one of the ugly sisters, joining Jimmy Logan as Buttons, in a show that proved very welcomed by local audiences.

"A simply wonderful season," is how Carry On Abroad/ Girls star Logan remembered it in his weighty autobiography, "People couldn't get seats, and I kept getting stopped in the street by folk asking if I could get them a ticket." Both vying for prominence and in spite of their professional and personal differences, the two would work together again for the 1981/2 season.

Below: Actual theatre tickets from various shows starring Terry over the years.

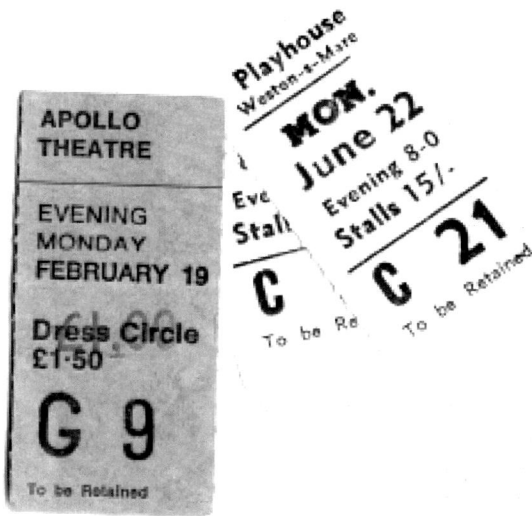

Terry in the 1970s

"When I see him, I really laugh and that wonderful baby face," giggled co-star Valerie Leon, leader of the female tribe in Carry On Up the Jungle, providing the accompanying DVD commentary to this the nineteenth Carry On film, "He was wonderful."

Terry stepped into the role of a Tarzan-like jungle man after series regular Jim Dale declined. This casting change was not unique, as Kenneth Williams was originally offered the role as ornithologist Inigo Tinkle but the part was to be played by the inimitable Frankie Howerd. However, Terry is all rugged and monosyllabic whilst Howerd 'Oohs and Arghs' fabulously in an amusing script provided by Talbot Rothwell. The two are both so convincing and provide so much enjoyment that how they arrived in being in the film hardly matters. Carry On producer extraordinaire Peter Rogers thought his performance excellent.

Terry is part of a sterling ensemble cast starring in the studio-bound romp. The characterisations of all of them are immaculate, Joan Sims as the comely Lady Bagley, soon to reveal a very close connection to Terry, Sid James as an uncouth guide, a returning Kenneth Connor as a randy assistant to Tinkle and Bernard Bresslaw, blacked-up as local guide Upsidaisi (he proves especially funny in shared moments with James). Released in cinemas in the same year as Carry On Loving, both pictures offered major contributions from Terry Scott.

Here, in Jungle, as a loin-cloth clad jungle man, somewhat rotund but highly amusing, during the film it transpires (Spoiler Alert) that his character turns out to be Joan Sims' long-lost son. But in real life, he was actually three years older than her!

A virginal Jacki Piper made her debut in Jungle as an assistant to Lady Bagshaw but finding love with Terry's character. Her initial meeting with him beneath a waterfall is a true classic Carry On moment, seeing her attempt to explain the differences between a man and a woman by way of a basic stick figure is especially amusing; especially when he innocently adds a certain appendage! Coincidentally, this scene was shot during Terry's first day of filming at Pinewood studios. Also sharing her memories on the DVD commentary, Jackie said that the two had rehearsed the scene earlier but were puzzled when the crew were all laughing during a take. It was later disclosed that Terry had inadvertently suffered a first sight of him, Terry peels off a tree and leaves a full body indent.) Unable to speak, Scott has to express his thoughts via facial gestures, which he does wonderfully. Indeed, he would have been a great success in silent pictures. As the jungle man, Terry in no way resembles Johnny Weissmuller but seems happy living above the tree tops until he spots the lovely Miss Piper. But even this primitive can see that there are striking differences between his physique and that of hers or the shapely Joan Sims.

Jungle offers little subtlety in his comedy but approached with an easy-going vibe there is much enjoyment to be found and even a pure farce sequence (with tents rather than bedroom doors). Look out for the dinner party scene involving a snake and Joan Sims demonstrating why she is the true Queen of Carry On.

Terry was recorded as acknowledging that on lots of film sets people do not necessarily talk to each other but this not being the case on Jungle. Filmed across October - November in 1969, there could be no place for temperaments on a Carry On set, "you get sent up rotten [14]," offered co-star Bernard Bresslaw.

"Well, it's like getting back into the fold," explained Terry in an on-set interview recorded for a Film Night special called Carry On Forever. "Getting back into a film-type Crazy Gang. You're all friendly and you don't have to establish relationships. We all know who plays cards. We all know who likes bacon sandwiches in the morning: it's Joan Sims." Whilst Joanie allied it to going back to school. Sid James favoured the family metaphor himself.

THE RANK ORGANISATION PRESENTS
A PETER ROGERS PRODUCTION
The Carry On team in STARKEST Africa
CARRY ON UP THE JUNGLE.

"If you're no good, you won't do another one," remarked Terry bluntly. By this point, Terry had been in Carry On Sergeant, Khyber; a businessman that would prefer a holiday in the sun rather than under canvas in Camping and then here in Jungle.

"I think the audiences of the Carry On films they're growing but the nucleus is the same. And they know how to shut up when a funny line is being said...they don't laugh through many laughs, you can work pretty fast on a Carry On film. Whereas possibly in other films you are inclined to have to wait and imagine, "will they laugh?" whereas in a wardrobe mishap, hence the giggling! June (Ms Piper) wants to share a kiss with his but he has no idea as to what he is meant to do but seeing the pretty actress, it cannot have been difficult to muster the enthusiasm. Both actors shared the same representation: a certain Richard Stone and would work together again in the theatre.

Wittily, Rothwell makes his character the worst ever 'Lord of the Jungle', as he constantly crashes into trees and falls about (in our Carry On film you are pretty certain they will laugh." Terry tongue-slightly-in-cheek, added, "They are well-trained."

Both Terry and Jackie Piper suffered for their art during filming due to the painful harness that they were attached to, for the sake of a sequence where they swing along together. At the film's close, we see Terry returning home in a suit; bowler hat and umbrella ala Carry On Camping, only when the camera pans down, we see that he has no shoes on. Heading towards the plush white exterior of a house (with a real location in Windsor being used), he turns and

Ⓐ🅱️Ⓒ①②③④

Cast

Sid James...Bill Boosey

Frankie Howerd...Prof. Tinkle

Joan Sims...Lady Evelyn Bagley

Terry...Ugh, the Jungle Boy

Charles Hawtrey...Tonka the Great/ Walter Bagley

Bernard Bresslaw...Upsidaisi

Kenneth Connor...Claude Chumley

Jacki Piper...June

Valerie Leon...Leda

Edwina Carroll...Nerda

THE RANK ORGANISATION PRESENTS
A PETER ROGERS PRODUCTION

CARRY ON UP THE JUNGLE Ⓐ

clambers up a rope ladder to a tree house and is greeted by June and their baby. Both actors would be seen again very soon, as Carry On Loving would follow the same year.

"The people involved in the team were proper, real professional actors and actresses who really, really knew their craft and were brilliant at what they did." Jacki Piper, March 2008 at the 50th anniversary of the Carry On films at Pinewood studios.

For the next Carry On, Loving, scriptwriter Talbot Rothwell took a playful look at the world of matrimony agencies in this rather slight entry in the series. Eric Rogers makes his rousing music score gel perfectly and it is a delight to see the likes of a returning Kenneth Williams, Patsy Rowlands and Hattie Jacques. Youngsters Richard O'Callaghan and Ms Piper play out a fun storyline in a movie that was well-received by cinema audiences. The film poster exhibited outside theatres featured a comic illustration of Terry and company "Doing their bit for laughter!" in this 'A' certificate feature. On future VHS and DVD covers, he was pictured with the delectable Imogen Hassall.

Cast in the role of the jovial Terence Philpot, a jolly type with a natty line in bow ties, Terry looks a bit different here, with his hair brushed forward accompanied by some furry sideburns. He is seen on screen immediately, exchanging a bit of fluff with a fellow rail passenger after departing from station Much Snogging-on-the-Green and remarking upon to his friend about the merits of his own wife.

In Loving, everybody is looking to find a partner, including the naïve and softly-spoken O'Callaghan, son of Terry's work colleague Patricia Hayes, who eventually falls for the sweet Sally (Piper) following some initial confusion generated in the mischievous word play contained in the amusing script.

It is at the Wedded Bliss Agency run by phoney couple Sid and Sophie (a tangerine skinned Sid James and a needy Hattie Jacques) that the characters visit in search of a mate. Popping in and out of the story, around eighteen minutes in, Terry returns and is sent to meet his new match, a plain Jenny Grubb (a fragile Imogen Hassall). Visiting her at her family home proves hilarious for the audience, as he is met by her mother, played by Joan Hickson, and introduced to the numerous other, non-expressive family members, of whom resemble the dour figures seen in a Norman Rockwell painting. Terry does a nice bit of physical comedy by accidentally sitting upon one of the relatives then on some knitting needles, spills his tea and knocks over a table before making his excuses to leave the "one, big happy family" by destroying a cake stand and all its contents! Jenny smiles broadly and we will see them together again as the story progresses.

Whereas Terry's character admits to simply wanting a bit of fun, confirmed bachelor Snooper (Williams) is forced to find a wife after making a mess of things whilst counselling estranged married couple Patricia Franklyn and Bill Maynard. Bill, Terry's former comedy partner, has belittled his involvement with the Carry Ons but has softened his opinions in more recent years.

Originally titled Carry On Courting, quite a large cast is used for this film, many of the names or faces familiar to Terry previously.

SIDNEY JAMES KENNETH WILLIAMS CHARLES HAWTREY
JOAN SIMS HATTIE JACQUES TERRY SCOTT
RICHARD O'CALLAGHAN BERNARD BRESLAW
JACKI PIPER IMOGEN HASSALL star in

THE 20th 'CARRY ON'... "Carry on Loving"

Returning to the plot, the neglected Sophie feels that Sid is more interested in their female clients than her and so employs feeble detective Charles Hawtrey (in a nothing role, sadly) to record his whereabouts and see what mischief he gets up to. This primarily involves chasing after a certain Esme Crowfoot (Joan Sims), whose big, burly boyfriend 'Gripper' (Bernard Bresslaw) unexpectedly returns after a spell away wrestling.

Resplendent in a ponytail, coincidentally Bernie would talk of being a wrestler in another Terry-related film project, Too Many Crooks (1959) but here he demonstrates his prowess.

Furious with Sid for his past matches, Terry returns to the crooked agency and demands a refund. Not wanting to lose his fee, penny-pinching Sid tries to find him an alternative before a radiant Jenny (Ms Hassall, living up to her 'Countess of Cleavage' label) walks in. Dazzling

them both by wearing a figure-revealing canary yellow dress, she wants her details removed from the agency has life has changed for her via a new job and independence gained by joining Sally (Piper) and Gay (Janet Mahoney) in a flat share. Both men fawn over her and Terry changes tact, offering her a lift and telling Mr Bliss that he is absolutely delighted with his match; looking at her, it is hard to disagree. Sid and Terry, having worked together a lot, exude warmth in their moments onscreen.

Taking him back to the flat, imagining that her fellow flatmates are out for the evening, the couple begin canoodling on the sofa until they are interrupted by a casual Sally in her underwear. A running gag occurs, the sound of Jenny's dress zip going up and down, depending on who is around. As the frustrated love birds try again, a rowing Gay and her boyfriend Adrian (a funny Julian Holloway from Carry On Up the Khyber) storm into the flat. With frowns covering their faces, Terry is again interrupted when Bertie (O'Callaghan) calls to pick up date Jackie Piper. Unfortunately Terry and Jenny's amorous adventures are continually thwarted and they simply cannot have the privacy to "get down to it." The script is full of such innuendo and it all works perfectly, flowing much easier than in other Carry On features. Co-star Patsy Rowlands was very complimentary about Terry's bit of sofa comedy, mentioning it during a DVD commentary.

Meanwhile back in the story, Sophie suggests to Mr Snooper that she is his ideal match and following an unbearable meal at his home, constantly interrupted by his infatuated housekeeper Miss Dempsey

Ⓐ①Ⓒ ①②③④ East st BRIGHTON 27010

Cast

Sid James...Sidney Bliss

Kenneth Williams...Percival Snooper

Charles Hawtrey...James Bedsop

Joan Sims...Esme Crowfoot

Terry...Terence Philpot

Richard O'Callaghan...Bertrum Muffet

Bernard Bresslaw...Gripper

Hattie Jacques...Sophie Plummett

Jacki Piper...Sally Martin

Imogen Hassall...Jenny Grubb

Patsy Rowlands...Miss Dempsey

Julian Holloway...Adrian

Janet Mahoney...Gay

Patricia Franklin...Mrs Dreery

Bart Allison...Grandpa

Joan Hickson...Mrs Grubb

Bill Pertwee...Barman

Ronnie Brody...Henry

Valerie Shute/ Mike Grady...Snoggers

Tom Clegg...Trainer

Alexandra Dane...Emily

Derek Francis...Bishop

Bill Maynard...Mr Dreery

Gordon Richardson...Uncle Ernest

Anna Karen...Wife

Kenny Lynch...Bus conductor

Fred Griffiths...Taxi Driver

Amelia Bayntun...Corset Lady

No unaccompanied children admitted after 7pm
ALL PROGRAMMES MAY BE SUBJECT TO LATE CHANGE

(Ms Rowlands) an agreement is made; although he offers little possibility in the line of any carnal activities between them.

Naughty Sid, concerned about losing Sophie at the agency, sets a successful plan in motion to scuttle the union and poor Kenneth receives the full wrath of Gripper until Miss Dempsey duffs him up!

Sophie returns to him after the above events but is infuriated with Sid upon hearing Hawtrey's report of the previous night's escapades with Esme. Under duress, Sid agrees to marry her.

On the day of their wedding reception, Terry and Jenny, the doting Sally and Bertie, Gripper and Esme, and many other sour-faced couples are in attendance. Chaos soon reigns forth, Gripper realizes that Sid was the man at the Rogerham Mansions flat belonging to Esme. Confronting him, he receives a bash on the head with a champagne bottle (Hattie's character does this to Sid, previously). Laughing at this, Esme lobs a blancmange at the "little squirt" Bertie as a mass pie fight erupts all around them. Look out for Laurie Lupino Lane, someone that worked many times with Terry, as the man seated to Imogen Hassall's immediate left in this scene. Terry ends up face down in a gateaux, inflicted upon him by a giggling Jenny in a wordless scene straight out of a silent comedy.

Another run of the Scott On... show was presented with six episodes of the popular BBC 2 offering commencing its run on Wednesday 2 September at 9.20pm. Now into its third series, the show continued until 8 October, with its two final episodes switched to a Thursday evening. A short, five minutes mini-show was included in the festive Christmas Night with the Stars programme which was broadcast Christmas Day. Sadly only excerpts from the series seem to have remained in the BBC archive, with an off-air audio recording of this episode exists in the archive.

The episodes order consisted of Scott On Progress (there now only exists segments of this episode in the archives); Scott On Law (completely lost episode but there is an audio-only copy of the recording); Scott On Industry; Scott On Communication (no recording exists of this "Televised in colour" episode); Scott On History and Scott On Nature (June Whitfield featured in this episode, originally airing on Thursday 8 October, and again, now lost).

Terry starred in the Robin Hawdon comedy The Mating Game, at the Ashcroft theatre (part of the Fairfield Halls banner), Croydon for a week commencing Monday 29 June. It then made the long journey north to be presented at the Grand theatre, Leeds from Monday 6 July. Directed by Maurice Stewart, Terry (as James Harris) was joined by Aimi Macdonald (as Honey Tooks), Nicholas Parsons (Draycott Harris) and Amanda Barrie (as Julia). The play would also enjoy a stay at the Playhouse theatre in Weston-super-Mare from 22 June, where a seat in the stalls was 15/-. Returning to the Grand, Terry would later venture back there to star in another comedy; A Bedfull of Foreigners.

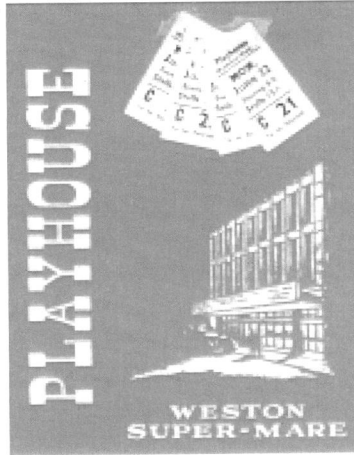

Parsons, forever associated with Sale of the Century and radio show Just a Minute, was also represented by Richard Stone, as we know Terry was. However, writing in his autobiography, he found little to reminisce positively on, "Many comedians have some personal neurosis that can make them delightful, a bit eccentric and off-the-wall or else they can be bloody difficult. Terry Scott was one of the latter, as far as I am concerned." Nicholas had his acting ability undermined by the demands of his co-star. "Terry eventually got rid of me." reflected the silky-smooth panel show host, "I have no idea why, and even though he later admitted to Stone that he had made a mistake, it was no consolation."

Game, Hawdon's third play, was directed by Maurice Stewart, "a consummate theatre professional...stage manager, company manager and director in many parts of British theatre, working on operas and West End productions of American musicals.[15]"

It also gave a role to Joanna Henderson, later to feature in more than a dozen episodes of "the epitome of middle class suburbia[16]" Terry and June. Terry would return to the play in 1972 when it transferred to London's West End. He would also take it to the "English Riviera" aka Torquay, for a summer season.

Broadcast by ITV on Christmas Eve, Carry On Again Christmas continued the comedy brand's TV foray. After being spoilt by the first seasonal special in colour, this second instalment was shown in black and white (due to a technicians strike) and seems to have been made on an equally as limited budget as the first one. But the cast highlighted by Sid James, Terry, Charles Hawtrey, Bernie Bresslaw and Barbara Windsor, do get to wear some lovely costumes in this pirate-themed episode which was co-written by Sid Colin and Dave

Freeman. Also, each is given a fair bit of dialogue and centre-stage.

Putting a fun spin on the Robert Louis Stephenson classic novel Treasure Island, Sid is Long John Silver with Terry, second billed, as Squire Treyhornay. An unfunny Kenneth Connor joins the gang but we have lost Terry's mate, Peter Butterworth in the process. Ms Windsor and Charles Hawtrey are particularly good, too. The special was both produced and directed by Alan Tarrant. Wendy Richard, to be seen alongside Terry in Carry On Matron and Bless This House (both 1972) has a nothing role.

CILLA BLACK LESLIE CROWTHER
ALFRED MARKS
TERRY SCOTT
ALADDIN
SHEILA BERNETTE
STACEY GREGG
LUPINO LANE
TV'S **BASIL BRUSH**

Singer Cilla Black plays the title role of Aladdin this year at the world famous London Palladium, previously regarded by Terry-Thomas as "without doubt the British Mecca of variety*" with Leslie Crowther as Wishee-Washee, Alfred Marks, Terry as Widow Twankey, Sheila Bernette, Billy Tasker, Bertie Hare, Jack Francois, Stacey Gregg, Sheila Melvin, Milton Reid, Tom Chatto, Johnny Hutch and Co, Lauri Lupino Lane, Irving Davies Dancers, Bel Canto Singers and "TV's Basil Brush".

Directed by the panto veteran Albert J.Knight, the show was performed twice daily; at 2.45 and 7.30pm, with seats ranging in price from 10/- to 30/-. Owned by Moss Empires Limited, the opening night performance was Tuesday, 22 December. Cilla, who had previously performed at the Palladium as a singer, received top billing followed by Mr Crowther, Alfred Marks and then Terry, all above the title. Leslie would appear on June Whitfield's 1976 tribute This is your Life show, as would Terry.

It was Terry's second stint at the Palladium after his recent appearance the previous year. Cilla was pregnant this year and gave birth before fulfilling her involvement in the panto!

An early-evening Christmas Night with the Stars was introduced by Cilla Black, with Terry appearing alongside June Whitfield in a segment of the BBC television show written by Dave Freeman. David Croft had moved on to co-creating Dad's Army and Clodagh Rodgers, a panto co-star of Terry's, also featured in the festive show.

Terry appears as himself on the 1971 BBC show It's Lulu. Based around the Scottish singer that performed on Gonks go Beat (1965) and sang the opening title song, also featured here was singer/composer Buffy Sainte-Marie and girl group The Breakaways.

Thursday 23rd September found Terry returning for another outing of his Scott On...series only this time with an increased quota of 8 episodes. Scott On Travel was the first; broadcast at 9:20pm, again on BBC 2, in a regular Thursday evening slot. It was followed by Scott On Wealth, Scott On Dress, Scott On Entertainment, Scott On The Home, Scott On Rebellion, Scott On The Supernatural and Scott On Food (the latter subject had previously been looked at during the initial series). This time around, Terry is aided by June Whitfield in a series of programmes seemingly all written by Dave Freeman.

Scott On...Travel sees Terry and his team discuss the merits of travel in a show which was shown on 23 September. If you think Mr Scott only slipped into a comfy cardie during his latter sitcom heyday, then you are mistaken, as he sports a nice line of them in this sketch/music show which opens with him speeding along in a sport car before finally ending up falling down an open lift shaft!

A smashing supporting cast is led by June Whitfield, Frank Thornton and Colin Jeavons with Terry again speaking directly to the audience and at the camera before joining in sketches related to the subject matter.

After a weak start, highlights include Terry and June singing together, the former utilising his Penfold voice (see Danger Mouse: 1981) in an amusing highway man scene, and the couple experiencing a disastrous barge holiday with Terry falling in the water on five different occasions (something that would return in episodes of Terry and June).

The very pretty Ms. Whitfield proves most appealing here, especially in the sing-song with Terry all about various city locations. Watching the show, it looks that it might have been great fun to be a participant in, especially when the closing sketch; a Star Trek musical spoof. Cheryl Kennedy, Jacqueline Clark and Sue Bishop also join in the fun. Many had already established working relationships with Terry including series regular Jacqueline Clarke, who would act in a tour of A Bedfull of Foreigners with Terry and Colin Jeavons (who would also tour with him in Foreigners).

Gonks go Beat actor Mr Thornton appears in three of the episodes this year and he would act again with Terry on a single episode in the following, with both featuring in the film version of Bless this House (also 1972). In her pictorial autobiography, June Whitfield presents photos of Terry dressed as an angle for one of the episodes partly filmed in Ravenscourt Park, London. Guests Peter Butterworth and Thornton were also dressed as women for the story and all three went out for a pub lunch still dressed in their outfits!

There is another photo featuring Peter and Terry with an unknown actor with each of them in outrageous drag.

Wealth seems to have been a two-hander with June Whitfield.

Dress saw comedy great Peter Butterworth joining Terry, supported by Stuart Sherwin, Frank Thornton, Dilys Watling and June. Stuart had worked with Terry back in the early-1960s on some Brian Rix comedy shows. He would also feature in the 1972 episode Scott On The Sex War plus a couple of episodes of Happy Ever After and Terry and June.

Entertainment: Ronnie Brody, Peter Butterworth, Rose Hill, Colin Jeavons, Frank Thornton, Dilys Watling and and June Whitfield co-starred. Brody acted in Carry On Loving (1970) and would feature in episodes of Terry and June. Rose Hill was in a 1964 episode of Hugh and I in 1964, and would return in 1976 for Happy Ever After.

The Home: Terry and June co-starred in this story and in Rebellion.

The Supernatural aired 16 December and the series closed with Terry and June in Food on 30 December. On the cinema screen, Carry On Henry proved a major box office draw.

Interviewer: "Terry Scott doing Cardinal Wolseley?"

Terry:"Not doing him, no. That's charming, oh no; have a bit of reverence...I am portraying Cardinal Wolseley as best I can." That was Terry (pictured below, in costume)quoted during a brief, on set interview when filming Carry On Henry across October - November of the previous year. This was often the usual shooting schedule because it allowed the principal cast to be free for pantomime work.

Playing the role left quite an impression, in real life was a lay preacher, he would recall, "Playing Cardinal Wolsey left me with one burning ambition unfulfilled. Every time I got into the splendid red robes of the Cardinal, I had an irresistible urge to sneak them out of the studio and wear them to my local church on Sunday morning."

Following up a double dosed of fun in 1970 with Carry On Up the Jungle and Carry On Loving, Sid James would excel in the title role of Henry VIII for which, back in the mid-1960s, Goons fool Harry **165** Secombe had been suggested for the part.

James portrays the woman-chasing king, magnificent with mutton chops, in another excellent period romp for the gang. Ably supported by Kenneth Williams, dear Charlie Hawtrey and Terry as Wolsey, Henry proves to be an engaging frolic in another male dominated feature with female characters including the ample Margaret Nolan through to a feisty 'Bet' portrayed by an over-excited Barbara Windsor. She and Sid would present their trade mark bubbly giggle and yak-yak-yak laughs, respectively, in overdrive. Joan Sims has the best role and is a delight as Henry's garlic-munching French Queen whom Sid just cannot bare to get close to.

Talbot Rothwell supplied the screenplay for this the 21st Carry On feature film, where it is a pleasure to see the team in period costume. Terry, looks magnificent in his flowing red robes, complete with a

A GREAT GUY WITH HIS 'CHOPPER'!

ALL NEW!

A PETER ROGERS

CARRY ON HENRY VIII

When the Honeymoon was over he gave 'em the axe!

comedy shuffle walk, frequency to cup his hands combined with an eye for the ladies. "He was a very clever man Terry Scott," remembered series cinematographer Alan Hume when discussing the film during a DVD commentary session.

Kudos should be given to the film makers for giving the project such a lavish look whilst maintaining their usual economical budget and strict shooting schedule.

Always known for its strong casting, actors queued up for parts in a Carry On and here we see brief but welcome appearances from Peter Butterworth, Bill Maynard and Kenneth Connor.

An added bonus is finding Terry in scenes with Sid, Hawtrey and Kenneth Williams, the latter proving most enjoyable alongside him as lackeys to the fickle monarch. Just as in Don't Lose your Head,

films and filming

june 1971   30p   AT CANNES

◄ My Swedish Meatball   Carry on Henry ▲

ALAN BATES Interviewed

New Italian Films   ★ Pasolini ★

Picture previews   The Go-Between   The Decameron

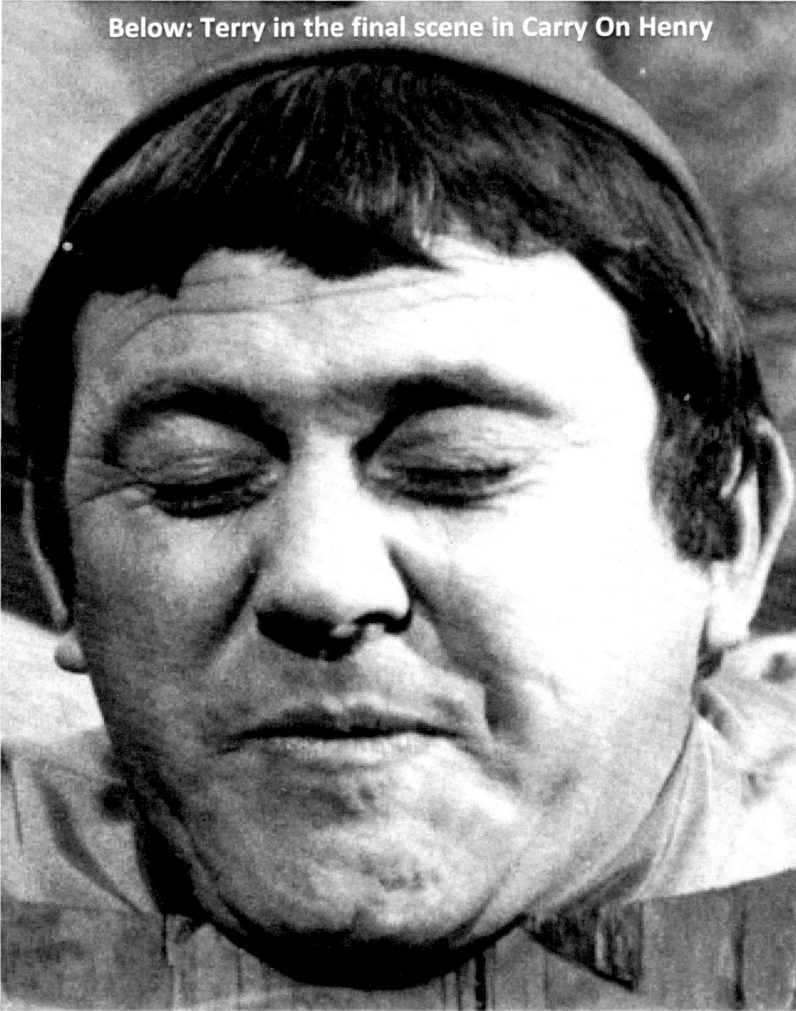
Below: Terry in the final scene in Carry On Henry

Williams (and Terry rather than Peter Butterworth) make an exit via the guillotine, with a writer clearly running on empty; it was Mr Rothwell's final Carry On feature film.

Peter Gilmore also arrives before the end as the French King, keen to see his newly-married cousin, Marie (Sims). Henry finds his interest raised by many females and to struggles to consummate (or "consume" as Wolsey mispronounces it) his new marriage due to her garlic obsession and insistence upon having it added to everything. Cromwell (Williams) and Wolsey (Scott) support and advise their king, with the Cardinal bound by the Vatican's rules.

So it is not easy for the union to be annulled especially as France would be an undesirable enemy. However, when Henry becomes interested in Bettina (Barbara Windsor), things become complicated further still.

Double-crossed when trying to help the King, both Cromwell and Wolsey find themselves about to meet their deaths via the guillotine when Henry rushes forth to stop it. Asking again for their guidance in his affairs, in unison they say, "Carry On Executioner, Carry On!"

Terry would be absent from the next one, Carry On at your Convenience (also 1971) after seeing his role hit the cutting room floor due to the overlong running time of the film. He would return one more time for Carry On Matron in 1972. In the guise of Cardinal Wolsey, Terry was included in the poster/brochure promoting a season of all the Carry On films screened at the prestigious Barbican Centre in London, in 1995.

At Christmas, Terry returned to the Palladium for the third time, here in Cinderella and was once more directed by Albert

ⒶⒷⒸ ❶❷❸❹

Cast

Sidney James...King Henry VIII

Kenneth Williams...Thomas Cromwell

Charles Hawtrey...Sir Roger de Lodgerley

Joan Sims...Queen Marie

Terry Scott...Cardinal Wolsey

Barbara Windsor...Bettina

Kenneth Connor...Lord Hampton

Julian Holloway...Sir Thomas

Peter Gilmore...King Francis of France

Julian Orchard...Duc de Poncenay

Gertan Klauber...Bidet

David Davenport...Major Domo

Margaret Nolan...Buxom Lass

William Mervyn...Physician

Norman Chappell...First Plotter

Derek Francis...Farmer

Bill Maynard...Guy Fawkes

Douglas Ridley...Second Plotter

Dave Prowse...Bearded Torturer

Monika Dietrich...Katherine Howard

Marjie Lawrence...Serving Maid

Patsy Rowlands...Queen

Billy Cornelius...Guard

Alan Curtis...Conte di Pisa

Leon Greene...Torturer

John Bluthal...Royal Tailor (uncredited)

Peter Butterworth...Charles, Earl of Bristol (uncredited)

J.Knight in a Louis Benjamin and Leslie Grade presentation. Comedy man Ronnie Corbett, in the role of Buttons, received top billing, followed by Clodagh Rodgers as Cinders, then Terry as Teresa, an ugly sister, all before the title with support from David Kossoff, Julian Orchard, Dorothy Dampier, The Wychwoods, Bertie Hare, Bill Tasker, Douglas George Ponies, Brian Hills, Bel Canto Singers, Patton Brothers, Tommy Shaw dancers, Jack Francois, Georgia Jee, Peggy O'Ferrell children and Malcolm Roberts.

Ms Rodgers had chalked-up almost a half-dozen chart singles and had represented the UK in Eurovision.

Devised and produced by an ever enthusiastic Knight, he had previously staged Aladdin at the Palladium back in 1964 with the book written by David Croft, whilst working on over forty pantomimes by this point. This time around, its comedy scenes were written by Bryan Blackburn, Barry Cryer, who had previously acted alongside Terry in an episode of The Gnomes of Dulwich and a writer of a non-Terry television Carry On episode (and theatre project), Dave Freeman and Spike Mullins.

One night, all the lights went out during a show and the audience was given a chorus of There's a Tavern in the Town before the cast went off to their dressing rooms in anticipation of returning.

Julian Orchard played Julia, sister to Terry's Teresa, and part of the terrible step-sisters to Cinderella. His name might not be recognisable but his persona will be once you see, and hear, his distinct plumy tones. His CV is extensive, encompassing film, theatre and television across many years and crossing paths, professionally, with Terry most recently this year with the cinematic release of Carry On Henry. It would continue with both having roles in the film version of Bless This House (1972) after starting back in 1962 in an episode of Hugh and I and on film in 1964 with Father Came Too! Julian sadly passed away due to cancer.

Terry's role as Mr Allcock in Carry On at Your Convenience regrettably failed to make the final cut but he still received his £500 fee for what transpired as a poorly-received entry in the series (it has since become a firm favourite amongst fans). His character was a union manager and he featured in scenes with Kenneth Williams, Sid James, Kenneth Cope and Richard O'Callaghan. If you find a copy of the DVD, a still from the lost scene is included in the extras.

In complete contrast to his more adult roles, Terry acted in a short, twenty two minutes long children's feature called Mr Tumbleweed. Teaming up again with A Ghost of a Chance director Jan Darnley-

Smith, he was cast as "The Bosun" in a little film which saw a youngster discovering a string puppet that magically comes to life. Made at Bray studios, Berkshire, the project was also known as Mr Tumbleweed: Jump Off. In amongst its smashing cast was Carry On lovely Margaret Nolan, who had worked with Terry in an episode of Hugh and I.

Cast

Harry Secombe...Mr Tumbleweed

Terry...The Bosun

Richard Beaumont...Paul

Jan Butlin...Mum

Eric Chitty...Art Gallery attendant

Jennifer Lewis...Janet

Katy Manning...Bride

Lance Percival...Leading seaman

Terry's daughters were growing-up rapidly, with Sarah 15, Nicola 13, Lindsay 11 and Alexandra 7. By 1972, he was appearing in the West End, at the Apollo, Shaftesbury Avenue, in another production of The Mating Game. Dating back to the early-1900s, a then-present day ticket for the Dress Circle cost £1.50. This time directed by his old Whitehall associate, Ray Cooney, Terry was cast alongside Aimi Macdonald (returning in the role of Honey Tooks and Clive Francis (the Carry On Abroad actor was playing Draycott and is pictured below with Terry and Ms Macdonald), funny woman Avril Angers (Mrs Finney) and the gorgeous Julia Lockwood was cast as Julia Carrington.

The first performance of the show at this particular theatre occurred on 14 June and it closed the same month in the following year, 1973. Terry would leave after nine months to make the now-forgotten Son of the Bride for BBC 1.

Returning to Game, its synopsis was as follows, "Set in a smart Mayfair apartment full of gadgets with minds of their own, the comedy zeros in on a trendy television personality whose romantic interludes are always interrupted by accidents, fate or his own incompetence. His bedroom fiascos are especially remarkable in light of his reputation as a notorious stud."

Snippets from newspaper reviews classed it as a popular success. "Audiences nearly raised the roof!" said the Daily Telegraph; "Bright, frothy knockout nonsense," waxed the Daily Mirror and Financial Times, renowned for its theatre section, offered, "Audience laughed fit to bust."

Clive Francis is still acting today and on his official website, he remembers working with the star name, "I played opposite Terry Scott who taught me the art of timing by constantly squeezing my knee rather violently!"

Terry is also seen on BBC2 in what will be the finals series of Scott On… the first episode being screened at 9:55pm on Monday 9 October in the Show of the Week slot. This show looked into The Sex War and combined a mixture of sketches and flashbacks after the original entries would often end with a mini-opera and apologies to Gilbert and Sullivan.

Scott On…Language/ …Culture/ …Success followed. But it would be Scott On…The Permissive Society that saw June Whitfield join Terry to delve into a very topical issue so concerning to the British public of the time. This episode, shown on Monday 11 December, would be the final one in the series. However, a special edition, Scott on Courage would be shown in 1974.

On the big screen, in one of his most recognisable Carry On parts, in Carry On Matron Terry is the randy Dr Prodd; a man with an unsavoury reputation amongst the medical staff at Finisham Maternity Hospital, who gets more than he bargains for when dallying with 'nurse' Kenneth Cope. The fourth

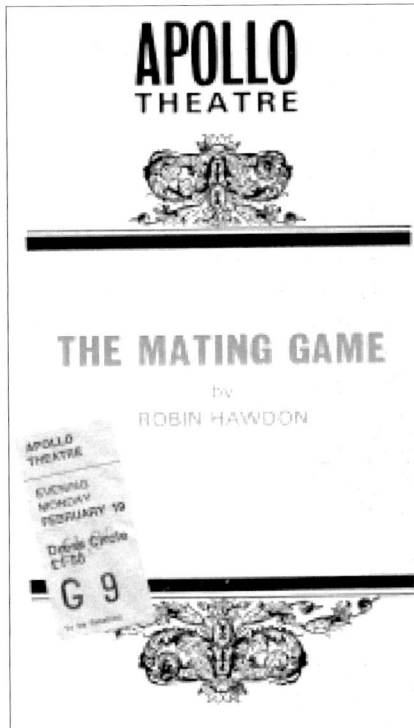

APOLLO
THEATRE

THE MATING GAME

by
ROBIN HAWDON

medical outing for the series, Kenneth Williams is perfectly cast as the snotty hypochondriac head surgeon, ably supported by Matron Hattie and bubbly nurse Babs Windsor.

In a gang with dad Sid (Sidney James), Ernie (Bernie Bresslaw) and Freddie (Bill Maynard), Cyril (Kenneth Cope) is given the task of infiltrating the hospital to steal a stash of contraceptive pills stored in the basement. Sid hits on the idea of sending him in disguised as a female student nurse and Cope is amusing especially when he catches the eye of the lascivious Prodd (Terry). He first meets 'Cyrlle' when she is rearranging her troublesome underwear in the gents!

Terry appears some six minutes into the film, wearing medic whites, with his hair longer than usual (this was filmed in late 1971). He works in paediatrics, consulting with numerous patients that come to see him, from a Sally Army lady, the hard-of-hearing Mrs Jenkins (Amelia Bayntun being very funny), Miss Smethurst (Valerie Shute) and Margaret Nolan. Whilst on the wards he is kept busy by Mrs Tidey (Joan Sims), seemingly more interested in eating than giving birth, while Kenneth Connor anxiously awaits news of their overdue delivery. Other new mothers at the maternity hospital include Wendy Richard and the exquiste Madeline Smith.

On night shift, the smitten Prodd reveals that he has a map of the hospital, not realising the nefarious ends of the newcomer. Cyrlle wants the map and agrees to collect it from his room. Unfortunately, he is confronted by an amorous doctor and has to fight him off. Pushing Terry away, he sends him flying over a sofa only for the medic to sigh, "What a woman!" Fans might recall similar escapades on a sofa, with Imogen Hassall in Carry On Loving (1970). That film gave Jacki Piper a larger role than the one as ward sister in Matron, the twenty fourth in the series.

The pneumatic Valerie Leon plays film star Jane Darling, an expectant mother given V.I.P treatment, with Dr Terry being sent to collect her in an ambulance. Needing a nurse to assist, he grabs the unenthusiastic Cyrlle. On the journey back, after instructing her to fill a syringe with pethidine meant for the patient, due to the motion of the vehicle, he accidentally gets a jab into his bum, "You've given me the lot!" sighs Terry in a very funny moment, before he is rendered unconscious. Arriving at the hospital, everything works out fine, with Ms Darling having had triplets delivered by Cyrlle!

Suffering the after effects of a sore posterior, the following day finds Dr Prodd back at work. Meanwhile the gang plans its night time raid whilst the disguised Cyril has to distract Terry away from the hospital lobby. He does this by asking him to walk 'her' back to the nurses' accommodation. Still keen, Prodd agrees but is knocked unconscious and has his hands tied to an ambulance steering wheel, so as to keep him out of the way.

As the story reaches a close, there follows the hilarious sight of the gang all wearing disguises and bringing in a pregnant, drag cloaked Bernie Bresslaw. He proves a delight in voicing his emotional support to Cyril earlier and here when his character plays the part of an expectant mother with relish.

Unable to locate matron's key to the storage room, and raising suspicions all around, they decide to blow the lock off. However, the noise only succeeds in waking up the patients and alarming the staff (it also starts Mrs Tidey's labour!)

Grabbing boxes, the boys attempt to escape but struggle to do so, as Sir Bernard (Williams) has ordered all the doors to be locked. Pursued around the hospital, they end up surrounded in the reception area.

Meanwhile Terry wakes up and accidentally starts the engine of the ambulance and sends it careering through the main entrance doors.

Sid and the others are allowed to leave after calling Sir Bernard's bluff, stating that the hospital's reputation would be damaged if it was publically revealed that their star nurse was in fact a man.

In the final scene, Kenneth Williams and Hattie Jacques are married and Terry is one of the invited guests there to see them off outside the church. And in a last gag, Bernie and Bill Maynard are seen running off after hearing of Sid's plans for a new and revealing job.

Matron proved hugely successful, making its production budget back only a few weeks after release. It was to be Terry's final outing in a Carry On film but not the last occasion that he would cross paths with legendary team members such as Sid James.

"Even when he plays straight parts or character roles, comical or otherwise, one of the most difficult things for a comic is persuading critics and journalists to describe him as an 'actor'."

That was Terry interviewed during the making of the Bless this House film which was released in cinemas this year.

Speaking of the Carry Ons, Terry was a guest on breakfast television show TV-AM in 1987, "We didn't make any money out of it but it's nice to be remembered."

Advancing to the movies, popular sitcom Bless This House made the step up into a feature-length film using many of the actors already familiar to each other through their Carry On connections. Sid James and Diana Coupland were the leads as Sid and Jean Abbott.

Indeed, Sid was the king of the comedy film series and a number of the cast had or would, appear in the Gerald Thomas/ Peter Rogers movies. Filming on Carry On Abroad had just been completed before the duo advanced onto Bless.

Terry was joined by June Whitfield as Ronald and Vera Baines, new neighbours to the Abbots (Sid and Diana joined by screen son Robin Askwith and daughter Sally Geeson). Whilst Trevor (Peter Butterworth) and Betty (Patsy Rowlands) are friends/ neighbours.

Departing residents Janet Brown and Julian Orchard are set for a new life in Bournemouth and the Baines arrive and are soon joined by their sexy daughter, Kate (Carol Hawkins). "He's alright," declares Ms Brown about Terry, "bit pompous."

Of course, the scene is set for Mike (Askwith) to fall for Kate especially once they both get summer jobs at a local café run by George A.Cooper. He would soon appear alongside Terry in the sitcom Son of the Bride.

Scripted by Dave Freeman, with a single screenplay credit behind him but a multitude of television experience, Terry's old comedy partner Bill Maynard, himself to appear in four Carry Ons, features as the randy owner of an indoor market where Jean and Betty set-up an antiques stall. After seeing three of his Scott On scripts broadcast the previous year, Freeman would write a film script for a full-fledged entry in the series in 1978: Carry On Behind.

Returning to Bless, things between the new neighbours do not start well, with Sally managing to soak Terry with a hosepipe, the Abbots damaging their living room wall and bodging a repair job in a smashing bit of slapstick involving Sid, Ms Coupland and Ms Geeson.

Ronald (Terry) is revealed as being a Customs and Excise duty collector, Sid and Trevor (a warm performance from Peter Butterworth) have to be careful, as their home brewing adventure in the shed sees them attempt to turn wine into brandy, an illegal practice.

As Mike and Kate's relationship develops, both sets of parents are keen to meet the other person that their son / daughter keeps mentioning; however, neither know their true identity.

On the evening of Sally's birthday producing a house full of guests at the Abbot's, Sid and Jean decide to visit the cafe and see who Kate is, not realising that Terry and June are planning to do likewise.

Spotting them, Mike hides behind the counter only for Terry and Sid to approach. Rebuffed by Mr Wilson (Cooper), the latter flings an egg and hits Terry in the eye. He retaliates, Sid joins in and another food flight erupts ala Carry On Loving.

Arrested and released, the two fathers bond after their experience and Terry informs their wives that he and Sid have agreed to allow the couple to become engaged and perhaps get married in due course. Jean informs them that a wedding is arranged and is happening soon!

Come the day of the wedding, a formal affair with the men dressed in top hat and tails, Mike accidentally hits the power supply to the illicit booze still and it subsequently blows up after most of the guests have made their way to the church. Terry attends to the shed fire, later joined by Sid, but both end up covered in muck as the fire brigade eventually arrives to help. Meanwhile at the church, the

THE RANK ORGANISATION PRESENTS A PETER ROGERS PRODUCTION

BLESS THIS HOUSE

ⒶⒷⒸ ①②③④ East st **BRIGHTON** 27010

Cast

Sid James...Sid Abbot

Diana Coupland...Jean Abbot

Terry...Ronald Baines

June Whitfield...Vera Baines

Peter Butterworth...Trevor

Sally Geeson...Sally Abbot

Robin Askwith...Mike Abbot

Carol Hawkins...Kate Baines

Janet Brown...Annie

George A.Cooper...Wilson

Patsy Rowlands... Betty

Bill Maynard...Oldham

Wendy Richard...Carol

Marianne Stone...Muriel

Julian Orchard...Tom

No unaccompanied children admitted after 7pm
ALL PROGRAMMES MAY BE SUBJECT TO LATE CHANGE

service goes ahead without the participation of either the bride or groom's father. Blackened by the fire, Sid and Terry grab a ride on the rear of a fire engine, siren blaring, and are dropped off outside. They get there just in time to be included in the photographs outside.

Released as a 'U' certificate, Bless this House, was a part of a trend in the early-1970s to turn TV comedies such as Steptoe and Son, On the Buses and Man about the House into full-length cinema features. It featured many familiar faces: Tommy Godfrey, Ed Deveraux, Johnnie Briggs, Frank Thornton, Norman Mitchell, Patricia Franklin, Brian Osborne, Marjie Lawrence, Lindsay Marsh, Michael Nightingale, Myrtle Reed, Molly Weir, Margaret Lacey, Michael Howe, Georgina Moon, David Rowlands and Billy Cornelius.

Terry acts in Macbett at the Belgrade theatre, Coventry, in a short run from Tuesday 3 July through to Saturday 14 July 1973. Written by Eugene Inoesco, this version was translated and directed by American playwright Charles Marowitz after originally being published in 1972. With Steptoe and Son actor Harry H.Corbett, Victor Spinetti, the brilliant Frances Cuka and Terry, the play was also performed at the Bankside Globe theatre, London 17 July - 4 August.

Also in the cast, Malcolm Storry, David Henry, Marshall Jones, Jacqueline Morgan, Clive Belman, David Trevena, Tim Brown, Michael Greatorex, David Delve, Maeleine Orr, Gypsie Kemp, Ray Callaghan, C.A Ford, Basil Clark, John Pollendine, Ian McDiarmid, Graham Seed.

Reviews proved positive, "Terry Scott's performance as Duncan emerges triumphantly as a subtle blend of horror and humour, and an unlimited source of witty and perceptive comment upon the mutations of the character." That summation was from E.Victor, writing in The Tablet (28 July 1973), "This fine comedian is an actor of considerable ability; there is here a formidable combination of intellect, technique and talent."

On 14 August comedy fans could see Terry Scott in the spotlight on BBC television in their "An hour with..." series. The Scott On Entertainment episode was shown first followed by an interview with Cliff Mitchelmore.

Terry was back on the TV in Son of the Bride on BBC1 at 7.30pm. The Daily Mirror featured him with his onscreen mother, Mollie Sugden, a co-star from Hugh and I. "This one sees him as a bachelor whose comfortable home life is threatened when his widowed mother says she wants to re-marry. Mollie Sugden plays his Mum and George A.Cooper is the bridegroom-to-be who takes one look at his intended stepson and decides he doesn't like him." June of that year saw a set of six episodes written by John Kane. Here's a newspaper summary, "Neville Leggit, a middle-aged man, has never left home and his mother is a major part of his life. When she meets Stan and introduces him to her son as her fiancé, Neville's world appears to be collapsing but he is determined to make sure that the wedding never takes place."

Episode one: *Mother Rocks The Boat*

Broadcast on Wednesday 6th June. Neville has been happy living with his mother all his life but things are about to change. No longer will he be the only object of affection in her life...

Cast

Terry Scott...Neville Leggit

Mollie Sugden...Mum

Stan...George A.Cooper

Josephine Tewson...Miss McDowdie

Olivia Hamnett...Angela

Episode two: *A Hostile Engagement*

Broadcast a week later it saw Terry's mother announce her engagement, infuriating Stan (Terry) who takes evasive action and decides to leave home. All five cast members from the opening episode return, aided by a guest appearance by Robert Keegan as a copper.

Episode three: *Of Unsound Mind*

Terry visits a psychiatrist with the intention of getting his mother certified, so as to postpone her wedding.

Cast

John Warner...Rev. Pollock

Anthony Sharp...Doctor Culthorpe

Dorothy Frere...Mrs Quail   David Rowlands...Mr Winston

Peter Hawkins...Mr Cuthbertson

Carolyn Jones... Receptionist

Ted Valentine... Anderson

Episode four: *Anything but the Truth*

Shown on 27 June, this story finds Neville in a cunning mood to discover if Stan (Cooper) has anything to hide from his past. To discover this, he hires a private investigator played by Dave the bar man from Minder, Glynn Edwards.

Cast

Glynn Edwards... Cutler

Dan Jackson... Preacher

Vie Ruby James & Rosetta Hightower... Singers

Episode five: *Blue Movies always make me Cry*

A slightly unsavoury title for this offering set during the day of Stan's stag do. Neville's presentation of a home movie doesn't turn out to be what he expected it to be, in this the penultimate episode of the one and only series of Son of the Bride.

Cast

John Warner...Rev Pollock

Kenneth J.Warren... Bookshop man

Pat Coombs... Mrs Beadle

Eric French...Stan's friend

Episode six: *The Best Man always wins - Sometimes*

And so to the final instalment in the show and broadcast on 11 July with a mischievous Neville (Terry) determined to spoil the wedding day. Series writer John Kane and producer Peter Whickham join in proceedings with acting roles.

Cast

Reg Lye... Man in shoe shop

Edward Dentith...Police Inspector

John Kane...Freddie

Ralph Watson...First pall bearer

Richard Blomfield...Second pall bearer

Peter Whickham...Expectant father

Jack Le White...Porter

Rosemarie Reeves...First mother

A feature film of the popular stage farce Not Now, Darling is released in cinemas. The role of Arnold Crouch was originally intended for Dudley Moore but he was signed to star in a film in the States and so it was then offered to Terry who had to withdraw from the role. Director Ray Cooney then assumed the part himself in a piece that had started out as a stage play in 1970, co-written with Hugh and I creator John Chapman.

After having a novelty hit single, My Brother, back in 1962, Terry deviated slightly from his little boy act to head an advertising campaign for Cabury's Curly Wurly bar. Wrappers featured a carton version of him as an over-sized school boy dressed in his full school uniform and school cap. He featured in television ads for the product, including on the Ghost Train at a fairground, "My brother and my friends are very bright, Mr Ghost Train driver. But don't worry, they won't be able to scream, 'cos I've given them a Curly Wurly. All those miles of chewy toffee covered in creamy Cadbury's chocolate will keep them quiet. Ooh, aargh, help — oh crumbs, let me out of here!" There was also a tie-in with teen band Bay City Rollers (the One Direction of their day) and a photo ad campaign which used Terry in his uniform holding a Curly Wurly.

On to the panto season and Terry made a very late return to the New Theatre, Oxford, in a 1,800-seater complex with a long-established history, in the heart of this academic town. Terry was in the Babes in the Wood cast that included Martin Dell, Blaye Barrington, and double-act brothers Gordon and Bunny Jay.

Opening Friday 21 December, evening shows commenced at 7pm, with the dreaded matinees at 2.30pm. The cast also had to incorporate a special Saturday morning matinee at 10.30am! The crowd was well-catered for across eight scenes in Act I followed by a further nine in the second, after the interval.

Terry topped the bill and even had special material written for him by Eric Merriman in a busy production with an extensive cast of artistes and dancers. Of interest: it was the first time that Roger Redfarn had directed Terry but his name will reoccur as we advance through Scott's career.

Cast

Martin Dell...Sheriff of Nottingham

Richard Prelow or Philip Longford... Thomas, his nephew

Melanie Hazel or Denise Birkett... Jane, his niece

Terry...Nurse Teresa

Paula Hendrix...Maid Marian

Gordon and Bunny Jay.... The Robbers

Blayne Barrington...Robin Hood

John Arran...Friar Tuck

Philip Booth...Little John

John Denton...Will Scarlett

John Lavelle...Alan

Tim Brown...Much, the Miller's son/ Geerbocks

Emlyn Wynne...Will Stutely/ King Richard the Lionheart

Keith Thomas...Roger

Elizabeth Grahame...The Forest Fairy

Keith Thomas...Screwloose

On television, Terry was cast as the Good Robber (to Hugh Lloyd's, Bad) in the BBC's production of Robin Hood. Co-written by John Morley and Austin Steele, with a running time of ninety five minutes, a Christmas Day broadcast went out on BBC1 at 4.20pm, that Tuesday afternoon. A strong cast included Trevor Adams soon to make his mark as the nervous Tony in Reggie Perrin.

Alan Curtis was in Carry On Abroad and Carry On Henry, Billy Dainty would, like Terry, also be interviewed about the pantomime dame in a 1982 TV documentary whilst Anita Harris as Robin, acted in Carry On Follow that Camel and Carry On Doctor. She had achieved success as a singer/ actress and dancer and would work with Terry in the 1980 season at Richmond.

Cast

Trevor Adams...Will Scarlet

Alan Curtis...Sir Robert

Billy Dainty...Nurse Trumpet

Dana...Maid Marion

Sheila O'Neil' Dancers

Freddie Davies...Samuel Tweet

Denis Dove...Babe

Richie Stewart...Friar Tuck

Anita Harris...Robin Hood

Hugh Lloyd...The Good Robber

Terry...The Bad Robber

Bowles Bevan Singers

"Facetious filibuster Terry Scott..."

Leonard Sachs

Shown on 1 February 1974, Terry performed a routine to a live audience on the popular BBC show The Good Old Days. Recorded at the historic City of Varieties hall in Leeds, he gave the audience almost ten minutes of his over-grown schoolboy Knocker act and finished with a song that he messed up the second verse of! The audience roared and he asked the conductor to start again, getting back into character and adding "cos it's very good when I can come in with you!" Also on the bill, Georgia Brown, Ray Allen and others were introduced by Chairman Sachs at a venue that has more than 140 years presenting various shows.

Married to Maggie, Terry and the family were based in Godalming, Surrey. Enjoying gardening and playing crib at his local pub, Terry worked hard this year and teamed up with screen wife June Whitfield for a one-off TV special: Scott On Courage. This forty five-minute show was screened on BBC2 at 9pm on Thursday 7 February.

One night in March, travelling back to his Middlesbrough hotel after playing a show at the Billingham Forum, Terry narrowly escaped death when driving to give a radio interview nearby. His route took him on the Middlesbrough Transporter Bridge.

Resembling a gondola-type contraption, it carries passengers and cars from a suspended device on rails from an overhead structure. Terry mistook this for a conventional toll bridge and accidentally drove through the safety gate on the approach road andoff the riverbank. Luckily, he landed in the safety netting below. He was headlining a touring production of A Bedfull of Foreigners which played in Stockton-on-Tees between 4 - 9 March. Also in the cast was future Open all Hours favourite Lynda Baron, Tim Barrett, Anna Dawson, who had worked with him in Mother Goose on television back in 1965, Colin Jeavons, Richard Marnor and Carole Turner.

Barrett had already been in panto with Terry and would soon join him in the new sitcom Terry and June. Situated in the Tyne Tees area, Billingham is an isolated industrial town and a venue then well-known for struggling to attract an audience. Tickets for the play ranged from 60p-90p, with reductions for pensioners and students.

After working together in 1973 on the short-lived Son of the Bride, Terry and producer Peter Whitmore reteamed for the first series of Happy Ever After, a new domestic comedy. The Radio Times summary was brief, "When you start on a voyage of rediscovery after 25 years of married life, there are all sorts of pitfalls..Reds under the bed, liqueur chocolates, a second honeymoon."

Whitmore was a producer/director known for his work on The Two Ronnies, and later, Yes, Prime Minister and Terry and June. In the latter, he would produce thirty nine episodes across four years whilst on Happy, he produced 36 episodes. Peter also worked with Terry the previous year on the Robin Hood TV pantomime; and performed the same duties on some Scott On episodes He was also involved in the 1970 festive treat A Christmas Night with the Stars and would advance to direct a total of seventy six episodes of Happy Ever After and Terry and June, collectively.

Coming under the acclaimed Comedy Playhouse banner, Happy Ever After joined other shows that received their first try-out included such subsequent classics as Steptoe And Son, Till Death Us Do Part, The Liver Birds and Are You Being Served? The show would typically have recurring characters and stock 'types' common to sitcoms of the time: police officers, workmen and bureaucrats that Terry and June would inevitably come into contact with.

Its pilot episode went on air on Tuesday 7 May, at 9.30pm on BBC1. It was the first of a total of forty one across five series (including Christmas specials) running through to 1978.

Terry was once more thrust in front of a BBC audience with the first full series with John Chapman and Eric Merriman providing the scripts. However, in 1974, the pilot and five episodes of series one, commencing on Wednesday 17 July were broadcast.

Written principally by Kane and Merriman, Happy Ever After would be the lesser remembered precursor to Terry and June. Here, long-term couple Terry and June Fletcher (Terry Scott and June Whitfield) have their family home to themselves after having raised three children who have now flown the nest.

One of their two daughters, Debbie (Caroline Whittaker) returns from university for a visit and broaches the subject of June's Aunt Lucy coming to stay for a couple of weeks: cue some physical comedy from Mr Scott, as he bangs his head under a piece of shelving!

Lucy (Beryl Cooke) arrives laden with loads of stuff including a talking mynah bird called Gunga Din, as we spend time with the Fletcher family in their Ealing home.

Not quite done with the comedy shenanigans, Terry manages a prat fall up the stairs and gets pecked by the bird, too.

Cast

Terry...Terry Fletcher

June Whitfield...June Fletcher

Beryl Cooke...Aunt Lucy Villiers

Caroline Whittaker...Debbie Fletcher

Pippa Page...Susan Fletcher

Paul Greenwood...David

Roger Davis...Gordon

David Carter...driver

Philip Ryan...driver

Episode one: *The Hotel*

June "Darling, are you awake? Where did you put that list of faults?"

In bed late one evening, Terry is shocked to discover that his wife is a Liberal supporter and not a Conservative, like himself. After many years together June also reveals that she dislikes chocolate liqueurs; a gift that her husband has presented her with throughout their marriage. Learning of this, by the following morning at breakfast, Terry's mood proves frosty as their relationship enters into a new phase of discovery. Away from his job as a company rep, Terry wears another cardigan, this time one that matches his peach shirt and tie, whilst June is a home maker. Agreeing to share a list of faults, home-maker June describes Terry as a hypochondriac and of not displaying much sense of romance anymore. Asking him to be spontaneous, she suggests that they return to their honeymoon hotel. He doesn't at first realise that she means to go immediately but he eventually agrees. A smashing moment sees Terry carry June over the threshold watched by elderly night porter Michael Ripper, an actor who will make a welcome return in another three episodes. He regrets that they only have two single rooms available, of course, and Terry knocks on the wrong door before returning to reception and locating the right room.

Noel Coleman, a fellow hotel guest, would feature in a 1976 episode and later in a Terry and June storyline in 1979. This episode includes a slightly modified opening credits seeing Terry and June joined by Aunt Lucy and less photos of the grown-up children.

Episode two: *Terry's Church Sermon or Jumble Sale Terry*

Terry. "Ever since the kids left home, you've done nothing but work yourself into a frazzle."

Terry proves an absolute delight in this second story, arriving home to find June sorting out prospective donations for the church jumble sale. Just as Terry and June would feature a vicar, Happy Ever After had its own, Reverend Parker, with Preston Lockwood making the first of his three appearances here.

After Terry talks his way into facilitating the reading at his church, he proves hilarious when practicing next to a disturbed-looking June. Pleading with him not to embellish the biblical text with accents and yell the words out quite so much. His eventual reading proves a delight for the watching audience even when he moderates his dramatic interpretation by placing an emphasis on key words. Hiccups and treading upon his reading glasses offer more than a touch of Hancock. Great fun.

Cast

Betty Cardno...Mrs Phillips
Beryl Cooke...Aunt Lucy
Eric Francis...Mr Curforth

Preston Lockwood...Rev Parker

Ronald Mayer...Verger

Episode three: *Amateur Dramatics*

Coming after the pleasure of the previous installment, June welcomes her am-dram chums Graham (Robert Dorning) and Peter (Chris Sandford) to the Fletcher home for an evening rehearsal.

A disinterested Terry is about to leave them to it until he answers the door to late arrival Sally (the gorgeous Madeline Smith). Instantly smitten by the shapely younger woman, Terry agrees to play a supporting role in the play, which somebody sums up beautifully as consisiting of involves "six lines and a grope on the floor [with Sally]."

The best scene is an exhilarating visualisation of Terry's imagination: speeding along in a Sports car, hopping in and out of a helicopter and demonstrating his martial arts prowess whilst attempting to rescue the young lady. Alas, he is rudely awoken upon falling out of bed: it was all a dream!

Thinking that Sally has fallen in love with him, Terry, now having morphed into a theatrical 'luvvie', all cravat and delusions of grandeur, confesses his predicament to a rather tolerant June.

Come the evening of the show, Geoffrey forgets his lines, only for June and Sally to prove the star performers. That is until an unrestrained Terry eventually manages to enter the proceedings, after some doors prove sticky, wherein he immediately falls off the stage in a superb piece of comedy. Terry and Madeline Smith would later appear on a real stage together, in a production of The School for Wives.

Cast

Beryl Cooke...Aunt Lucy

Robert Dorning...Graham

Chris Sandford...Peter

Madeline Smith...Sally

Episode four: *The French Businessman*

Cast

Beryl Cooke...Aunt Lucy

Neil Hallett...Jean Paul

Episode five: *Keep Fit*

The concluding episode in an enjoyable first half-dozen offerings of Happy Ever After was broadcast on 21 August.

So what of the audience? An IMDB review offered by 'ShadeGrenade' gives a good nsight. "...Possibly because it was the target of a hate campaign in the 1980s by the alternative comedy crowd, Terry and June is the better remembered of Scott and Whitfield's sitcoms. Yet Happy Ever After, which preceded it, is superior, mainly thanks to Eric Merriman and John Chapman's scripts [other writers who worked on the show included John Kane, Jon Watkins and Christopher Bond].

The Scott character was like an overgrown schoolboy in that he would come up with daft ideas and try - unsuccessfully - to implement them. He was also a bit of a snob - when he got a phone call from a member of the aristocracy, for instance, he got of bed and stood smartly to attention. June was the more level-headed of the two. The disruptive presence of Lucy and her bird in the Fletcher household added to the comedy. Daughters Debbie and Susan were played respectively by Caroline Whitaker and Pippa Page (Lena Clemo, in the pilot). One episode landed the BBC in hot water; it featured Terry having a nightmare in which he imagined himself in a health farm run like a World War II P.O.W. camp. On the night it went out, BBC1 screened the latest instalment of the American mini-series Holocaust. Viewers complained the sitcom was in bad taste."

Happy Ever After would run across an impressive five series, and would have gone on longer had not the writers decided they had had enough. As it was pulling in phenomenal audiences, the B.B.C. refused to let it go, and after a brief legal skirmish, Terry and June's characters returned under the re-titled Terry and June banner. The Fletchers became the Medfords, and poor Aunt Lucy was dropped (Terry went on kids 1980's TV show Multi-Coloured Swap Shop and during a phone-in, had to explain to a caller why Aunt Lucy was no longer in the show)."

With a popular television series on air, for the summer season Terry appeared at the Pavilion Theatre, Torquay, in the stage farce well-known to him, The Mating Game (see the next page). The show premiered on Friday 31 May and was directed by Roger Redfarn. Terry had played the role of James over 400 times in the West End and down by the seaside, he was joined by Ian Masters, Anita Graham, Carole Turner and Joanna Henderson (all of whom had or would work with him elsewhere).

Having appeared with Irish singing star Dana the previous year in the BBC pantomime Robin Hood, Terry was the guest on her chat show, with his appearance being seen on 15 December. It was the third of six shows that this popular singer, then making her mark as an established panto performer, particularly as Snow White following her success in the Eurovision Song contest.

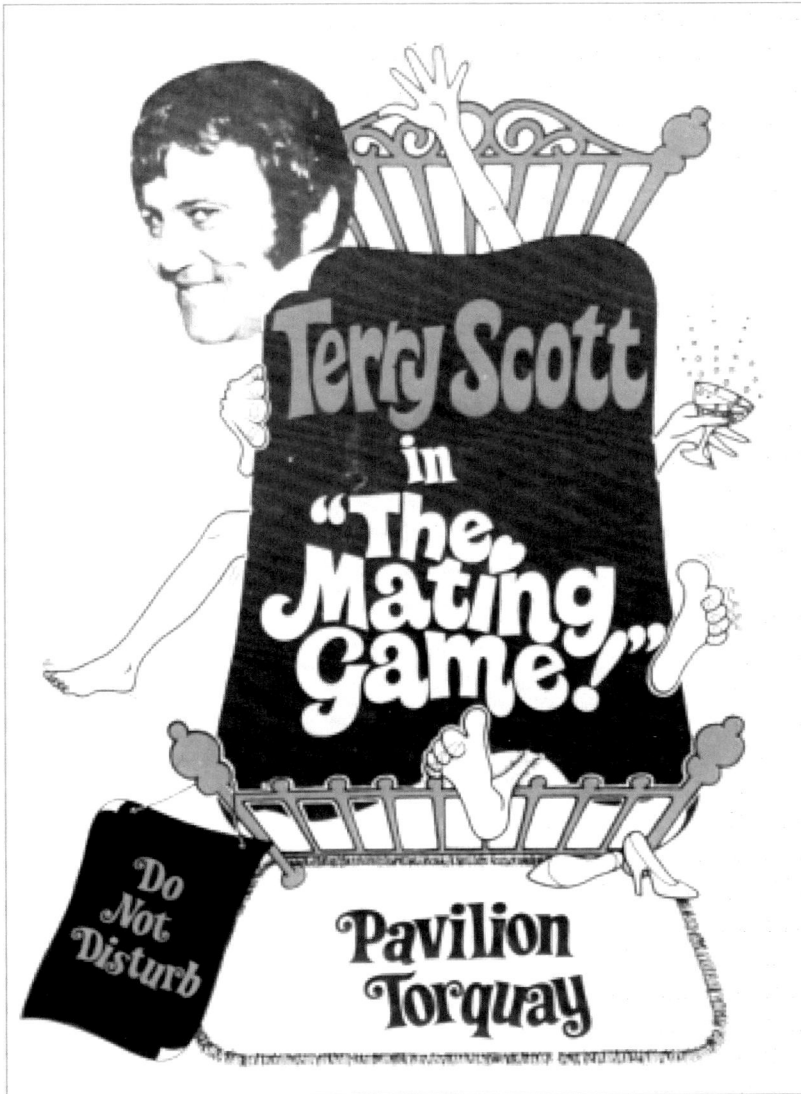

TERRY SCOTT in "The Mating Game!"

Do Not Disturb

Pavilion Torquay

This year Terry was at the Richmond theatre, Surrey in the starring role as Mother Goose for a run starting on 20 December. Actress/ dancer Joyce Blair, sister of Lionel, was joined by Desmond Walter-Ellis (Squire) and Ed 'Stewpot' Stewart headlining with Terry. Supported by Gemma Craven (as Jill), Peter Greene, Ian Lindsay, Jeffrey Holland (as the Bailifs), Kay Lyell, Mary Ashton, Robert Aldous, a superb villain, the Doreen English Babies, Jeffrey Holland was also in it. Directed by Terry's familiar theatre man, Roger Redfarn, Mother

Goose was made for Paul Elliot and Duncan C.Weldon and was a Triumph (Productions) Ltd. Walter-Ellis had a role in The Great St Trinian's Train Robbery (1968).

Terry joined musician David Nixon for a TV edition of It's Norman, a festive comedy sketch show made for ITV with Norman Wisdom.

Not sure if it was this year, but he appeared on Celebrity Squares.

Terry guests on Peter Butterworth's 1975 This is your Life show where a clip of Carry On Camping featuring them with Betty Marsden, was shown. Oddly, the studio audience barely registered a laugh. Also in 1975, he made another contribution to Mollie Sugden's tribute on the same show.

He would also tour South Africa with A Bedfull of Foreigners. It was a true family affair, with both Terry and co-star June Whitfield seeing their children join the travelling cast, also. The tour began in Cape Town at the Nico Malan theatre, then known as "The Nico" which had only opened in 1971 but by the time of the Bedfull tour arriving, the theatre there had become the first to allow mixed-race audiences. Foreigners also played in Durban and would seem to have played Grand theatre, Leeds in September of this year.

The cast consisted of amongst others, Terry, June, Lynda Baron, Peter Bland, Colin Jeavons and Julia Sutton. Jeavons appeared on Ms Whitfield's original This is your Life tribute and also in three episodes of Terry's 1970s series Scott On and a 1983 Terry and June show.

On television, Terry made the first of two guest appearances as a panellist on the ITV murder mystery game show Whodunnit? Airing in September, the programme was devised and partly written by Jeremy Lloyd and Lance Percival; Lloyd had a role as a naïve young medic in Doctor in Clover back in 1966 within which Terry appeared as a rather camp hairdresser.

In this episode, Worth Dying For, Terry was on the panel alongside actors Patrick Mower, Anouska Hempel and the lovely Dilys Laye, who shared some screen time with Terry in The Bridal Path, a genteel comedy set in Scotland and both had roles in a St. Trinian's comedy.

This particular entry also included a part for Victor Spinetti, an actor who had in recent times worked with Terry in the theatre. The plot for the guest panel to discover the killer is as follows: a gun is found after a cleverly planned shooting has occurred but as usual, there would be various red herrings and clues to be found by the panellists after watching a short film within which a murder is committed. Doctor Who star Jon Pertwee controlled proceedings as the host, after making the show his own from the second series onwards. The show proved a popular success and would run until 1978. With its notable invited guests/ participants the programme proved to be a who's who of 1970s British film and television stars.

Back on stage, for a full account of the storyline to A Bedfull of Foreigners, stageplays.com offered the following, "Stanley and Brenda Parker are driving about France on their vacation when they find themselves in a village near the German border on the eve of a local festival, they consider themselves lucky on finding a hotel room. But this kind of luck, no one would want to endure for long. In less than an hour with Brenda absent Stanley finds himself lowering an attractive, stark naked girl from his room's window. Confusion turns to chaos with the arrival of Claude Philby, the girl's husband followed by the arrival of Claude's girl friend, Simone. By the second hour, almost everybody is in the wrong bed!

Figures dressed as nuns and monks rush in and out. Seductions and confrontations run rampant. And when the dust finally settles, a weary and dazed Stanley wishes they had have spent their vacation at a nice, quiet English seaside resort."

Whilst britishtheatreplayhouse.com added, "Adding to the confusion, are a hotel porter, who may or may not have been born in Lapland and subsequently joined the Foreign Legion and a lustful German hotel manager in Renaissance costume and a strangely high singing voice! Beautiful girls undress on stage, middle aged women climb out of third floor windows, radiators fly to the ceiling and bicycle chains find new uses." A Bedfull of Foreigners also plays at the Wimbledon theatre in December with its principal cast enhanced by Jean Ferguson and Morgan Sheppard.

Terry stars in Goldilocks and the Three Bears at the Bradford Alhambra alongside Golden Shot girl Anne Aston, dandy wrestling star Jackie Pallo, Geoffrey Hughes, Keith Harris and Cuddles and Blayne Barrington.

With its distinctive corner tower entrance and lettering above, the Alhambra makes a stunning discovery to those seeing it for the first time. The lettering might have gone but it still stands majestically on since opening back in 1914. A large scale venue able to host 1,400 theatregoers, the Alhambra saw the panto still running in March 1976 after opening on Boxing Day (a Friday) after a five day rehearsal period. To promote the show, whilst appearing at the theatre, Terry made a public appearance at nearby Pudsey to open a Save the Children Fund sale. He also met Bradford Telegraph and Argus prize winners on 22 December at Santa's Grotto somewhere in town.

"I met him in about '76; he was coming out of what was Kells Lane Bingo Hall in Low Fell (Gateshead) after a gig. Seemed like a nice chap." Anon.

The second and third TV series of Happy Ever After both air this year, with an added Christmas special, too. With its theme tune sounding similar to It's a Knockout, series two commenced on 8 January 1976 and the show will run through to 11 March with the tenth episode, titled The Novel, being broadcast.

Episode one: *A Country Cottage*

Cast

Beryl Cooke...Aunt Lucy

Jillianne Foot...Stable Girl

Damaris Hayman...Peggy

Bill Shine...Arnold

Episode two: *Old Folks' Party*

June. "Well there are some very peculiar men about these days: what? How's daddy?"

June Whitfield gets to deliver a lot of funny lines in a very well executed script from John Chapman and Eric Merriman. Daughter Debbie (Caroline Whitaker) returns home and persuades Terry and June to volunteer within the community. Visiting the Social Srvices office, Mrs Henderson (Joan HIckson) initially assumes that the couple need help before realising their true purpose for visiting. The Flecther's decide to welcome a group of pensioners into their home for a travelogue lecture to be presented by Terry. In an episode where none of the older characters seem to have first names, there are many faces known to Terry from his past here including Larry Noble, another artiste from the Brian Rix stable.

Hugh and I star Jack Haig does another old git characterisation, adding a bit of randiness but otherwise seemingly the same man from the earlier sitcom. The evening proves a disaster with the guests being very difficult to control and Terry's lecture flopping.

Cast

Eric Chitty...Mr Calthrop

Beryl Cooke...Aunt Lucy

Jack Haig...Mr Bartram

Joan Hickson...Mrs Henderson

Larry Noble...Mr Dingley

Patsy Smart...Miss Ackroyd

Mollie Maureen...Mrs Turner

Caroline Whitaker...Debbie Fletcher

Episode three: *Lucy's Premium Bond*

Cast

Noel Coleman...Hubert

Beryl Cooke...Aunt Lucy

Episode four: *Telemania*

Cast

Beryl Cooke...Aunt Lucy

Episode five: *Terry in Court*

After previously having seen Terry on screen as a policeman asked to give evidence in a succession of films it is a delight to see him back in court but no longer in uniform. This time around, he decides to represent June in a compensation claim against their local council after being bamboozled by the legalese spouted by a lawyer. June thinks it a bad idea but Terry wants to take a stance and stand up for the 'little man' after she has a bump in their car involving a council dustcart.

Throwing himself wholeheartedly into the project, both June and a bumbling Aunt Lucy are called as witnesses and the whole thing proves a delight. Showing off, Terry enters the courtroom in full Barrister's outfit, wig and gown before being ordered to remove it by the judge (Basil Dignam). Immediately confused by the terminology used, an early example sees Terry asked to present his case and so he hilariously and quite literally, shows his briefcase to the adjudicator.

Using a bellowing tone, Terry eventually wins the case after grilling driver Grubb (the much-loved character actor Harold Goodwin who had been in Nearly a Nasty Accident), to admit liability. However, in a final gag, Terry manages to reverse his boxy Austin Maxi into a parked dustcart. Much of the script/ plot would resurface later in an episode of Terry and June, the natural successor to Happy Ever After.

Cast

Ralph Ball...Court usher

John Cater...Mr Smith

Beryl Cooke...Aunt Lucy

Basil Dignam...Judge

Robert East...Opposing Barrister

Harold Goodwin...Mr Grubb

Nicholas McArdle...Taxi driver

Episode six: *The Flower Show*

A frequent co-star with Terry Scott, Dennis Ramsden appears in this episode and William Moore, Mollie Sugden's husband, is all in it.

Cast

Beryl Cooke...Aunt Lucy   William Moore...Mr Cooper

Dennis Ramsden...Col Sutcliffe

Episode seven: *June's Day in Bed*

Cast

Norman Bird...Mr Fletcher

Pearl Hackney...Mrs Fletcher

Beryl Cooke...Aunt Lucy

Also starring: Anita Kay, Lorna Nathan and Patsy Blower.

Episode eight: *Frank's Return*

Cast

John Alkin...Frank

Beryl Cooke...Aunt Lucy

Pik Sen Lim...Nancy

Episode nine: *Filming the Fletchers*

Cast

James Appleby...Licence Investigator

Beryl Cooke...Aunt Lucy

Pippa Page...Susan Fletcher

Ralph Watson...Tristram

Caroline Whittaker...Debbie Fletcher

Episode ten: *The Novel*

The final show was broadcast on 11 March.

Cast

Neville Barber...Head waiter

Beryl Cooke...Aunt Lucy

Neil Hallett...Philip

Jay Neill...Waiter

Anita Sharp-Bolster...First lady

Beatrice Shaw...Second lady

Away from television, Terry and his theatrical co-stars Lynda Baron, June Whitfield and Dennis Ramsden were pictured together on stage at the famous Victoria Palace Theatre, London during a rehearsal of their farce A Bedfull of Foreigners on 7th April, a day before its opening night. Julia Sutton and Colin Jeavons and Peter Bland would also join them in the cast with Roger Redfarn directing.

The Victoria Palace, across the road from the train/ tube station, had housed the Carry On stage show whilst Foreigners was specially written for Terry by his old colleague Dave Freeman.

Here's the synopsis according to the latter: "The play is set in a French village near the German border on the eve of a local festival. When an English couple, Stanley and Brenda, obtain a room for the night...they consider themselves lucky – but not for long. In Brenda's absence less than an hour later, Stanley finds himself lowering an attractive girl stark naked from the window. The arrival of Claud, the pretty girl's husband followed by his girlfriend, Simone, causes further chaos. By the second hour, almost everyone is in the wrong bed, as figures dressed as nuns and monks rush in an out and seductions and confrontations run rampant."

I think that the play was initially performed back in 1973 but it did not run at the Victoria Palace until April 1976 before being transferred to the Duke of York's by October.

Scott and Ms Whitfield were very busy at this time, rehearsing during the day for their Happy Ever After sitcom and in the new farce in the evenings. Occasional cast changes would occur, Anna Dawson being one. She would subsequently work with Terry many years later in another popular stage farce; Run for your Wife!

Cast

Terry...Stanley Parker

June Whitfield...Helga

Dennis Ramsden...Claude

Lynda Baron...Simone

Colin Jeavons...Heinz, the hotel manager

Julia Sutton...Brenda

Peter Bland...Karak, head porter

Act I saw the characters in a hotel bedroom whilst the interval was followed by Act II, with the action returning a moment later.

Terry and June make a record Nicholas the Clown/ A Bedfull of Foreigners this year (DJM label).

Terry is also a guest on June's This is your Life tribute show from Thames television. The show, recorded on 19 March and broadcast 14 April, offered Terry taking great delight in telling of June and A Bedfull of Foreigners co-star Lynda Baron recording his sonorous snoring whilst in his dressing room during the South African tour. "I now know what my wife and this other wife have to put up with while I'm asleep," snorted her TV husband before adding with a glint in his eye, "and I hope that she doesn't mind!" Many of the invited guests that day had acted in projects with Terry also, namely people like Pat Coombs, Peter Jones, Reg Varney, Norman Vaughan, Ronnie Barker, Leslie Crowther and Peter Butterworth. Bob Monkhouse was the last to be presented to June and mentioned their working association which stretched back to 1952. He and Terry's career paths had of course crossed (albeit unsuccessfully) at the BBC many years back.

Foreigners co-star Lynda Baron would later tell the tale involving the touring cast of the show when they were in South Africa. It was on Terry's birthday, 4 May, when the company had been joined by Charles Prince, an old pal of his, for drinks whilst they were in Durban. Having a lovely time, swigging champagne, they decided to give Terry the bumps before throwing him in to the pool where he managed to lose his shorts (no, Brian Rix was nowhere in sight). Spying a photographer and someone that they thought a reporter, also, they then threw him into the pool but the man in question turned out to be the Mayor of Durban! Cousin Quintin, known to Terry as 'Tiny', in a letter to the author, remembers an earlier mishap, "Owen (Terry) used to come to our house regularly, especially at weekends. And we would go swimming in the canal at Grove. On one occasion there were about twelve of us, including a number of girls. They boys were in the water and the girls were on thebank, sunning themselves. The swimmers were messing about, as you do, when suddenly there was a cry from Owen: his trunks had come off. After diving and searching but not finding them, he had no option but to leave the water naked. But the girls, well they said that they would not look but as soon as he was out they allturned around! He never came swimming again."

Devised by Denis Gifford and presented by Denis Norden, Terry was an invited guest on Looks Familiar, alongside Peter Sellers, actress Stella Tanner and actor/composer Ray Ellington. In the programme, guests would talk about their careers and I wonder if Terry and Ms Tanner recollected working on the Miss Marple film?

After being a guest on series three, Terry rejoined his old Prince of Wales theatre co-star Jon Pertwee for another episode of the murder mystery show Whodunnit? This one, titled Time to Dye found Terry and fellow guest actor Gareth Hunt joining others to attempt to identify the murderer of a model. His appearance aired 12 July.

Following a bit of a gap, series two of Happy Ever returns on 9 September, again with the Chapman and Merriman writing team. A few actors utilised in the new series had or would work with Terry at other times in his career e.g. Colin Jeavons, Michael Ripper and Josephine Tewson. Also, Joan Benham and Terence Alexander would both advance to be cast in the initial series of Terry and June.

Episode one: *Foster Parents*
Cast
Beryl Cooke...Aunt Lucy
Stephen Galloway...Anthony
Colin Jeavons...Mr Truscott
Episode two: *Restoration Piece*
Cast
Beryl Cooke...Aunt Lucy
David Gooderson...Mr Lawton
Rose Hill...Mrs Parker
Preston Lockwood...Rev Parker
John Ringham...Mr Marchmont
Michael Ripper...Mr Cobb
David Woodcock...Soldier
Episode three: *It's All In The Title*
Cast
Joan Benham...Countess of Buckleigh
Beryl Cooke...Aunt Lucy
Anthony Howard...Earl of Buckleigh

Pippa Page...Susan Fletcher

Michael Ripper...Mr Cobb

Martin Wimbush...Lord James

Episode four: *Mistaken Identikit*

Some familiar faces in this one including Josephine Tewson, a comedic actor making quite the name for herself via comedy roles and worked with Terry both on television and in the theatre.

Cast

Ralph Ball...Policeman

Charles Collingwood...Policeman

Beryl Cooke...Aunt Lucy

Robert Gillespie...Station Sgt

David Rowlands...Policeman

Josephine Tewson...Mrs Robins

Corbet Woodall...Newsreader

Episode five: *The Car Rally*

Cast

Patrick Connor...Farm labourer

Beryl Cooke...Aunt Lucy

Tony Sympson...Old man

Peter Tuddenham...Lollipop man

Episode six: *Holiday Plans*

Cast

Beryl Cooke...Aunt Lucy

Neil Hallet...Philip

Toni Palmer...Angela

Episode seven: *The Protest*

Cast

Jacqui Cook...Mrs Groves   Beryl Cooke...Aunt Lucy

Joseph Greig...Mr Addison

Nelly Griffiths...Old lady

Betty Impey...Mrs Addison

Robert McBain...Mr Groves

Geoffrey Palmer...Mr Critchley

Robert Vahey...House of Commons attendant

Episode eight: *The French Student*

Student. "Tell me Mr Fletcher, which one do you like the best?"

Terry and June's daughter Debbie goes to France on a month's language exchange and in return, a super sultry Francoise Pascal comes to stay with them in this none-too-subtle episode which starts off poorly but improves immensely.

A Euro sceptic, Terry soon sways gazing upon the delectable Michelle (Ms Pascal). There follows a fabulous piece of slapstick after they are introduced, seeing his new greenhouse collapse all around him (after being poorly erected by Terry in his vain efforts at D.I.Y).

Invigorated by the arrival of the beautiful visitor, Terry gets into the spirit of things by adopting a 'Johnnie Onions' outfit of stripy jersey, beret and a soon-to-be problematic cravat. June has many lines of dialogue responses to Terry's fawning, in a witty Groucho Marx stylee.

Intending to show Michelle the London sights, he knocks on her bedroom door only to discover her in a state of undress, flustered, as indeed we all would, she asks Terry which dress she should wear today. Holding them out in front of her and revealing her stunning figure: the scene is pure farce and very funny. Watch Ms Pascal as on a couple of occasions you will notice that she laughs in scenes. After having Madeline Smith to paw over in another episode, Terry is a lucky man at getting close to the stunning Francoise.

Having decided upon what to wear, the young lady goes to find June to ask her to zip up her dress at the back. However, with only Terry there, he offers to help but in the meantime manages to attach his cravat in the zip. There follows another comedy highlight, involving the couple attempting to free themselves from the compromising position. Flopping on top the bed, June arrives and Terry says than he can explain everything! It is the type of scenario that Terry would work with on stage across a number of plays, such as in A Bedfull of Foreigners and Run for your Wife.

Another enjoyable sequence sees Terry and June showing Michelle the London landmarks before she returns home.

At the close of the episode, an exhausted Terry is surprised to see Debbie again so soon and asking if they could put up some students that she met on the way home. They enter and it is revealed that they are a trio of foxy young women. Terry is delighted and switches in to overdrive in his excitement. Coincidentally, one of them is played by Lena Clemo, who had been one of the original Fletcher daughters.

Cast
Beryl Cooke...Aunt Lucy
Caroline Whitaker...Debbie Fletcher

Kirsten Hiern-Cooke...French student

Francoise Pascal...French student

Donna Scarf...French student

Lena Clemo...French student

Barnie Gosney...Waiter

Episode nine: *Lucy's Present*

The debonair Terence Alexander appears in this episode, he would advance to be cast as the original Malcolm in Terry and June.

Cast

Beryl Cooke...Aunt Lucy

Terence Alexander...Norman

Jane Downs...Sybil

A Christmas Special was shown on 23 December.

Cast

Charlie Caine (Simon Beal)...Carol singer

Beryl Cooke...Aunt Lucy

Pippa Page...Susan Fletcher

Tracy Plant...Carol singer

Caroline Whittaker...Debbie Fletcher

In Jubilee year, Terry joined his former Carry On up the Khyber co-star Roy Castle, here as host, as a celebrity panellist on ITV's Whose Baby? Its format found the panel quizzing the children of a famous parent to guess the guests identity. Terry participated in two episodes, recorded on the same day, and going to air on 16 February and 23 February 1977.

Both featured in That's Carry On, released in cinemas this year, it was the first compilation feature comprised of clips from the various films in the series. Terry could be seen in a half-dozen scenes taken from the likes of Henry, Khyber, Loving, Jungle and Matron.

A fourth television series of Happy Ever After consisting of seven episodes and a Christmas special would also be presented. Guest cast members Donald Hewlett would later tour with Terry in The Wind in the Willows whilst Ian Masters acted in a number of projects with him and Brian Oulton had been in Hugh and I and in the Carry On films.

Episode one: *Hello Sailor*

Cast

Beryl Cooke...Aunt Lucy

Donald Hewlett...James

Ian Masters...Robin

Pippa Page...Susan Fletcher
Philip Ryan...McGregor
Caroline Whittaker...Debbie Fletcher

Episode two: *Talk of the Devil*

Cast

Beryl Cooke...Aunt Lucy
Arthur Howard...Mr Braithwaite
Preston Lockwood...Rev Parker
William Moore...Mr Cooper

Episode three: *You've Got to Have Art*

Cast

Dave Atkins...Delivery man
Peter Bayliss...Sir Frank
Ian Burford...Mr Whitaker
Beryl Cooke...Aunt Lucy
Mary Henry...Miss Butler
Michael Ripper...Stonemason

Episode four: *A Proper Choice*

Cast

Beryl Cooke...Aunt Lucy
A big cast included Beatrice Shaw, Stuart Sherwin, Barrie Gosney.

Episode five: *He Who Excavates Is Lost*

Cast

Beryl Cooke...Aunt Lucy
Brenda Cowling...Mrs Robinson
Valerie Griffiths...Woman on beach
Gypsie Kemp...Telephonist
Mike Kinsey...Policeman
William Moore...Mr Cooper
Robert Vahey...Man on beach

Episode six: *Never Boring*

Cast

Beryl Cooke...Aunt Lucy
Terence Alexander...Norman
Jane Downs...Sybil
Brian Oulton...Mr Thornton

Robert Urquhurt...Sir Andrew

Episode seven: *Never Put It In Writing*

Cast

Sheila Brennan...Mrs Hewitt

Beryl Cooke...Aunt Lucy

A Christmas Special, titled June's Parents, co-written by Eric Merriman and Christopher Bond was shown on 23 December. Bond had written a number of the earlier Brian Rix television farces, some of which had Terry in.

Cast

Joyce Carey...June's mum

Anthony Woodruff...June's father

Beryl Cooke...Aunt Lucy   Pippa Page...Susan Fletcher

Caroline Whitaker...Debbie Fletcher

In September a touring production of A Bedfull of Foreigners arrived in Hong Kong after the play had enjoyed a fifteen month stint in the West End. The show was staged at the plush Hilton Hotel's grand ballroom throughout the month as an expensive dinner-theatre offering remembered by Bouree Lam on timeout.com.hk, "Years ago...the Hilton Playhouse theatre had luxurious dinner entertainment shows over a multi-course meal, events that were extremely popular."

Joining Terry were June Whitfield, Aimi Macdonald, who had previously worked with him in The Mating Game, Dilys Laye, Dennis Ramsden, Anthony Morton and Jimmy Thompson. Lynda Baron was no longer attached to "Dave Freeman's spicy bedroom comedy" which had been pigeonholed as being "Classically funny" (Daily Telegraph) and "Genuinely hilarious" (Guardian).

Its plot was summarised as "He's supposed to be on a business trip but is actually with his French mistress. Problems ensue when his wife pays a visit." Postscript: the Hilton has since been demolished.

"Panto at its very best."

www.its-behind-you.com

Aladdin at the Alexandra theatre, Birmingham, was where audiences had a history of enjoying a funny production this Christmastime was competing for an audience with the neighbouring Hippodrome which was staging Cinderella.

Here, however, bubbly Barbara Windsor ably filled the title role alongside her old Carry On team mate. Alfred Marks, who had performed with Terry at the London Palladium. Also in Aladdin, was Abanazar, crooner Ronnie Hilton as Wishee Washee and Terry once again donning his glad rags as Widow Twankey, Aladdin's mother. Jeffrey Holland fulfilled dual roles, most notably as the Genie in a show that featured David Davenport from Carry On Henry, Nita Gavin, David Auker and Dave Atkins (later to delight as the slovenly barman in Men Behaving Badly who this year had also played a delivery man in an episode of Happy Ever After. The show was directed by Roger Redfarn, opening Tuesday 22 December.

Ms Windsor, never one for subtlety, is now a veteran of many pantos and interviewed by Eileen McCarroll-Outram in the Daily Express, she was able to offer her considered opinion on the role-reversal tradition, "Christopher Biggins is an excellent dame. The great Jack Tripp was wonderful, so precise. John Inman was funny and a very dainty dame. And he was a joy to work with. Terry Scott was brilliant but not a nice company man. We all say June Whitfield should have got a medal for Terry and June."

Roger Redfarn once again directed proceedings. It ran from 22 December through to February 25th 1978. Written by John Morley, a theatre writer/ historian with more than 250 panto scripts to his name, Jeffrey Holland, who did a lot panto work with Terry, had the dual role here and he would take a great deal from watching and performing alongside him. Advancing to playing a Dame himself, Jeffrey observed, "I try to play it the way I saw it played as kid," the actor told whatsonstage.com, "the greats like Arthur Askey and Cyril Fletcher. I worked with Terry Scott a few times during the late 1970s and early 1980s, and he was an incredible Dame. Not such an easy man to get on with, he could be quite difficult sometimes, but you cannot take away the fact that he really was a superb pantomime dame, and he taught me a lot. The great Jack Tripp, who I worked with once too, also taught me a lot. I've learned from the best..."

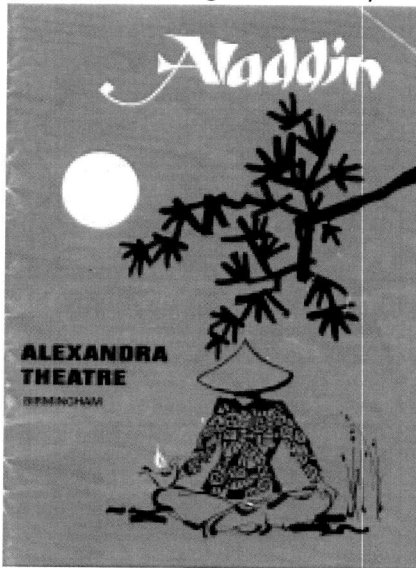

As himself, Terry was a guest on the BBC's Saturday Night at the Mill. Presented by Bob Langley and Tony Lewis, he appeared in the late evening show alongside resident house band Kenny Ball and His Jazzmen and Glenda Jackson. The show aired on 28 April 1978.

"Just a minute, I said when I'm 60 and not before!"

Terry is pounced upon by Eamonn Andrews clutching his bed red book as the recipient of a tribute on This is your Life. With events in his life dealt at breakneck pace by the host, Terry had been doing a personal appearance at a department store in Camberley when the Irishman struck! A frowning Terry watches as Andrews emerges from a rack of clothes to surprise him as he hands out signed photographs to the crowd.

A clip from Happy Ever After is shown, with Terry seen repeatedly banging his head within the confines of a boat (and not proving to be at all amusing, alas). His first guest was Beryl Cooke, who had been co-starring in the show with him and June Whitfield for the last five years. Ms. Cooke, Aunt Lucy in the sitcom, had been cast by producer Peter Whitmore in the show which ran from 1974 until 1978. Dedicated to her craft, Beryl left Happy Ever After to join the cast of Tenko (alongside Stephenaie Cole).

June regaled the host with a tale of some members of the public being unable to distinguish their onscreen life from off; often believing that she and Terry were married. Next came his real wife Maggie and daughters Sarah (then aged 20), Nicki (18), Lindsey (16) and 12-year-old Alexandra.

Jimmy Murray and his wife reminded Terry of a sketch that they used to work, with him as a plumber's mate and Jim as a jealous husband.

They were followed by older sister, Joan, fondly remembered by many in Watford even today as a local midwife. She told of her brother pinching her clothes for his act and trying out his routines in front of her friends!

Next on came cousin Ron Butcher, revealing that he was the begrudging inspiration behind Terry's "Knocker" character. Ron was always called this by Terry but he wasn't too enamoured by the tribute as Terry made quite a name for himself as the "obnoxious and rotten" schoolboy and played it throughout his working life.

Aged eleven, Terry won a scholarship to Watford Grammar school, as Owen John Scott, playing Pilot in Henry V across three days in March 1942 (26/27/28) and in the following year he was the lead in Macbeth from 1-3 April. The drama class had quite a reputation and when Terry joined, he took part in many productions including The Importance of Being Earnest and those listed above. His performance warranted a review in the local press which said, "He will be wonderful if he knew what he was talking about." Terry reradily agreed, "I said it loudly but I didn't know what I was saying."

Actor Garard Green was in the former production alongside Owen and would later tell Andrews that even then Terry demonstrated great promise as a serious actor. Indeed, this was one of his unrealised ambitions, admiring as he did, people like Rex Harrison for being able to play the more serious roles. Even as an 8 year-old he was performing; as Mr Bumble in a school production of Oliver Twist.

A joyous Bill Maynard was next introduced and he told of his partnership with Terry back at Butlin's holiday camp in 1950 before their Great Scott, It's Maynard TV co-star Shirley Eaton made a brief, smiley appearance. Former working partner Hugh Lloyd appeared via a filmed tribute as he was appearing in the West End at the time of the recording of the show. "Of all the pairs, we've been 2 babies; we've been 2 kids; 2 robbers; 2 old ladies; 2 ugly sisters; 2 gnomes. Of all of them, I think I enjoyed being the Parsons best." Offered Hugh before launching into the tale of both of them being invited to perform for the Queen and the fun they had dressed in their religious garments.

Old pal Charles Prince told of an incident whilst on tour in South Africa, something that his co-star Lynda Baron continued on with.

Small screen co-star Mollie Sugden told of Terry's love of gardening, revealed by his dashing off after rehearsals. Then a bit of an awkwardly contrived gag about him recording the dawn chorus was offered before she produced sincere insight, "I'm sure you'll agree that comedy is a very exacting business. But it's always been a great joy to work with you; 'cos you're not only a very funny man but you're also a very nice lad."

Next up came farceur extraordinaire Brian Rix. Knighted in 1986 and later to become Lord Rix, Terry was able to express his thanks to him for allowing him the opportunity to get into theatre work after flopping on television, "...he is one of the key factors why I managed to keep going. Otherwise I may have had to pack it in because I couldn't get the work." Rix passed away in August 2016.

Senior nurse Mollie Avis was presented next. From the Godalming nursing home she told of Terry's support for the place across the last twenty years. The final guest was singer/songwriter Sue Kelly Christie. Now living in India, she regaled of meeting Terry in South Africa where he shared his philosophy that we are all really kids that never grow up.

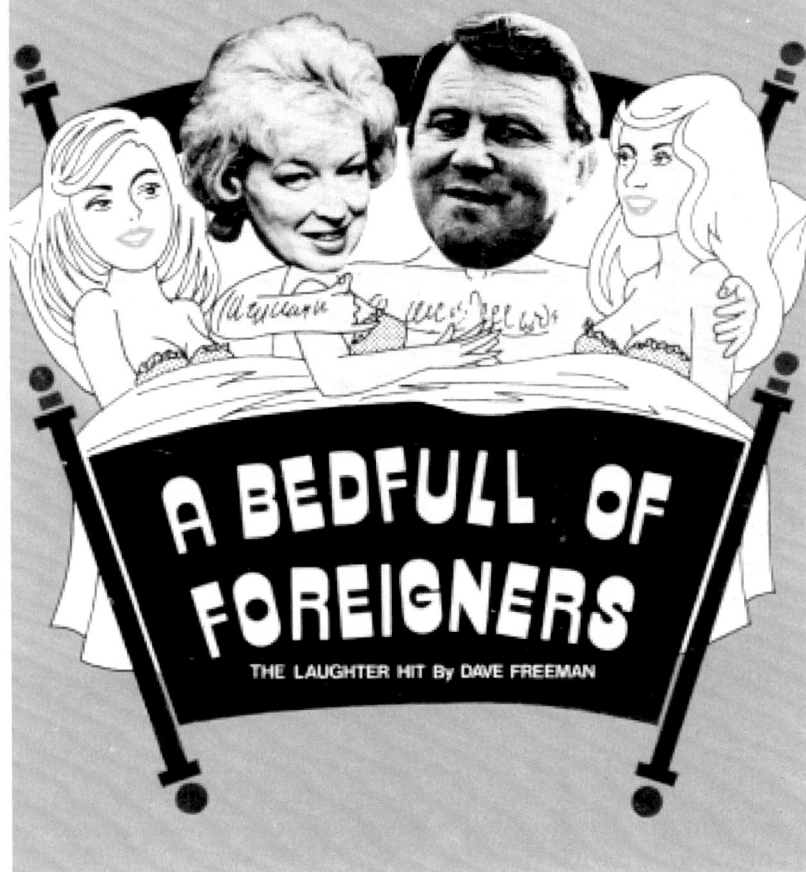

PIER THEATRE
Bournemouth

A BEDFULL OF FOREIGNERS

THE LAUGHTER HIT By DAVE FREEMAN

It inspired her to write a song for him.

The tribute was broadcast on 22 November.

Terry was at the Pier Theatre, Bournemouth with June Whitfield for a summer run of A Bedfull of Foreigners running from 26 June – 14 October prior to a spell on Jersey (see photo on previos page). The actors engaged in a number of charity fundraising activities including publicising the RNLI national lottery and the duo enjoyed a trip in a lifeboat. Directed by Terry, the cast consisted of: Dudley Owen (Karak), Barry Howard (Heinz), himself as Stanley Parker, Josephine Tewson (Brenda Parker), June (Helga), McDonald Hobley (Claude) and Anita Graham as Simone. In actuality, Scott had or would, play the same venue in a different production of this same show. Directed by David Warwick, Anita Graham, Jacqueline Clarke, Jeremy Bulloch, Carry On Loving/ Up the Jungle associate Jacki Piper, theatre co-star Barrie Gosney and Barry Howard had featured in what must have been a great production.

A year since its last outing, Happy Ever After returns to television, with its fifth and final series commencing on 5 September. Made up of a half dozen episodes plus a Christmas special, episodes were written by future Terry and June creator John Kane. Terry's comedy colleague Julian Orchard appears in episode two.

Episode one: *Watch Your Weight*

Cast

Beryl Cooke...Aunt Lucy

Pearl Hackney...Mrs Danvers

Christopher Lawrence...PT instructor

Episode two: *The Hut Sut Song*

June. "Oh Terry, how wonderful after all these years your love-making still breaks records!"

There is much to enjoy in this seies and The Hut Sut Song has to be one of its finest. Directed by Peter Whitmore from a John Kane script, a bit of office politics features in this storyline. June and Terry have to endure a home dinner date with withthe oddly-accented Ralp and his chatterbox wife, Cynthia (future Terry and June co-star John Quayle and Janine Duvitski). Alas all Cynthia can do is talk about how efficient her hubby is, whilst Terry subsequently finds himself dangling from an attic hatch after mislocating the ladder. Terry and June would see him in a similiar position, only in a church belfry.

The reason why he was up there was to locate an old 78 record after displaying little knowledge of the current music scene to his guests. The vinyl, an infectious bit of infectious Swedish gibberish called Hut Sut Song, has special meaning to the Fletcher's as it reminds them of their courting days.

A novelty recording from the 1940s, Terry visits a record shop which sells collectible vinyl. Here he meets the rather snotty Julian Orchard, who asks him to sing it but soon becomes annoyed with Terry, as he thinks he is on a wind-up from his friend.

Losing heart, Terry's enthusiasm returns when sales assistant Miss Sneed (Damaris Hayman) joins in with him and the two dance together in a delightful moment. After explaining that he wants the disc for his oncoming wediing anniversary, Miss Sneeds delivesr it personally on the special day. It costs Terry quite a lot, as he also has to re-emburse her for the taxi fare.

Meanwhile June, after hearing of the same store buying old records, sells them them their scratched copy only for Terry to subsequently be unaware that this is the same one that he buys! She gives him another gift, an lp of the Melba Trio's greatest hits, which includes their version of the song. Embracing, they flop onto the sofa and Terry accidentally sits on the album.

Cast
Beryl Cooke...Aunt Lucy
Janine Duvitski...Cynthia
Damaris Hayman...Miss Sneed
Julian Orchard...proprietor
John Quayle...Ralph

Episode three: *Business and Pleasure*

Another John Kane-inspired episode full of tongue-twisting dialogue finds Terry off to a business conference. Only this time, he is taking June rather than indulging in a lads weekend with colleagues such as Eddie (David Lodge). Terry does attempt to put June off after receiving a call from him but she knows whathe is doing and delights in teasing him about it.

Driving to the hotel in their Austin Princess, the author wonders if the BBC had a sponsorship deal with the company as Terry also drives one in the latter show. At reception, Mary Healey is delighted to see Terry return, after detailing his notoriety for his antics there the previous year. Upon discovering that Fletcher has brought his wife, Eddie and the others blank him.

Venturing out later to fix things, Terry finds them in a club but decides to return to the hotel and June. She teases him again, saying that his associate Stubbins and his partner have invited her out (to the very sam venue that he has just left). They finally stay in and Terry manages to put his back out whilst pushing the beds together. r David Lodge, seen here, played the doorman in the 1961 film No! My Darling Daughter and also a cameo in I'm All right, Jack (1959)."

Also starring: Mary Healey...Receptionist

Gordon Peters...Stebbins

Bella Emberg...wife

Episode four: *The King and June*

Written by Christopher Bond and Eric Merriman.

Cast

Beryl Cooke...Aunt Lucy

Also starring: Norman Atkyns, Gordon Salkilld, Stuart Sherwin, Sarah Tamakuni.

Episode five: *A Woman Called Ironside*

Cast

Lindy Alexander...Mother

Richard Bartlett...Policeman

Beryl Cooke...Aunt Lucy

Kim Fortune...Shop assistant

Jeffrey Gardiner...Mr Bennett

Michael Napier-Bell

Philip Ryan...shopper

Patsy Smart...Old lady

Joyce Windsor...Traffic warden

Episode six: *The More We Are Together*

Jon Watkins takes over the writing duties for this closing episode in the fifth series. It contains some familiar faces including Sabina Franklyn, soon to return in an episode of Terry and June, and super sexy Carry On lady Valerie Leon.

Cast

David Hayward...Barman

Roy Holder...Milkman

Geoffrey Palmer...Bob

Murder in a Bad Light, the 'new comedy thriller' created by Dave Freeman, saw Terry starring in it at the Yvonne Arnaud Theatre, Guildford. With its premiere taking place on Tuesday, 28 November and running until Saturday 16 December. Mr Freeman would create both Carry On Behind and Carry On Columbus and lots of the TV Carry Ons and Carry On London show. His daughter Deb Boultwood (nee Freeman) offers, "I have looked through my box of memorabilia as although we all remember the play we couldn't recall any details. I found a few old programmes and flyers for the play and it appears that

Murder in a Bad Light did a short run outside London late 1978 and early 1979: Yvonne Arnaud Theatre; The Ashcroft Theatre, Fairfield, Croydon Monday 19 February for two weeks; Theatre Royal Brighton 5 March 1979 and Richmond Theatre Monday 19 March for one week. There may have been other dates that we have no record of. I did meet Terry Scott a number of times as my father was a scriptwriter on many of the series that starred Terry and we often went to recordings of the shows. They first worked together on Great Scott, Its Maynard in the 1950's and then again in the 1960's/70's with Scott on... followed by some of the Terry and June sitcoms, plus many other smaller bits.

A Bedfull of Foreigners was written with Terry in mind and being hugely successful, led to my father writing Murder in a Bad Light which ultimately became Kindly Keep it Covered. Personally I always found Terry to be friendly, a strong personality with forthright opinions and very much a family man."

Such was the popularity of Terry and June Whitfield, that in 1978 they were named joint Personalities of the year by the Variety Club.

Also this year, Terry could be seen in six episodes of a now-forgotten show made by Southern television called Tell Me Another. Devised by prolific comedy writer Dick Hills, Terry and work colleagues Roy Castle, Alfred Marks, Clive Dunn and Leslie Phillips amongst many others, spoke about their lives across some forty four episodes. Terry participated in the following: Stories about their careers/ Stories about how they started in showbusiness/ More stories about their early days/ General Stories - How Terry Scott became a knocker at a séance.../General Stories/ More stories about their careers and General Stories.

At Bournemouth, Barry Howard was in the cast and this was the first time that he had worked with Terry and June, he would once again work with them in the next year and at Bristol in panto with Terry for the 1982/3 season, whilst being one a Hi-De-Hi! star.

Another role in pantomime was chalked up by Terry, this time at the Sussex seaside at Eastbourne as Widow Twankey, in Aladdin.

Terry had an emergency brain operation to combat a haemorrhage and in the midst of this, it was revealed that he also had an aneurism, which could have proven fatal if it had not also been operated upon immediately.

June visited him during his recovery and Terry said to her that the surgeon has simply let some hot air out of his brain! The two paired up again for their new BBC sitcom Terry and June, which would be broadcast in October.

ASHCROFT THEATRE Fairfield, Croydon

General Manager: Michael Tearle T.M.A., F.I.M. Ent.

Fairfield Box Office: 01-688 9291, Open Mon. — Sat. 10.30 a.m. - 8 p.m.

Credit phone: 01-681 0578 (Access & Barclay Card)

Commencing Monday 19th FEBRUARY for 2 weeks

Nightly 7.45 p.m. Saturday 5.00 & 8.15 p.m. Wednesday matinee 2.30 p.m.

Prices: £2.50, £2.25, £2.00, £1.75, £1.50. Sat. 8.15 p.m.

Tickets: £3.00, £2.50, £2.00, £1.50; Saturday (8.15) £3.25, £2.75,

£2.25, £1.75. Wednesday Matinee first Monday (Preview) £2.00, £1.50.

Duncan C.Weldon & Louis I.Michaels
for Triumph Theatre Productions Limited

present

TERRY SCOTT
JOHN BIRD
DILYS LAYE

and

ANTHONY SHARP

in

MURDER IN a BaD LIGHT

A New Comedy
Thriller by
DAVE FREEMAN

with

BARRY HOWARD   JEFFREY HOLLAND

and

JUDITH ARTHY

Directed by **ROGER REDFARN**

Designed by **TERRY PARSONS**

An Yvonne Arnaud Theatre Guildford Production

As previously stated, Murder in a Bad Light plays at the Ashcroft Theatre, Croydon from Monday 19 February for two weeks before moving on to the Theatre Royal, Brighton, from 5 March 1979 and then Richmond for a week from Monday 19 March.

In the cast alongside Mr Scott was satirist John Bird, The Bridal Path co-star Dilys Laye, Anthony Sharp, Barry Howard, Jeffrey Holland and Judith Arthy in another production directed by the resounding Roger Redfarn. Mr Sharp was known to Terry, as he had acted in a couple of episodes of Hugh and I, and coincidentally, was also in Doctor in Clover (1966).

Happy Ever After special The Go Between was shown on 25 April 1979, after being postponed from its original Christmas scheduling.

It was another co-written by Christopher Bond and Eric Merriman and had some smashing actors in it: Ballard Berkeley (later seen in Terry and June) and Dilys Laye, one of Terry's theatre / film co-stars.

Cast

Beryl Cooke...Aunt Lucy

Noel Howlett...Lucy's suitor

George Moon...Lucy's suitor

David Rowlands...Religious caller

John Scott...Lucy's suitor

This first series of Terry and June later received quite a backlash from alternative comedians in 1980s but as Peep Show star David Mitchell questioned, "It's a simple situation and it stands or falls on whether or not you give a damn about the characters: and I've always liked them, you know, from when I was a little boy." TV Heaven - Telly Hell interview

"Even nowadays, you know, people write and they say 'I hope that we're not going back to the days of Terry and June' and that kind of thing. But an awful lot of people liked it, at the time, and it did last. Overall, we did it for about thirteen years so we must have done something right." June Whitfield

That was Terry and June co-star Ms.Whitfield interviewed a couple of years ago when asked why the show is often so heavily lambasted.

In another TV chat, this time with Alan Titchmarsh, she added, "Too middle class, too middle of the road, too middle anything-you-can-think-of. The critics didn't like it. It wasn't edgy. I mean, when you get to the edge, you sometimes fall over, don't you!"

Consisting of a half-dozen, thirty minute episodes all written by John Kane and produced by BAFTA-nominee Peter Whitmore, the first series was broadcast between 24 October-28 November, 1979. Having recently worked together across sixty episodes of Happy Ever After, copyright problems with that show meant that Terry Scott and June Whitfield needed a new project and hence the creation of Terry and June. They retained their first names, with their onscreen surname now changed to Medford but not a lot else was that different.

According to radiotimes.com, the now-classic theme tune to this new situation comedy was never actually commissioned exclusively for it; "Music libraries still make a mint from selling generic tunes to production companies...Terry and June was just that – mood music, filed under 'comedy.'" This jaunty tune was composed by former pop star John Shakespeare and went by the curious name of Bell Hop.

Yet like Only Fools and Horses or Coronation Street, it is impossible to imagine any of these shows without hearing the music too.

Terry. "I've got a couple of lumps here the size of ostrich eggs."

June. "I think we ought to get a carpenter in."

Terry. "Don't worry, they'll go down eventually."

That's the best gag in Long Weekend, our introduction to the Medford's, Terry and June: otherwise known as Terry Scott and June Whitfield. Recently-promoted sales manager Terry, content at seeing his and June's children having grow-up and moved out, they decide to relocate to a smaller house after making a tidy profit from the sale of their family home which they had lived in for twenty six years. With a move to their new home found at number 26, Elm Tree Avenue, Purley (which is in the London Borough of Croydon), they stay overnight there in advance of their possessions being delivered the next day.

The episode sees lots of physical stuff for a fifty-two-year-old Terry to endure; carrying lots of things at once and banging his head under the kitchen sink and even having a toilet cistern hit him on the head! Whilst writer John Kane also gives him and the other cast members some tongue-twisting dialogue.

Their chatty new neighbours invite themselves in and joyfully recount the various odd bods that have lived in the house before the Medford couple. Tina is played wonderfully by old Terry associate Anita Graham and here she (over)dresses in a multi-colour fashion, head-and-shoulders above cocky husband, Brian (Roland Curram).

Terry is keen to remove the estate agents sign outside which still has its 'For Sale' notice on and in a slightly jarring scene he answers the door to an Indian gentleman who asks if the property is still available. This being the 1970s, the interaction is a little awkward especially after closing the door, Terry is almost audible in calling the uninvited caller a "wog" to wife June. You know this is what he is

saying but I have to wonder why the studio-audience thought it amusing (perhaps a sign of those particular times). He removes the sign by pulling out of the ground whilst driving his car and this being a sitcom, Terry speeds into his garage and accidentally smashes a pane of glass there with a ladder as a consequence. A truly amusing moment sees the new arrivals discover a hidden lavatory connected to the kitchen and Terry being hit on the head by it falling onto him, as mentioned. He also fails miserably to do some wallpapering.

By the end of the episode, Terry ends up in hospital, where the medic attending to him only happens to be the caller from earlier: now revealed as being Doctor Ramur (Tariq Yunus). Brian and Tina pay a visit and say they will be happy to call-in on him every day but this soon assuages him to leave!

Above: Terry with his screen wife June Whitfield at the peak of their popularity in Terry and June.

Cast

Terry...Terry Medford

June Whitfield...June Medford

Roland Curram...Brian Pillbeam

Anita Graham...Tina Pillbeam

Tariq Yunus...Dr Ramur

Sarah Lesley...Nurse

Episode two: *On the Move*

Terry. "I'm not unpacking the van looking for a bible. They'll think I'm a religious maniac!"

In actuality, Terry Scott was a lay preacher but the quote is still an amusing one, taken from the second episode. Packing up their things from the old house Terry and June try not to get sentimental but all removal man Mr Ridge (George A. Cooper) wants is to get moving as his team do not work later than 3pm on a Saturday. Cooper often played pedantic parts such as this and had recently worked with Terry and Mollie Sugden in another BBC comedy, Son of the Bride.

Just about to set off in convoy across London, things come to a halt as daughter Wendy arrives outside, crestfallen at partner Roger's perceived infidelity with a co-worker. It transpires that it was all a simple mix-up and that nothing actually happened. Watch out for a scene-stealing Beatrice Shaw, the Medford's neighbour at their old address, as her numerous attempts at waving them off are repeatedly halted. Ms Shaw had the distinction of being in two episodes of Terry and June; here and in a 1983 one. She can also be seen in a couple of episodes of Happy Ever After, the aforementioned precursor to this.

Cast

Roland Curram...Brian Pillbeam

Anita Graham...Tina Pillbeam

Jessica Turner...Wendy

Kit Thacker...Roger

Beatrice Shaw...neighbour

George A. Cooper...Mr Ridge

Adriene Burgess...Marjorie

Harry Fielder...Maurice

Ridgewell Hawkes...Ronnie

Episode three: *Flying Carpets*

Terry. "Do you think if I grew a moustache, I'd look like Burt Reynolds?"

June "I think you'd look like Debbie Reynolds."

Regarded as the First Lady of British Comedy (what a great opposite number June Whitfield proves to be in this show) delivering the above repose with aplomb and being very funny, too. When Terry returns home rather merry after enjoying a drink at work to welcome in the new executive suite, he and June are soon to be entertaining his boss and his wife at their new property. Unfortunately, their new lounge carpet has not been delivered in time but irritating neighbour Brian knows a man that can sort this out for them. In comes dodgy Nigel and Uncle Vern (Colin McCormack and a super Leslie Dwyer of Hi-de-Hi! fame) to deliver and fit one for them. Chastised for not stacking the furniture away in advance of their arrival, Terry goes to bed.

Come the visit, his boss Malcolm (Terence Alexander) apologies for being late, relaying that a thief has burgled the new office suite and stolen the plush carpet that Terry was so enamoured with! And yes, it is the one that has been laid in their living room. With the supposed help of Tina and Nigel, Terry and June attempt to return it via an external window cleaning pulley due to a Commissionaire standing guard in the reception area. He was played by Stuart Sherwin, a name associated with Terry since the early 1960s. Of course, they get stuck and spend a chilly night marooned high above the office block until Malcolm comes to work the following morning. But after all their hard work, the carpet was not stolen after all. In an enjoyable episode, Terry gets more tongue-twister dialogue from Mr Kane and Anita Graham grows more endearing.

Cast

Roland Curram...Brian Pillbeam

Anita Graham...Tina Pillbeam

Colin McCormack...Nigel   Leslie Dwyer... Uncle Vernon

Terence Alexandra...Malcolm

Rosemary Frankau...Beattie

Stuart Sherwin... Commissionaire

Episode four: *A Bridge too Far*

Terry."What this job needs is somebody with fire and energy, imagination and flair and poise and charm in abundance."

June. "Oh well, darling, better luck next time."

That's just one of the pithy exchanges between Terry and June in possibly the best entry in the opening series. A chirpy Medford returns home to find wife June attempting to make Taramasalata in the kitchen. After having a fruitful day at work, he reveals that he is close to gaining a new promotion but that he needs to continue to impress the big boss Sir Dennis (Reginald Marsh). A little older than Terry, Marsh makes his entry into the show and he would become an established character in the series, returning for the Disco Fever episode in series two. The two would also co-star in a couple of pantos together, one with June.

Returning to the story, Terry learns that Sir Dennis needs a partner for his Bridge team and so volunteers; the only stumbling block being that he has no idea how to play! Off screen, Scott was a keen Crib enthusiast and would compete at his local public house. Sir Dennis calls Terry at home and suggests that the duo meet up for a practice session that same evening. Shocked and unable to cry off, Terry is forced to learn the rules of the game by using a book and with the help of his attractive wife.

The couple try to follow the rules but are baffled by the many game play regulations and so hit upon a plan for Terry to receive a phone call during the evening which would require him to leave. This back when a house phone or call box was your only option, June provides much mirth in trying to find a vacant box to call home on. Meantime, the game starts and Terry hasn't a clue about all the terminology used by his guests and manages to end proceedings by bashing his head under the table.

Cast

Reginald Marsh...Sir Dennis Hodge

Anthony Coleman...Major Pritchard

Noel Coleman...Admiral Boyd

Heather Bell...Lady in phone box

Episode five: *Writing on the Wall*

As is often the case in the acting profession artistes sometimes end up appearing in things together on multiple occasions and in Terry and June this seems to be true. Whether or not Terry recommended certain people, I am unsure, but some names would crop up again and again. In this show, the excellent aforementioned Anita Graham was used a lot and Barry Howard would also make a brief appearance in this episode. Although only acting with Terry in a single scene, they had played in theatre shows before this time and would extend their working relationship.

Usually each episode started with Terry returning home from work and finding June at home. Perturbed at some fruity graffiti daubed nearby, he tells her all about it before Tina (Graham) arrives with her shy nephew, Magnus (Wayne Norman) asking Terry for possible fancy dress ideas for the local church fair. The mumbling lad wants to go as a pirate but 'Uncle' Terry talks himself into helping him go as Spock from Star Trek, complete with Enterprise spaceship which Mr Medford has to build!

His initial attempt to do this proves a disaster and to let off steam, Terry decides to go out for an evening stroll. Here he literally stumbles upon the graffiti artist outside the home of new neighbour Barry Howard. Picking up the spray can, Terry blubs that he isn't responsible for the vandalism as he has been making a spaceship in his kitchen: cue a puzzled look from future Hi-De-Hi! star Howard who died in 2016.

On the night before the fair, Terry completes a new ship for Magnus not knowing that the lad will never utilise it, as he is revealed next day by Aunt Tina, as the 'filthy phantom' responsible for the naughty graffiti.

Terry refuses to let his own hard work go unused, so he ends up manning the thing himself, after an amusing exchange with the 'King of Poland', a sharp youngster played by Tommy Barnett. Given a helpful push by June, he begins making his way to the fair behind a group of children but things are never so simple for Terry, as he ends up being pulled along a main road after accidentally becoming hooked-up to a works van. Master Barnett is a real find and he would make a return in Series two.

There is a clip of Terry fluffing his lines during a scene in the kitchen from the Friday night recording made before a live studio audience.

Wayne Norman was still a teenager when he was cast as Magnus in this episode, and here he relates his experience of working on the show, in a letter to the author. "I can remember about four or five of us in Director Peter Whitmore's office and we took it in turns to read the part. It was a two page monologue about how he wanted to go to this fancy dress parade as a pirate but we had to mumble all the lines. I remember Peter laughing out loud when I did it, he must've liked the way I mumbled I suppose, I still do. It was the usual set-up, we had a read through on the Monday morning and rehearsed through 'til Thursday in an old church hall somewhere in Chiswick, I think. Terry Scott was very professional and we worked on the scene many times to work out when he thinks Magnus has finished speaking to get the timing perfect. On the Friday we had the whole day at the at the old BBC studios in Wood Lane. We just ran the episode a few times during the day and recorded the show in the evening in front of a live audience. I had done a few live TV recordings before but for the first time I had my parents and Nan in the audience. They have a warm up comedian to get everybody in a good mood and the cast are then introduced before filming.

It was quite a long scene, maybe seven or eight minutes and it was all done in one take. But I could hear my Nan laughing all the way through; they were sitting in the front row underneath the microphone. So that set me off, I tried to stop going by pinching myself. After we had finished I thought they were going to redo the scene again maybe because of my laughing but they were happy with the take and moved on to the next scene (it was all filmed chronologically and they played the recorded film clips in the story). The whole evening would have taken a couple of hours, Terry said "Well done, lad" afterwards and that was it.

I watch it occasionally because on a personal level it is really moving because I can hear my Nan laughing through the whole episode, she only died eighteen months ago and it is a lovely timeless reminder of her too and she loved Terry Scott.

I can't really remember too much about him in the rehearsals. He kept himself to himself I think but June Whitfield was lovely and took time to talk to me. I obviously knew of them before even at that age, I was a big film and comedy fan and loved all the Carry on series too."

Cast

Roland Curram...Brian Pillbeam

Anita Graham...Tina Pillbeam

Barry Howard...Cochrane

Wayne Norman...Magnus

John Warner...vicar

Tommy Barnett...King of Poland kid

Episode six. *Animal Crackers*

Terry "Oh you know me; I've always had a way with the birds!"

Even June Whitfield audibly sighs at the dialogue that she has to deliver in this the final episode of the first series all written by Scotsman John Kane.

Relaxing in bed; June with a horror book and Terry being sent to sleep by his work-related manual, the title of the episode proves apt as the Medford's get lumbered by friends with a menagerie of pets to look after whilst they are away. Guinea pigs, a rabbit, ferret, parrot, snake and more take over their living room and a little Yorkshire Terrier, by the name of Boobalinka, rounds of the collection! The tiny mutt causes Terry a lot of problems, running away and seeing him disturb a courting couple, then a policeman and his dog and householders that mistake him for a burglar.

You have to give it to Mr Kane for his imagination in creating this storyline but the wordy dialogue lets down the series close. "You hold Boobalinka whilst I put Starsky (the snake) in his hutch," that's about the best line in this episode. For those unfamiliar with 1970s TV, Starsky and Hutch was a hugely popular American cop show import.

The series might have ended but it would return for a new batch by September of the following year.

Cast

Peter Stenson...Leonard

Sue Lynne...Moira

Derek Martin...PC dog handler

Brian Jameson and Deborah Fairfax...young couple

On Christmas Day, Terry made a guest appearance on popular ITV game show 3-2-1. Hosted by comic Ted Rogers, a former Butlin's holiday camp worker, like Terry, the show ran from September 1978 through to November 1987 and produced 147 programmes. Terry's involvement saw him dressed as Bill Sykes in one of the sketches in this specially-themed 'Dickens' show, number thirteen in the second series which was broadcast at 5.15pm.

The format of the show was that partners would compete against each other to initially answer questions before one remaining team would watch four brief sketches and attempt to decipher the cryptic clues. Terry featured in the first one, as Bill Sykes, observed coming down a ladder after burgling a house. Here he is confronted by a Bobby on the beat (Chris Emmett) before being duped by the so-called officer who takes his bag of goods, prior to revealing that he himself has just left a fancy dress event. Meanwhile Terry is back up the ladder and unable to do anything to prevent him from making off with his loot. The scene is over in less than three minutes, followed by Terry meeting the contestants, Angie and Eugene, and revealing a clue to Rogers. Also playing in the other three sketches were Steptoe and Son star Wilfrid Brambell and Terry's old mate Bill Maynard.

The couple failed to win any significant prizes such as a luxury holiday and instead ended up going home with £320, a furry Dusty Bin (a sort of Mr Potato head character held in great affection by the audience) and a radio cassette player.

This year's October proved to be a momentous period for Terry as he suffers a brain haemorrhage whilst preparing for a part in a stage production of the Ray Cooney/ John Chapman farce Not now, Darling in the West End. Let theatricalia.com explain, "The original casting for 'Arnold Crouch' was Terry Scott (opposite June Whitfield, of course), but at the end of the first week of rehearsal he was rushed into hospital for an emergency brain operation, from which he later recovered. This led to the last-minute replacement of Andrew Sachs, who... joined the cast for the third (and final) week of rehearsal, before opening direct at the Savoy Theatre. Understudy, Mansel David, rehearsed with the cast for the whole of the second week of the three-week rehearsal period, which paid dividends later when he had to play some performances the following February, after Andrew Sachs succumbed to the inevitable exhaustion of the busy schedule brought about by the circumstances." The production was set to play at the Savoy theatre, London and author Ray Cooney played the role at some point.

Below: Terry and June became an instantaneous success and here Terry answers a fan letter regarding the show.

Terry in the 1980s

Writer/ actor/ musician James Bryce, was in amongst the cast with Terry in A Bedfull of Foreigners this year and still working today, he remembers a great deal from his involvement, some of it not so positive. The play was Scots-born Bryce's fifteenth theatre role in a career dating back to 1977. Now living in Midlothian, I have quoted James directly from a lengthy correspondence with the author, to allow a rare insight of an actor's life on tour.

"I haven't kept all the programmes, and didn't keep a diary at the time, so the period of the tour between 4 - 27 October isn't clear." Begins James, "I know we played Wilmslow...or at least lodge there...(author note: see entry below for update). Assuming that it was one week in each venue, this means that there are two weeks missing before Bath (as above). I'm recalling that there were only two week's rehearsals. In London.

The first I was aware of Terry Scott – as a real person rather than a figure on the TV - was when I auditioned for him for a role in Dave Freeman's farce A Bedfull of Foreigners, which was playing the summer season in Weymouth and then touring.

After the audition, I received a phone call. "There are two types of directors," he said, "Those who sit sleeping in the auditorium and let the actors get on with it, and the other kind......."

A year earlier, I had worked with a certain type of "the other kind", who had been … to say the least...frustrating. I had a strong feeling that Terry would be of this kind, so made sure I was 'off-book' and well-charactered by the first day of rehearsals. Not only for my character, the handyman, Karak, but for the two other roles I was understudying.

Rehearsals went well. I had heard stories that he had been difficult to get on with, but that, after an operation, he was now much better. And he seemed OK."

14 July- 6 September: Weymouth Pavilion theatre

Cast

Terry Scott: Stanley Parker

Josephine Tewson: Helga Philby

Peter Byrne: Claude Philby

Barry Howard: Heinz

Nicola Hamilton: Brenda Parker

Fiona Douglas-Stewart: Simone

James Bryce: Karak (also understudied all the males).

Foreigners commenced its run at the Pavilion on Monday 14 July. "He [Terry] was always in the bar afterwards, drinking with Barry Howard. I tended to drink with one of the actors, Peter Byrne, who early on opined to me that Terry had it in for him. (Author's note: Byrne had been in panto with Terry in Worthing back as far back as 1955). He had been thrown when, in the first performance, Terry and Barry had inserted a planned corpse (fit of stifled laughter) while standing on each side of Peter, holding a ….lance I think it was....anyway a pole-like object between his legs . A situation which can leave one with egg on one's face; and seemingly did to Peter.

At one point, Barry came up to me and said "You're a fool." meaning that I should be drinking with Terry. Fact is I think that he had to be the centre of attention, and I wasn't good or easy with social canoodling. I wonder now if I didn't trust him somehow. That was certainly true later. There may have been a bit of doing people down, a trend I have seen in a couple of companies. But they are far from the norm in my experience. I noticed that he would drink a bottle of wine during each performance. He was a hard taskmaster, though I got off lightly – he seemed to accept what I was doing.

Being an understudy, we held an understudy rehearsal once a week. For the tour, Peter Greene was brought in to take over from Barry. It was the job of the company manager and the understudies to rehearse him in. We had I think, a couple of rehearsals with him before Terry came in to add the final touches.

Let me describe what happened. The curtain opens. Karak (myself) is sitting on a bed, Heinz (Peter) enters. The dialogue is supposed to go something like.

Heinz: Karak! What are you doing? I am downstairs with the guests and you are upstairs drinking.

Karak: What? You want 'em downstairs drinking?

At this first rehearsal with Terry, what happened was Karak (myself) is sitting on a bed, Heinz (Peter) enters.

Heinz: Karak! What are you doing? I am downstairs …

Terry: Is this acting? Do you call this acting?

Peter had been cast a few days earlier. His lines were perhaps a bit sticky. He certainly was just building his character; usually, this happens in rehearsals. Not here.

Terry: "I can't direct this!"

We tried to explain it was early days. I offered to go over the lines with Peter before the next rehearsal. Later, I picture him, hang-dog face, saying "I should never have taken the job. I know what he's like. I worked with him before. I was told that after the operation, he was better."

We never saw him again. Someone else was being found.

Barry had agreed to forgo his holiday at the beginning of the tour to help Terry out. At the final performance, Terry gave his post-show speech. He gave thanks to the council and staff, and offered particular thanks to Barry for foregoing his holiday, because, he explained. "We had another actor come in, but frankly he was terrible." James adds, "To say this to an audience ran like a shock through me. There was a frisson in many of the cast."

'The laughter hit by Dave Freeman' at Weymouth offered ticket prices from £2.50 - £1.50 and 80p for children/ pensioners. It was indeed after enduring four hours of brain surgery that Terry agreed to do the short summer run at Weymouth, "But he was brave, if foolish…" recounts his agent and friend, Richard Stone, "I went to the opening night, and in the car park, after the performance, he fell on my shoulder and said that, without me, he would not have wished to carry on in showbizz. That, to an agent, is worth a 'guinea a box'".

The Pavilion theatre is still open today, rebuilt on the site of a previous venue that was lost to fire in 1954. Construction commenced in 1958 and the theatre complex opened two years later. By 2013 it reopened after a spell of uncertainty that same year.

The run in Weymouth finished on 6 September.

9 - 13 September: Leeds Grand

I think Jan (Hunt) took over the part Helga Philby from Josephine Tewson and Anita Graham takes over the part of Simone from Fiona Douglas Stewart.

On one of her first performances she [Jan] delivered a line on stage to which Terry immediately responded. "That's not the right line. The right line is ……." (and quoted it).

Of course, this got a massive laugh from the audience.

This never happened again: after the performance, she immediately went to his room and gave him a bollocking, "No one! No one!" she reported to us, "Does that to me!"

15 – 20 September: Newcastle Theatre Royal

A photograph of a lingerie-clad Anita Graham with Terry was used in an interview with him ostensibly to promote their visit to the city. Anita, as you may remember, had made a mark as the aforementioned Tina in early episodes of Terry and June.

Retrospectively, the paper began with, "The production - very much of its time - saw Scott hopping in and out and out bed with a succession of beautiful 'foreign' women, and had audiences giggling at the stream of naughty bedroom and toilet jokes." Terry commented, "Nothing ever really happens in the play. It's all innuendo. In fact I would not be in it if it did because my daughters would not approve. And they are the most important thing in my life." Foreigners had enjoyed a tour of Hong Kong and South Africa, previously. Terry added, "Humour does not vary much the world over. People still like naughty jokes."

James Bryce adds, "It must have been here that David Morton took over from Barry, although the Newcastle programme advertised Peter Greene in the role. We understudies had already rehearsed him in. In fact, I don't actually remember Terry coming in to direct, but I must be wrong in that. After an early performance, Terry came up to me, a little desperately, "Would you like a drink?" I was immediately on guard, thinking "What's this about?", but went for the drink. After delivering it, Terry said in my ear, "Well, what do you think?" which I interpreted as referring to David. Immediately I knew there was no correct answer. If I said he was terrible or I prevaricated to ease Terry, then that would be bad. Anyway, I thought he was good, so I said so, "He's good." In rehearsals, the understudies and company manager had found him great. Writing this now, I realize that Terry must have had some faith in me to ask me. On the other hand, he may have asked everyone else too. He always gave the impression of needing reassurance, or to be above everybody.

David's first performance took place on a Wednesday matinee. Often, these are filled with an older audience, some of whom may have hearing difficulties, and this seemed to be the case here. Terry was the only one getting the laughs. I'm standing in the wings watching during one of the few scenes Terry isn't on. He comes up to me and hisses, "Where's your funny man now?" I felt a rush of annoyance and anger. I replied, "It's a bloody bad audience and you know it."

22 – 27 September: Glasgow King's Theatre and 29 September- 4 October: Edinburgh King's Theatre

"At the Kings in Glasgow, the show was slated. We then went on to the King's in Edinburgh. Again, the show was slated, apart from, ironically, David and I. Terry came up to me on stage during the show and muttered "Did you see the review?" I don't recall what I said, but think it was probably merely, "Yes".

This was the year that he was invited to appear on the Royal Variety show. When he got the news, he went round the cast several times to announce it. Jan left it for a few nights before revealing to Terry she was giving a private performance for the Queen. There was no love lost between them."

Then James thinks that the tour possibly moved on to Wilmslow. There was a well-established venue there called the Rex, which had started its life as a cinema back in 1936 but had become a venue for shows prior to a possible West End booking. Terry associates Eric Sykes, Sid James, Kenneth Williams and David Jason had all played there, usually across a week. Former stage manager at the Rex, Anthony Riley, recalls local audiences patronizing the venue when the star names visited but that they were equally appreciate of amateur productions, too. The beautiful building has remained but is now in use as an elegant furniture store.

13-18 October: The Rex Theatre, Wilmslow

As detailed above, the author has since discovered that the show did indeed stop off here.

27 October- 1 November: Theatre Royal, Bath

"(Whilst) in Bath, we were taken out by Terry to a Chinese restaurant. During the performance he would come up and say "Remember we're going to the Chinese tonight?" The assistant stage manager claimed that he saw a whole line of Chinese in the audience that night, and wondered if they'd been given comps. So it went on.

3 - 8 November: Birmingham

After the final performance...the cast had planned to go to see Danny La Rue, but without Terry. After our show, the girls went off to get ready. Terry came up to me and said quietly, "I've got stage-side seats for Danny La Rue. Would you like to come?" It was an embarrassment, so I confessed that we were going already. So what this meant was that half of the cast sat well away from the stage, while Terry and his close circle sat by the stage. Afterwards, those by the stage went to see Danny in his dressing-room. JH and I and Mike, one of the stage management sat together at the back.

After a while, I elected to go to Danny's dressing room. I don't think I ever met him. We sat in the in the sitting room adjoining his dressing room. Later, JH enters, floats past Terry and the rest of us (and Noele Gordon, who was there also) directly into Danny's inner sanctum. It turns out she had worked with Danny before.

Anyway, the upshot is that it transpired that Danny had given tickets to the whole company to see his show, and Terry had made it look as if he himself had got them.

In spite of having been honoured by Terry saying as we parted "you're very good, you know", when I was offered the season for the same play the following year in Blackpool, I decided against it. I sort of regret it in a way. I know, looking back, find him a curious character. Not happy... at least, certainly not at ease. Was most surprised to read recently that he was a lay preacher.

The next year, my agent said that Terry and Jimmy Logan were doing panto together in, if I recall alright, Newcastle. I had heard about Jimmy, and wondered how two such egos would get on. Years later, in the early 90s, I worked with Jimmy, and asked him about working with Terry (I knew I should have kept my mouth shut, but was intrigued.) His face wasn't happy. It transpired that, in spite of being in the same panto, they never actually appeared on stage together. In summary, I felt he was a sad man.... no, not sad...a sense of desperation about him. He HAD to be at the centre of things."

Life in the world of television situation comedy continued for Terry with Terry and June back for another six episodes from September plus a Christmas special, with Mr Scott and Ms Whitfield presenting more of the same, with even the opening titles of the show remaining unchanged. Writer John Kane scripts most of the episodes apart from a couple and the house used for the exterior shots seems to be different; as is the interior set for the Medford home. The first episode was transmitted on 5 September and the sixth went out on 10 October. Terry and June really were proving popular, and were presented to the Queen Mother at this year's aforementioned Royal Variety Performance (but did not perform on stage).

Episode one: *To Catch a Thief*

A gentle return for the Medford's finds Terry excited about his new company car (replacing his large Ford Granada for a green 'Princess' model; a car with a laughingly poor reputation for reliability). Fussing over it with June, whilst adjusting his seat he accidentally hits the accelerator and shoots out into the road outside the driveway, where a police sergeant spots them (John Junkin).

John had worked with Terry previously, contributing additional dialogue to Hugh and I as well as making an un-credited appearance in Doctor in Clover.

The following morning and Terry is distraught to discover the car has been stolen. Meanwhile chirpy milkman Dickie (Roy Holder) tries to get to know his customers better but only succeeds in irritating Terry. In a later morning moment, dressed in his pyjamas, Terry is locked out and seeing the 'Milkie' again, manages to fall through the unlocked front door with great theatricality!

Off to report the theft at his local police station, Terry is reacquainted with Sgt Tucker (Junkin) alongside his colleague and forgetting the registration number, he goes through the motions of trying to remember via a memory technique taught to him by June. P.C Winthrop (Geoffrey Morgan) joins in whilst the perturbed Sergeant looks on aghast.

Come the next day and the car has miraculously been returned with a note saying that an expectant father took it to get his wife to hospital but this turns out to be a trick. It seems the Medford's are given theatre tickets for a West End show as a thank you but whilst they are out they are burgled.

About to drive home, Terry forgets that he has a new car alarm and when it goes off, he cannot remember how to disable it. Another copper arrives & doesn't believe him, stating that the vehicle is listed as stolen. Eventually getting home, the Medford's discover the house has been completely emptied before a knock at the door sees the dour Sgt Tucker explain that this has happened to others in the locality. Not to worry, those responsible have been apprehended and all their possessions will be returned.

Cast

Roy Holder...Dickie

John Junkin...Sgt Tucker

Geoffrey Morgan...P.C Winthrop

Michael Sharwell-Martin...P.C Brody

Episode two: *Words of Love*

Terry. "You keep your hands to yourself: I might get hurt!"

Often seen about to go to bed, Terry in snazzy pj's and June in her 'nightie', apart from a kiss on the cheek or showing the occasional bit of affection, Terry often eludes about sex but we never usually get to see him and June in a real clinch. But in this episode they do indeed engage in a bit of hanky panky!

After watching Bette Davis in Now, Voyager (1942) June questions Terry about the lack of romance in their relationship; something which he takes great umbrage to and hence the spontaneous coupling.

Speaking with Malcolm (Terence Alexander) at the office, he quizzes him about romance in his marriage but the latter comes across as a bit of a letch and always speaks down about his own wife, Beattie (Rosemary Frankau).

Today being June's birthday, a busy Medford asks his secretary Miss Coolidge (a funny Janie Booth) to get his gift engraved for her but he is uncertain as to what to write. Malcolm overhears them thinking out loud and completely gets the wrong idea.

Meanwhile June is at home making starters for the evening meal when Tina (Anita Graham in another multi-coloured outfit) tells her about her own husband being unfaithful with his secretary. This makes June paranoid as Terry is ticking all the tell-tale boxes of doing the same. Entering dressed in a white dinner suit, Tina makes a 'waiter' joke (he does resemble one). As do Malcolm and Beattie, invited guests for the evening. Of notice in this episode is the fact that doors on the set of the Medford's house do not close properly: firstly in a kitchen scene and then in the lounge, when Malcolm reveals to Terry that his wife found a letter from another woman on his person.

But returning to the plot, he then forces Terry to say it is his whilst Beattie comforts June following her perceived deception. It is later revealed that the note is from Miss Coolidge's long-standing fiancé Cyril (Robin Parkinson) and there is fun to be had when he calls into the house looking for her.

In a farce-like storyline, Terry and actress Janie Booth work well together; with Scott forcing her into a broom cupboard under the stairs to avoid June discovering her having brought his engraved present to the house later than anticipated. June and Terry display a great deal of affection in this frantic episode which proves most amusing viewing.

Cast

Anita Graham...Tina

Terence Alexander...Malcolm

Rosemary Frankau...Beattie

Robin Parkinson...Cyril

Janie Booth...Melanie Coolidge

Episode three: *Uncle Terry and Auntie June*

Comedy writer Dave Freeman injects some old fashioned slapstick into this episode, all of which is ably performed by an adept Terry Scott.

228

The highlight seeing him lifted up a considerable height by a fork lift truck at a cash and carry warehouse (it really is as funny as it sounds). Terry also manages to be entombed by multiple boxes of washing powder in another moment of Medford misfortune. It was the first of a half-dozen episodes to be written by Freeman.

Perturbed by their latest electricity bill Terry believes that they have been overcharged and questions June on her excessive shopping. When nephew Alan (Roger Martin) pays a visit Uncle Terry is concerned, as he knows that the young man is nothing more than a sponger. In London on business, June invites him to stay but soon regrets doing so following a clandestine delivery of multiple boxes of smelly cheese which is dumped all around the hall.

Concerned that the goods might not be kosher, Terry and June visit a local cash and carry to see if they can gain any insight. Once there, Terry gets consumed by a desire to save a bit of money by multi-buying and manages to cause mayhem for the unfortunate manager (Colin McCormack in another of his three appearances in the show) and cashier Sarah Scott (Terry's real-life daughter). The bungling Mr Scott tips a bumper-sized pack of corn flakes over him after being unceremoniously finding himself shelved high up above the shop floor!

Utilising the business card of Alan's manager, an unseen chap that proves to be committing fraud, June has to deny knowing her husband in an identity mix-up. In a hilarious interchange, she has to adopt a terrible Welsh accent (after Alan tells her that his boss's wife is Welsh but then remembers she is Irish) upon visiting Terry at the police station after pleading ignorance about him. He reiterates his innocence but not wanting to get his nephew in trouble, just when he is about to be charged with fraud, Terry tells the truth. Back at home, a knock at the door follows, with men from the electricity board there to cut them off.

Cast

Alan...Roger Martin

Colin McCormack...store manager

D.S Bates...Norman Comer

Police Inspector...Michael Napier Brown

Lorry driver...Gordon Salkind

Electricity man...Anthony Arundell

Sarah Scott...cashier

Episode four: *Disco Fever*

Terry. "Middle age is when your narrow waist and broad mind switch places."

Coming after the delights of Uncle Terry... this episode could quite easily have been called Age is not an Issue, as the subject is at its core.

Sir Dennis (Reginald Marsh) makes a brief appearance here, whilst Terry and his other more mature work colleagues worry about their jobs after the arrival of the former's young nephew instigating changes at the company. The youngster books a venue for the annual staff party back when disco was still popular (remembering that this is 1980) and the more mature employees, including Terry and Malcolm try to learn some modern moves. The later attempts to do this via a book, caught, mid-move by June. "It's the disco meringue," exclaims Terry.

"Looks more like a couple of cream puffs!" deadpans Ms Whitfield.

Wanting to fit in, Terry drags her to a beginner's class in disco dancing but arriving at the venue early, the others have not yet arrived. In a delightful moment, the couple engage in a smashing bit of dancing which is applauded by the live studio audience. When the instructor arrives along with a prancing group of younger dancers, this causes the Medford's to want to leave: though the sight of a sexy girl (Susie Silvey), persuades Terry that perhaps they shouldn't be too hasty. They briefly join the class and prove reasonable dancers until Terry catches a glimpse of himself in a studio mirror.

The proceedings come to a close with a lame, laboured joke delivered by Terry; something that he is obliged to do in other episodes, and it flops equally there. The line feels like an exclamation mark or as if the actor is forced to hold up a sign to the viewer reading "The End".

Cast

Sir Dennis...Reginald Marsh

Malcolm...Terence Alexander

Steve...Tony Anholt

Stan...Frankie Cull

Al...Ken Rogers

Sarah... Susie Silvey

Episode five: *Workers Unite*

The first twenty minutes of this fifth episode, here with Jon Watkins taking over writing duties, proves challenging viewing even for the most undemanding viewer. However, its final third saves it thanks to the combined efforts of June and Terry, after having delivered some excruciating dialogue, initially. Watkins had recently worked with them in a 1978 episode of Happy Ever After and in total, he would script four episodes of this new project.

Watkins brings up important issues, such as gender roles in both the work place and marriage and he does get away with making the whole thing a lot of fun by the close.

"I'm sorry, I'm putting my foot down," squeals Terry, after June takes a temporary job as a Market Research interviewer.

"You can't;" returns June, "it's a 30 m.p.h limit!"

That is one of the enjoyable exchanges between the onscreen couple in Workers Unite but the wittiest had occurred previously; in the Medford's kitchen. After agreeing to take turns preparing breakfast, a distracted June spills luke-warm tea from the pot into her husband's lap. Minus his trousers, which were in need of repair, Terry hollers, "I can smell burning," and cue a nearby toaster smoking away in an amusing sight-gag. Terry stumbles a bit over his words here in the eleventh Terry and June outing.

Cast

Elizabeth...Angela Morgan

Rex Robinson...Rex

Episode six: *Only Two Can Play*

"Three weeks of this and it's driving me up the wall..." bemoans Terry to his cello-playing wife before she asks him what he said. "I said three weeks you've been practicing and it seems no time at all."

John Kane returns as writer and gives Terry and June hobbies: the first as a painter and the latter as a rekindled cello player. Unfortunately, June plays terribly and when she returns from a lesson with old school friend Millie (Shirley Dixon), an awful beginner on violin, Terry can't stand it. June decides to quit after speaking with Terry; he's delighted.

Cast

John Rolfe...Arthur

Shirley Dixon...Mildred

Christmas Special

Another John Kane script presents the Medfords at Christmas time in a slight storyline noticeable in that Terence Alexander has been replaced by Tim Barrett (in the role of Terry's boss, Malcolm).

A bit of light relief is provided by Patsy Smart and Daphne Oxenford, as a couple of dotty charity shop volunteers, visited by the June and Terry in their quest for Christmas cards. Patsy had already worked with Scott on television series Hugh and I and Happy Ever

After and she would advance to playing a recurring role in Terry and June, also.

The character of Malcolm does grate, as he is always making derogatory remarks about his wife or cheating on her with another woman. Here, he asks Terry to hide a mink coat that his now departed lady friend has returned and he plans to give it to his unsuspecting wife. Terry agrees and puts it under the bed only for June to accidentally find and assume that the horrid item is meant for her: this despite them agreeing on a £5 present limit.

Four of the worst carol singers call in at the Medford's and Terry shows them how to properly sing a carol.

On Christmas morning, returning from church, June reveals a new sound system that Terry wanted and thinks that he will soon give her the coat. He doesn't know this and proceeds to offer a kitchen timer, which is what she said that she would like as a present. With Terry still not getting her hints, June explains that she found the coat and that he can give it to her now. Malcolm and Beattie knock the door, the latter delighted with the new fur coat and poor June finally realises that she is not going to get one too. They chat in the kitchen and he promises to buy her one when his work bonus comes through. And with this seasonal special, this marks the close of series two.

Cast

Tim Barrett...Malcolm

Rosemary Frankau...Beattie

Patsy Smart...Miss Fuller

Daphne Oxenford...Renate

Tommy Barnett...carol singer 1

Gerry Dolan...carol singer 2

Vincent Pakosz...carol singer 3

Christopher Poole...carol singer 4

On 3 December Terry joined June Whitfield in a group shot to promote the BBC's Christmas programming schedule; also there on the day, Basil Brush (a co-star in panto with Terry!), Ronnie Barker and Mike Yarwood.

Richmond was to be Terry's panto location this season, in a production of Babes in the Wood. Known as "The Theatre on the Green" it started its run on 12 December co-starring a trio of Carry On faces: Terry as Nurse Teresa Glucose V.A.T, Anita Harris as Robin Hood and big Bernie Bresslaw as 'Bernard the Bad". They were joined by Christopher Timothy, a long term theatre stalwart best known for his role as James Herriott in All Creatures Great and Small, a youngster playing Maid Marion billed only as Hillie, The Three Squires, The Barbara Speake Babes, Canadian fiddler/ composer Ward Allen and the hugely experienced West End singing star Eric Flynn. The panto was directed by familiar name: Roger Redfarn.

With such an instantly-recognisable voice, Terry was snapped up by animation company Cosgrove Hall to play Penfold, the cowardly side-kick to secret agent Danger Mouse. Often mistaken for a mole in his thick glasses and a blue suit, he joined David Jason across 161 episodes spanning ten series. Commencing on ITV on 28 September 1981, the opening series ran through to 19 March of the following year. Danger Mouse, a white mouse that "fights off villainy wherever it rears its ugly head," was written by Brian Trueman, creator of Jamie and the Magic Torch and others. Coincidentally, David would also play Toad, as did Terry Scott. Both had previously co-starred in the 1965 TV panto Mother Goose (1965) and their theatre paths also crossed. There is a lovely interview with Terry, David and Edward Kelsey laying down their voices for an episode of the show. Working to a very tight schedule, five episodes would be recorded in a day. Terry playfully jokes that he must be daft to be doing the show when a young lad interviewing the trio says that his character (pictured below) is a bit silly.

Still working hard, Terry rejoined June Whitfield and the crew for series three of Terry and June on the the Beeb. Joanna Henderson, a

co-star from The Mating Game touring production from 1970, makes the first of her lucky thirteen appearances in the show and Sam Kydd, seen previously in two films which also gave roles for Terry, has a part in The Lawnmower episode.

John Kane was responsible for four scripts, including the Christmas special, whilst Jon Watkins and father and son team Dave and Greg Freeman completed the others. The series was shown from 13 November through to 28 December.

Episode one: *The Lawnmower*

Terry. "On a clear day you can see over Croydon…"

At the start of this new series the Freeman team present Terry and June with posh new neighbours Tarquin (Allan Cuthbertson) and Melinda (Joan Benham). Both well-travelled and a little conceited, June wants to be convivial but her husband struggles to hide his contempt when they are invited around for drinks.

The pedantic Tarquin declines to return Terry's lawn-mower, originally lent to former neighbour Frank, claiming that it was on the inventory of the house's contents.

Also making a welcomed return to the show is nephew Alan (the delightfully chirpy Roger Martin) who introduces his uncle to the peculiar Louis (Sam Kydd) a former lawyer who advises Terry to go and retrieve the said item. So a plan is hatched for Terry and Alan to seize the mower from within his neighbour's shed.

However, the duo are not the most competent of burglars and June phones the police whilst offering a running commentary, incorporating fireworks exploding, loud music and spotlights illuminating the pair before they abandon the scheme. The pairing of Terry Scott with Roger Martin is a pleasure to watch and we will see more of the latter later in the series. A witty and satisfying opening to the third series.

Actress Joan Benham passed away in June 1981 with her role as Melinda her last. She had acted in a 1976 episode of Happy Ever After, previously and was in The Bridal Path film (as was Terry). The ubiquitous Sam Kydd, here speaking in a very strange manner, had a working association with Terry stretching back to 1959.

Cast

Allan Cuthbertson...Tarquin

Joan Benham...Melinda

Sam Kydd...Louis

Roger Martin...Alan

Episode two: *Stars on Sunday*

Original writer John Kane returns for this one with the opening credits seeing the Medford's successfully enjoying their fruit drinks without any mishaps, as they also would in episode one.

The 54-year-old Scott is the shining star in this episode which begins with Terry and June visiting Malcolm in hospital. Here they meet Reverend Austin (John Warner making his second appearance in the show) who is involved with hospital radio. Terry talks himself into volunteering to interview visitors about the poor-quality food served-up at the place but he innocently ends up causing all sorts of problems. June is also to be involved, presenting a cookery spot.

It is during their visit that we meet jolly nurse McArdle (April Walker), who also happens to write plays in her free time. And it is thanks to this that the two funniest scenes occur; initially with Terry, June, Malcolm, Beattie and herself having a read through of one of her radio scripts. It is fun to see them do this together especially Terry and June Whitfield, as both had experience of doing this for real in their earlier careers. The proceedings end in chaos, naturally, with Terry performing the play alone and offering his bird song impressions before calling in June for a sing-song in a frenetic close to an amusing episode.

Cast

Tim Barrett...Malcolm

Rosemary Frankau...Beattie

John Warner...Rev. Austin Doyle

April Walker...Nurse McArdle

David Gillies...Bernie

Michael Walker...Martin

Robin Hopwood...Dell

Patrick Jordan...Eric

Episode three: *It's a Knockout*

Sir Dennis. "We don't want to set the world on fire, Medford, but by god, we're determined to put it out."

Mr Kane produces the funniest script of the series thus far in a surreal tale which sees Terry dressing-up as a life-sized rabbit, complete with over-sized carrots!

In a true blast from the past, young Alan turns up late one night and gets his aunt and uncle to agree to store some costumes that he has obtained from the adult comedy game show It's a Knockout. For those unaware of it, Knockout was massively popular on television from the 1960s through to the early-1980s and involved all kinds of nonsense. Uncle Terry proves right in being hesitant at allowing his nephew into their home but the possibility of earning a few quid by storing the costumes in the spare room soon assuages this.

In the meantime, Terry wants to impress Sir Dennis enough into offering him the sales position, based in Brussels, to sell their fire extinguishers to the European market which has been flooded by cheap Japanese imports (much to the irritation of his boss).

Inviting himself and trusted Secretary Miss Fennel (Joanna Henderson) to dinner, Terry might know how to say the right things to his chairman but he is often bullied by him. Expecting his imminent arrival, Terry is disturbed by Alan bringing around some Japanese business men interested in purchasing the outfits. Many farce-like moments ensue which eventually conclude with Scott being persuaded to put on a rabbit suit and demonstrate the game to the delighted visitors. He does this with detached aplomb by bouncing from one bed to another in the spare room where the items were being stored.

June is entertaining their invited guests downstairs when Sir Dennis mentions that his secretary had a drink problem and perhaps should not partake of any alcohol. This being a sitcom, she asks to use the bathroom and upon hearing the commotion next door, opens it and seeing Terry in his rabbit outfit thinks she his hallucinating and offers a scream!

In a delightfully constructed script, Terry manages to confuse the foreign businessmen into thinking that he wants them to put on the remaining outfits rather than help him off with his own which has a stuck zip.

Calling down to June for assistance, Sir Dennis answers and finds Terry has managed to remove most of the rabbit costume apart from the large ears. Terry quickly snatches this off and completely ignores the double-take of his visitor in a smashing comedy moment. Scott works hard in these scenes which are brilliantly concluded by the bizarre sight of the visitors coming down the stairs all dressed in the rabbit suits. The final gag is given to Terry having Sir Dennis quiz him about why they are doing this. In a naff close to another wise devilishly imaginative episode, he says that they have just come from the "Bunny club" presumably meaning the Playboy nightclub in London.

Cast

Reginald Marsh...Sir Dennis

Roger Martin...Alan

Joanna Henderson...Miss Fennel

Vincent Wong...Japanese gent

Hi Ching...Japanese gent

Elji Kushuhara...Japanes gent

Episode four: *Friends and Neighbours*

June. "I still don't think that it's a good idea Terry trying to solve your problems.

It's rather like asking a man with a lighted match to look for a gas leak."

It's Sunday and Terry Medford wants to do nothing more than laze in his armchair and read the paper. That is until a knock at the door reveals an attractive new neighbour called Cynthia (Jo Rowbottom) who asks if Terry could help her in her garden. Seeing how keen her husband is to help, June is concerned. After having bounced around in the previous episode, Terry is once more required to physically exert himself, here moving paving slabs for the sexy new divorcee before June finds him in the first of a couple of compromising positions with the newcomer.

Friends Malcolm and Beattie are having relationship problems and ask the Medford's for advice but the result is that the latter storms off and the former moves in with them for a week! Blabber mouth Terry tells him about the new neighbour and the randy Malcolm asks him to put in a good word with her. But being Terry, he manages to give the wrong impression and Cynthia thinks he fancies her. And who should arrive just as she kisses him? None other than his wife: June.

Cast

Jo Rowbottom...Cynthia

Tim Barrett...Malcolm

Rosemary Frankau...Beattie

Episode five: *The Chaotic Peaceful Weekend*

In the opening credits of this and the previous episode, Terry's chair falls backwards. By now up to the penultimate entry from series three, the Medford's leave suburbia and head off to the sticks to see nephew Alan's latest money-making endeavour: running a pub.

Upon their arrival, they see just what he has taken on; a ruin. Uncle Terry is not impressed in this rather slight story written by Dave and Greg Freeman. However, his enthusiasm is stirred upon being asked to open the pub whilst Alan goes off to collect his one and only barmaid, as played by a non-speaking Sarah Scott. The episode ends with Terry actually making money from his nephew, for once! Cast member David Rowlands had worked on a number of projects with Terry and June, previously, including Happy Ever After and the film version of Bless This House (1972).

Cast

Roger Martin...Alan

Michael Sharvell-Smith...Harris

Stuart Sherwin...Willis

David Rowlands...Barton

Jeffrey Segal...White

Tony McHale...Grey

Peter Schofield...Landlord

Sarah Scott...Barmaid

Episode six: *In Sickness and in Health*

June. "You know when George Bernard Shaw was ill he used to stand in front of the window stark naked.

Terry. "Well, it was alright for him, he'd got a long beard, ain't he."

Terry teases June about her baking prowess during the opening of this final episode in the series, here with John Kane providing the words. His happy mood is because he has been asked to attend a working conference at Eastbourne and that June can accompany him for the seaside break.

The only problem for Terry is that he is struck down with flu and decides to visit his doctor before things worsen. Here he meets the chatty Cath (Gretchen Franklin) and quieter Doris (Joan Newell) who amusingly talk at each other with poor Terry stuck in-between them.

Taking to his bed, he is cared for by June before recuperating enough after a few days rest, to want to go on the Eastbourne trip. Alas, June has picked up the bug and has the misfortune to receive clumsy care from her husband, with Terry managing to experience various mishaps both towards himself and the house.

However, they do eventually go on the trip and we see the actors on the promenade only for Terry to be revealed to have broken his leg and be in a wheelchair pushed by June.

Cast

Timothy Bateson...Mervyn

Gretchen Franklin...Cath

Joan Newell...Doris

Christmas Special

June "Seeing you two eat was like watching Jaws I and II."

After overindulging at Christmas alongside his Uncle Harold and Auntie Sybil (glimpsed in a photo montage sequence, a popular graphic at the time), Terry laments daughter Wendy's absence.

A distressed Beattie arrives early for their New Year's Eve bash prior to a blustering Malcolm's appearance. The couple have again fallen out and Beattie makes her husband furious by snogging a chap as the New Year countdown is observed. A jealous Malcolm responds by attempting to punch the man in question but only succeeds in accidentally striking Terry!

On the morning of New Year's day, June, Terry and Malcolm all believe that Beattie has spent the night in the Medford's spare room with another man. This is soon dispelled when an energised Beattie returns and tells the trio that she has been awake all night after making new friends.

It transpires that Wendy (Jessica Turner) and husband Roger (Kit Thacker) took the spare room and Terry is delighted upon discovering that their daughter made it to be with them after all. The character of Wendy makes only her second appearance in the show and would not feature again.

This festive edition closes with Terry and the cast looking into the camera and wishing viewers "a Happy New Year."

Cast

Tim Barrett...Malcolm

Rosemary Frankau...Beattie

Jessica Turner...Wendy

Kit Thacker...Roger

In March, Terry had returned to his home town to open the Watford Museum, in conjunction with the mayor of the town, Cll S.G Reynolds. "I went to Watford Fields school, just like Terry," remembers Paul Reynolds in correspondence with the author. Not a fan of his schooldays, he adds, "We had a fete every year and I remember Terry coming to one when I was ten or eleven, I think. It would have been 1981 or so. He seemed nice; gave an inspirational speech to us kids."

At Christmastime, Terry appeared at the King's theatre, Edinburgh in Jack and the Beanstalk in their 75th anniversary production. Meanwhile his stint as a guest performer on The Good Old Days, was broadcast on the BBC that Boxing Day. Also on the bill was little Arthur Askey, comedian Duggie Brown, smashing actress Sheila Steafel and singer Patricia Cahill. Sheila had previously worked with Terry in a witty episode of Hugh and I back in the 1960s.

In the panto, Terry co-starred with another man with a big ego, Scots comic Jimmy Logan. Also in the cast was Welsh actress Ruth

Madoc; a panto co-star in Bristol with Terry, Michael Kilgarriff and Derek Royle. Directed by Logan's pal Clive Perry, the Scot writes about his experiences of working with Scott in his aforementioned autobiography. "When Terry came to Edinburgh...I knew what to expect," remembered the performer, "But I must say that I never found him easy to deal with. He didn't turn up until the second day of rehearsals. So that was a bad start.[17]"

It seems that the two performers could probably not agree as to what day of the week it was and back stage concerns about routines and attitudes caused problems. "Terry Scott was a difficult man to get on with, and if that affects the mood of the company it can affect the production. And that can be obvious to the audience."

Richard Stone represented both men and with hindsight, wondered if he might have realised in advance that their professional union was going to be problematic. "I stupidly suggested Terry Scott, forgetting that Jimmy and Terry...both normally very easy to deal with, had been together before [in Newcastle, 1969] and hadn't exactly hit it off. The first of many problems was the billing..." It seems that up north, Logan was given top billing but down south, it was Terry whose name went first. Again in his autobiography, Richard elaborates further, "So I arranged that Terry Scott was to be billed on the left with his picture and that Jimmy Logan, with his picture, was to be on the right, but higher up on the poster. This simple artifice hopefully deluded both contestants that they had won the battle![18]"

Fellow cast member Michael Kilgarriff also found the working experience galling, as he outlined in a correspondence with the author, "During the first week's rehearsal I was having a drink with Nicola Lindsey, the Fairy, who puzzled me by saying, "I suppose everyone's talking about me because of my Dad." When I asked who Dad was she replied "Terry. Terry Scott..." I then discovered that another daughter was employed as Terry's dresser, her boyfriend was the deputy stage manager and the choreographer was Terry's wife, Maggie Scott. You had to be very careful what you said and to whom you said it.

Terry unquestionably had a massive star personality and instant audience rapport honed from decades in variety, but off stage his need to dominate verged on the pathological. Even in the local after show watering hole he had to be the centre of attention by; wait for it; performing card tricks!" As an aside, Terry had a long-established love of magic and was known to be a decent magician, something which he developed as a youngster. Let cousin Quintin aka Tiny elaborate, "One Saturday morning, me and my three brothers were home when he called in. We persuaided him to do some conjuring tricks. After taking coins from our ears and doing some other, simple tricks, Rowan (known as Knocker, a character that Terry would pinch for his act) said, "If you are so clever, make this disappear," giving him a housebrick. We were standing in line and I was wearing a very large, red handkerchief, this he took and covered the brick that he was holding. Asking Vivian (Bib) to feel if it was there, he next went to Michael (Bunty) and again to Knocker. All agreed it was still there and when we got to me, Terry whispered, "Take it quick." This I did; hiding it behind my back. Then he went to all three of them who were all flabbergasted that such a heavy brick could disappear like that. At the time, we were all in the North Watford Salvation Army Band. Terry would quite often try to blow the instrument that we each played. This was, I believe, the foundation of his love of brass bands."

Returning to Mr Kilgarriff, he added, "It was in this bar that I once mentioned I managed to save £500 to £600 a year by careful handling of my recently introduced VAT returns. "Oh well," he sneered, "if five or six hundred a year is important to you..."

Fortunately I only had one brief dramatic scene with him (I played the villainous Fleshcreep, the Giant's henchman) so he left me alone, but I saw him threaten a boy dancer who was slow in picking up some comedy business with dismissal. His relationship with Jimmy Logan became so toxic that the house manager told me he thought he would need to put barbed wire down the corridor between their dressing rooms, and after one heated disagreement between the two stars Terry muttered to me, "Fucking Scots comics...I've worked with them before..." Perhaps Jimmy Logan, Scotland's favourite son, resented Terry having top billing, but the whole experience must have been unhappy for Terry as well as those who suffered his scabrous put downs, for he declined to appear in the show the following season in Glasgow, as was customary. But despite his and Jimmy's antagonism I have never seen the Busy Bee routine better performed, though it took some while for the stage partnership to click. As Richard Mowe wrote in the Edinburgh Evening News on 8 December, "[Scott's] routines with Jimmy Logan's Simple Simon lacked the spontaneous spark which characterised the relationship of Francie and Josie in Babes in the Wood last year. But their rather subdued partnership can only grow as the production progresses."

Terry's intemperateness partly sabotaged another review, this time by Allen Wright in The Scotsman: "Terry Scott recently gave me a long lecture on the duty of critics. He said that, while they were entitled to express their own opinions, they should also say how the audience reacted. So, here is what I have to report about last night's performance of Jack and the Beanstalk at the King's Theatre, Edinburgh, where Mr Scott appeared in a succession of outrageously funny costumes. The ladies sitting in the row behind me were not much amused, and spent the entire evening finding fault with the show. On the other hand, the party occupying the front of the stalls were clearly having a whale of a time...The management cannot have been pleased."

Television documentary The Art of the Pantomime Dame sees Terry musing about playing in pantomime in an interesting documentary which also saw him on stage as Dame in Jack and the Beanstalk in Edinburgh. It had been thanks to seeing self-proclaimed "Lanchashire's ambassador of mirth," Norman Evans as Humpty Dumpty that made Terry feel that he could do the same. "It was that nosey parker friendship which I saw in Norman Evans. Because I was always surrounded by gossipy women in Tucker street, Watford. Mrs Carpenter, two doors down, would come in to my house and say 'What have you had for lunch?' All that warmth is there..." Seeing him transforming into character, we also get a glimpse of daughters Lyndsey (dresser/ assistant) and Nicola, in the panto as a fairy.

The BBC really milk Terry and June, offering a new, fourth series of the show from 5 January 1982 after using scripts from writers John Kane, Terry Ravenscroft and Dave and Greg Freeman.

Episode one: *A Piece of the Action*

If you know that Terry Scott was from Watford then the later series of Terry and June will make you notice that the town is mentioned on a number of occasions. John Kane's opener is an underwhelming start for this show coming under the BBC light entertainment banner.

A mega-stressed Malcolm (Tim Barrett) pressurises Terry into completing a much-needed report over the weekend whilst the latter is more interested in finishing a detailed jigsaw puzzle with wife June. With only a couple of pieces remaining, it is discovered that the final one is from another puzzle, so an embarrassed June returns the box to seek a replacement. Here the young, disinterested sales girls form the impression that June is actually then-Prime Minister Margaret Thatcher and we get to hear Miss Whitfield's above-average impersonation of the dreaded 'Iron Lady'.

Sir Dennis clearly has a soft-spot for June, forgiving her for accidentally damaging his valuable Rolls-Royce especially after they exchange the missing pieces from both the jigsaws that each had been unable to complete.

Cast

Tim Barrett...Malcolm

Reginald Marsh...Sir Dennis   Joanna Henderson...Miss Fennel

Debbie Arnold...Lorraine

Elizabeth Edmonds...Connie

Episode two: *Snookered*

Following a weak start to the new series, Snookered does not prove itself to be much of an improvement, despite being written by Terry Ravenscroft.

The strength of a sitcom like Terry and June is when the story focuses upon Terry's latest fad interest. Here, that is for snooker and some amusement is gained upon seeing Terry in his full 'pro' outfit complete with dickie bow tie and waistcoat. He definitely looks the part but unfortunately, he proves a lousy player and being derided by June, he decides to sell the small table that he bought from Joe (Jack Haig).

A mix-up in the advertisement that he placed in the local paper sees Terry mistakenly believing that the table is valuable and smelling a quick profit, along with June, he manages to buy it back.

Fed up at not being able to make any cash from it, Joe subsequently returns and buys it back from them. Jack Haig, a co-star with Terry in Hugh and I, plays the role.

Cast

Ray Fell...Mr Marsh

Jack Haig...Joe Davis

Stacy Davies...Dustman

Neville Barber...Mr Price

Episode three: *Camping*

Terry. "We're in for two hours of acute and agonizing boredom…"

The running gag anticipated by the viewer of a mishap occurring to either Terry or June during the opening credits always proves funny and here we see June's chair collapse after Terry brings them out a drink in the garden. His reaction is a joy to behold as the credits close!

Literally sent to sleep by the dullness of the holiday films recorded by next door neighbour's Melinda and Tarquin (Diana King coming in as Melinda, a role originally played by Joan Benham) and Allan Cuthbertson on good form as the super bores), the Medford's decide to try a camping holiday but nothing as awful as in Carry On Camping (1969).

As a trial, and after a great deal of difficulty, resulting in Terry being trapped inside, they manage to erect the large tent in their very spacious, sprawling back garden. However, June particularly struggles without her home comforts and is eventually followed back indoors by her disappointed husband. But not before he gets himself arrested for breaking and entering into his own house.

Cast

Allan Cuthbertson...Tarquin

Diana King...Melinda

Mike Lewin...Sgt

David Oliver...PC

Episode four: *The Cowering Inferno*

'The Firm is a family'

John Kane returns as writer following Greg and Dave Freeman's efforts on episode three with Terry and June away at his firm's conference where they meet a decrepit hotel porter (a scene- stealing Robert Locke).

Terry is always bullied by the over-bearing Sir Dennis, and so as not to keep his chairman waiting, poor Terry has to meet up with him and his colleagues after accidentally applying ladies perfume to his scalp rather than his usual hair tonic. After a few funny looks and a bit of homophobia, Terry is obliged to give the chairman's opening speech the following morning.

Being away from home and envious of June enjoying a night out without him, Terry struggles to sleep and accidentally takes multiple, super-strength, sleeping pills which render him almost comatose. Unable to give the speech but with his firm attempting to see themselves as a family company, June steps in whilst Terry snoozes.

Cast

Reginald Marsh...Sir Dennis

Robert Locke...Porter

Michael Bilton...Ernest

Clive Panto...Waiter

Episode five: *The Auction*

The Freemans writing team provide the fun for Terry and an

extensive cast in this penultimate episode of a vastly improving series. In the opening credits, this time the table holding their drinks collapses!

We get to see Terry's extensive cardigan collection given a good airing in this storyline which sees him taking on auctioneer duties at the local church hall.

Come the day of the event, a furious Tarquin confronts Terry, bitter after being usurped by his neighbour for the main duties of the event even though he is a trained sales auctioneer. Terry is delighted and equally pleased at his small victory as well as being able to embarrass him further via an uncomplimentary catalogue listing. Struggling to maintain order, Terry ignores Tarquin's fury at seeing his lot of two china dogs passed-by during the auction itself. Assisted by June, Terry gets distracted by the action of those present and accidentally destroys one of the dogs with his gavel. Actress Gilly Fowler had previously been in a 1974 episode of Happy Ever After.

Cast

Allan Cuthbertson...Tarquin

John Warner...Rev Austin Doyle

Joyce Windsor...Enid

Nicholas McArdle...Mr Bolton

Billy John...Mr Green

Walter Goodman....Mr Good

Eileen Brady...Mrs Pugh

Gilly Fowler...Mrs Good

Patrick Travis...Mr Jay

Follie Setches...Mrs Jay

Jean Campbell-Dallas...Mrs Whitehouse

Episode six: *Something to Get Alarmed About*

Things are often more entertaining for the viewer upon seeing Terry and June step out of the studio setting and in this closing episode of series four, Terry Ravenscroft's script takes them into a local park.

June wants to invest in a burglar alarm after Terry disturbs an attempted burglary but he worries about the excessive costs involved and seeks a cheaper solution. This will involve recording the sound of a dog's bark, the idea being that this will deter a potential intruder as it would be activated after a pressure pad is stood upon in the hallway. But actually recording a dog proves tricky; with Terry clambering up a tree to avoid the attentions of one canine and pensioners Bert and Gert (Eric Francis and Edna Dore) proving unhelpful after Terry learns that their dog is mute. Undeterred, his next attempt sees a hound chew up his microphone and a further occasion results in Terry once again falling into a canal. The series closes with Terry seemingly having rigged up an alarm but all he succeeds in doing is attract an excited pack of dogs that spill into the hall and jump all over him!

Cast

Christopher Johnston...Edwards   Christopher Ettridge...Evans

Eric Francis...Bert   Edna Dore...Gert

Charles Pemberton...Man with dog

Tuesday 19 October marked the start of another series of Terry and June, with fans spoilt this year with a double helping on offer.

In spite of now being in its fifth series, there is a great deal to be recommend in this new batch of episodes; beginning with a political theme, or rather seeing Terry standing for a seat on his local council. The opening episode was written by Terry Ravenscroft, who would contribute nine scripts between 1982-5. Still writing, Terry only met Terry Scott at script read-through's and on recording days. "I started writing Terry and June right at the end of the long series." He remembers, in a correspondence with the author, "At the time I was writing The Dawson Watch; Peter Whitmore was the producer of the show as well as being the producer of Terry and June. Using this very useful contact I wrote a TandJ script on spec, they liked it, and asked me to write another. Ultimately I ended up writing nine episodes of the final two series of thirteen, before Terry's untimely death brought an end to the series. As regards Terry as a person I found him very easy to get on with. He certainly had no 'edge', which you often get with 'stars'. He was never less than complimentary about my scripts (as was June) and on the very few occasions he wasn't completely happy about a gag here or a sentence there he would always talk to me about it rather than alter it himself (As some do!)"

Episode one: *No, Councillor*

Medford is Mad...

Scott was known for doing many of the stunts in the show and during this episode in a plot contrivance, has to be catapulted into the river from his car but for this he allowed the professional to do for him!

Due to a slump in sales at the fire extinguishing manufacturing company that Terry works for, Sir Dennis forces him to stand for a seat on the local council, so as he could then influence them better to help sell them their product. Nobody thinks much of his chance of being elected, least of all his posh neighbour Tarquin (Australian-born actor Allan Cuthbertson, who made a living via these kind of parts) who coincidentally is the party worker forced to assist him.

With the help of his always supportive wife, Terry is sat, boxed-in on top of their car with a loud hailer and banner beneath reading "Medford is made for the job." In a cracking first episode, Terry ends up catapulted into some water, as aforementioned. Following a sharp cut, he is seen flailing about, soaked right through. That's when a great gag involves him asking June to remind him to get a new banner after part of it is ripped off and leaving only 'Medford is Mad'.

More fun comes when the couple attempt to canvass in a public park but the only audience Terry has is a little lad and even he wanders off! Seeing an on-going football match nearby, they approach and decide to speak to the crowd during half time. Unfortunately, testing the faltering loud hailer, he startles the players and a goal is conceded. Furious, the players pick Terry up and stuck through a basketball hoop in the park in a very funny bit.

In a final push to publicise his vote, the couple canvas locally but even that proves a disaster, with Terry inadvertently pressing a woman's boob and making a baby cry, too. He loses the election by a single vote: June's before revealing that she voted for the opposition candidate also.

Cast
Reginald Marsh...Sir Dennis Hodge
Allan Cuthbertson...Tarquin
Ray Gattenby...Returning Officer
Richard Butler...Chelsea supporter
Harry Fielder...Goalie

Episode two: *Swing Time*
After a hugely satisfying initial episode, regular writer John Kane returns with the caterpillar-eye-browed Reginald Marsh as Sir Dennis, seeing his character involved a bit more than usual.

Using a company golf weekend as a setting, Terry gives him the impression that he is an adept golfer but in truth, he hasn't played for years. Malcolm, Beattie and June are also along for the trip, too.

A running gag sees Terry's cheap clubs and bag gradually disintegrate as he makes his way around the course, with a hard-of-hearing Colonel Culpepper (Ballard Berkeley, the Major in Fawlty

Towers) making up a foursome with Malcolm. Unfortunately, Sir Dennis is rubbish at the game and Terry stumbles a bit with his own but no one else would play as they do not want to anger the big boss by beating him and possibly jeopardising their jobs. As the round progresses, the Colonel polishes off his hip flask and is paraletic by the end. Watch out for an appearance from Terry and June scriptwriter John Kane as a golfer disturbed by the shouting Colonel.

Cast

Tim Barrett...Malcolm

Rosemary Frankau...Beattie

Col Culpepper...Ballard Berkeley

Joanna Henderson...Miss Fennel

Robert Briggs...Barman

Episode three: *Noise Abatement*

Terry. "June, I've got a screw loose."

Following the fun of the golf weekend in episode two, comedy writer Dave Freeman joins with his son, Greg, to concoct this story which finds the Medfords in the opening credits enjoy a drink on their patio with no accidents at all! (In the previous one, Terry's chair collapses).

There is not much that June could say to the above quote after seeing Terry put in a spot of late night silliness. Now aged fifty five, Terry takes up a new hobby of woodworking whilst his irritating neighbour, Tarquin, reveals that he is the newly appointed Chairman of the resident's committee. Sponging nephew Alan returns, in a welcome visit by the chirpy character portrayed by Roger Martin. Michael Sharvell-Martin makes one of his five appearances in the show, playing a different role in each, from a policeman to a butcher.

Cast

Allan Cuthbertson...Tarquin

Roger Martin...Alan

Michael Sharvell-Martin...Fred

Jay Neill...Policeman

Episode four: *Eyeball, Eyeball*

"He isn't any relation to Evel Knievel, your husband, is he?"

Script man Ravenscroft uses the popular Citizens Band radio craze as the background of this enjoyable entry in the series.

Terry gets enthralled with the 'C.B' fad and buys a radio set using the money he and June had put aside for "little luxuries", with a disappointed June thinking a trip to Paris would have been more appealing. In an entertaining, silly and juvenile outing that is a joy to watch, a distracted Terry manages to drive up into a removals van and be locked in, reminding the viewer of a similar moment in Some Mother's Do 'ave 'Em.

June decides to teach her hubby a lesson for wasting their money and allows Terry to remain in the van over night. This being a sitcom, the vehicle gets stolen but he manages to extricate himself (all occurring off screen). Returning home, he is not a happy bunny but agrees to take June to Paris. Ian Masters is good here, as a police officer visited by a worried June. The actor would be seen across three episodes of Terry and June, all as the same character.

Cast

Michael Stainton...Abbot

Ian Masters...PC Williams

CB voices...Roger Martin/ Norman Comer/ Jeffrey Segal

Episode five: *Playing Pool*

Terry. "The gentle plop of a frog..."

Written by John Kane, as would the next episode and the Christmas special, the sterling Peter Whitmore once again fulfilled the producer/ director roles in an episode with a special bonus feature: Carry On favourite Bernard Bresslaw. Making a brief but welcome appearance as an agitated garden centre work perturbed by the visit of Terry and June, he is always a joy to watch.

For some reason, Terry wants to impress Malcolm and Beattie by turning a dirty sand pit into a garden pool by the time they next visit. Paying a visit to a new garden centre, Terry manages to damage a fledgling display and get his finger stuck in a plant pot. This is where they come across Big Bernie, in a scene which concludes with Terry Scott engaging in a little stunt work. Soaked by a hosepipe whilst up a ladder, due to Morris (Bresslaw) being afraid of heights, Terry grabs at an overhead banner which collapses and causes him to fall onto the floor with it.

The writer has one more piece of discomfort for his star to endure; he ends up in the newly-installed pond! In the opening credits it looks like the Medford's will be able to enjoy their drinks until the patio umbrella folds over their heads.

Cast

Bernard Bresslaw...Morris

James Marcus...Bleeker

Episode six: *Bingo*

Terry. "Don't worry vicar; if the bingo's bent, we'll straighten it!"

Probably the most amusing offering from series five, Terry and June are roped into giving a talk to pensioners at their local church hall. Unfortunately, the audience proves miniscule until the bingo starts afterwards; which they will also have an involvement in and at which Terry proves a delight as an enthusiastic caller. Patsy Smart as the well-meaning Miss Sibley proves a scene stealer and plays a wonderfully funny part in an amusing script to close the series.

Cast

Allan Cuthbertson...Tarquin

Diana King...Melinda

Patsy Smart...Miss Sibley

John Warner...Rev Doyle

Kathleen St John...Mrs Edgley

Ronnie Brody...Mr Tinker

Eileen Brady...Mrs Barker

Harry Webster...Sleeping Man

Christmas Special

For this special, festive edition, new opening credits show the heads of Terry and June pictured on Christmas tree baubles.

At the office party, Terry is hoodwinked by Sir Dennis into being invited to the Medford's for Christmas lunch. And for good measure, he again brings along Miss Fennel. Meanwhile, "company crawler" Malcolm is furious with Terry for seemingly sucking-up to their boss. Not wanting to miss out on any chance to ingratiate himself, he invites himself and pretty wife Beattie along, too. June had wanted a quiet day with just the two of them but this clearly is not going to be the case and so lunch for six is arranged.

Gathering around the dinner table, Sir Dennis mentions that during the war he used to play charades so Terry takes on the task of trying to play out the film Close Encounters of the Third Kind. Funnily enough, both he and June Whitfield made appearances on the actual ITV show Give Us a Clue; a game of celebrity charades.

Cast

Reginald Marsh...Sir Dennis

Tim Barrett...Malcolm

Rosemary Frankau...Beattie

Joanna Henderson...Nora Fennel

Before the run of the latest Terry and June series had concluded, in November, Terry performed in a run of A Bedfull of Foreigners at the Theatre Royal, Windsor before he advanced to starring as Sarah the cook in Dick Whittington, at the Bristol Hippodrome from 20 December through to March 12 1983. In the same month, he attended the 30th anniversary of Agatha Christie's The Mousetrap in the West End, London.

This particular Theatre Royal had an established pantomime history since opening back in 1910. And coming up-to-date, this year's offering was co-written by John Morley and director Dick Hurran, Terry was in a cast full of popular BBC comedy stars from Hi-De-Hi; Paul Shane, Jeffrey Holland (who had worked with Terry previously, at Birmingham and elsewhere), Barry Howard as King Rat and Ruth Madoc, as Dick. It also included Terry Doogan, Susan Holland, old panto pro Len Howe, Brian Pulman, Dino Shafeek (from TV comedies It Ain't Half Hot Mum and Mind your Language), Sally Smith and numerous others making-up the cast.

Director Dick Hurran was a familiar name to local audiences at the time; this was his fourth pantomime in the region in recent years. Actor Christopher Farries, who worked with Terry in panto and in an episode of Terry and June, fills in a bit about how it was working with him, "Hurran was a tyrannical director but the results of his work were always spectacular. He wore a trademark red carnation in the buttonhole of his camel haired coat and if a disagreement ever sprung up, his one liner was always "you're starting an argument you can't win!""

Then living in Surrey, Terry's wife was a drama teacher and his eldest daughter was also in show business. Audiences flocked to the Hippodrome and came away well satisfied, "Dick Whittington is slick, professional variety pantomime at its best," reported David Harrison in the Exeter Express and Echo, "It has colour and spectacle, plenty of stars to recognise, every traditional cliché in the book and, above all, a cast that takes itself seriously. It must be tremendously hard work to keep up the pace and the humour but it rarely shows – and that is a mark of success. The storyline may be tenuous, the music a patchwork of second hand songs and some of the jokes almost as old as pantomime itself. But it doesn't matter, it's all part of the tradition, and seasoned practitioners like this team polish it all up like new. Terry Scott makes a superbly vulgar Dame, with a collection of ever more fantastic costumes to rival even Danny La Rue (one outfit included a gigantic bonnet with massive buttons on his coat coupled by huge lapels). After a low moment involving one of the cast singing, "...such embarrassments were happily offset by brighter spots, such as Terry Scott's hilarious striptease. Like all pantos with variety acts to squeeze between odd references to the story, it is too long, even with such consistently fine costumes, dancers and special effects. The Hi-de-Hi! input, was, thankfully, kept to a minimum, but the performers were really a lot better than the show itself." Mike Dolan, writing in the No. 18 edition of Venue magazine, enjoyed the show, "Terry Scott...gives a performance which captures the essence of the panto dame. Bashful, bumptious and alternating between being coy and vulgar, Mr Scott is superb. Many of the sets were impressive...but the best test of all is always the kids' involvement and I left with my ears ringing with shrieks and squeals of delight."

The sixth and seventh series of Terry and June arrives on BBC1 on 15 February 1983 and runs through to 22 March, with the latter commencing at the end of October.

For the sixth, main writer John Kane scripts the first three stories before Terry Ravenscroft (episode four and five) and Jon Watkins complete the remainder. Terry Scott and June Whitfield would both see old colleagues from other projects make appearances; namely Colin Jeavons and the talented Josephine Tewson.

Episode one: *Off the Record*

Sir Dennis. "I don't care what personnel say about you; in my book you're an absolute great."

John Kane provided the words for this underwhelming opening episode in the sixth series across a four year period. Plot wise, youngsters today will have little grasp of what it was like to have a video recorder, usually on rental due to the exorbitant costs of purchasing the early machines.

Taking advantage of a week's trial from their local electrical store, Terry foolishly offers to record a programme for Sir Dennis not knowing how the device works. A jealous Malcolm storms around after a misunderstanding with Terry at work, and we have the hilarious proposition of possibly seeing him and Terry having a fight! This is avoided when Terry locks him out of the house. Other highlights include June showing off her mimicry skills whilst in bed with Terry who had fallen asleep and missed much of the Bogart film that he had been watching.

Sir Dennis subsequently watches the show at his club, leaving the Medford's and Malcolm not needing to have gone to so much trouble to help him after all.

Cast

Reginald Marsh...Sir Dennis

Tim Barrett...Malcolm

Iain Ormsby-Knox...Mr Fraser

Episode two: *Wine, Women and So Long*

Terry. "Me teeth have gone soft..."

After seeing June's chair collapse on her previously, here Terry's sun lounger does the same to him in the opening credits.

Thumbs up to John Kane for creating a very amusing episode, seeing Terry develop his interest in home brewing. Disaster ensues, thanks to exploding bottles, undrinkable delights and Terry's 'Cock ale' making both himself and Beattie ill. Eventually he manages to create a coffee liqueur; a hugely palatable delight manly due to it consisting of lots of Polish vodka.

Ms Whitfield excels in this episode and there is a chuckle to be had with a briefcase spouting liquor all over an unsuspecting Sir Dennis.

Terry is talked in to being a wine judge by his boss but is overwhelmed upon receiving the two-dozen samples that he is obliged to test; not surprisingly, he gets inebriated, "Dandydile and bimbong..."

Kane sets up the story for Terry and June to head over to France by offering Malcolm and Beattie's ferry tickets to the Medford's. Embracing the language, as he does in other episodes, Terry is keen to take advantage of the hypermarket bargains, too.

Arriving at Folkestone, the ferry leaves without him and there are some nice moments of comedy running provided by Terry whilst holding a large suitcase watching as the ship departs.

Cast

Reginald Marsh...Sir Dennis

Tim Barrett...Malcolm

Gareth Armstrong...French Officer

Ben Howard...Railway man

Episode three: *A Day in Boulogne*

Recapping key moments from the previous programme in the opening credits, Terry finally catches up with June in Boulogne.

In a hugely creative scene, Terry mistakes a fellow traveller for a Frenchman and gets into a conversation with the man's wife (Josephine Tewson), who also thinks that Terry is French. It is an inspired piece of comedy based upon a really clever idea.

Location scenes about half-way through the episode show the Medford's in France. To avoid excess duty Terry takes evasive action by swigging from the bottle as they return home. June drives Terry home.

Coincidentally, Ivor Danvers, playing a Customs Officer, had been an un-credited army recruit in Carry On Sergeant (1958), Terry's first appearance in the long-running film series. The lovely Kirsten Cooke had previously appeared at the close of a 1976 episode of Happy Ever After and Peter Bland had played alongside Terry in A Bedfull...

Cast

Josephine Tewson...Brenda

Anthony Morton...Geoffrey

Gareth Armstrong...French Officer

Kirsten Cooke...Hostess

Peter Bland...Gendarme

Ivor Danvers...Customs Officer

Ben Howard...Railway man

Brian Jameson...Policeman

Fiesta Mei Ling...Waitress

Episode four: *Strictly for the Birds*

Tarquin. "The last person to have worn it must had the figure of a deformed orang-utan."

Terry Ravenscroft takes on the writing duties and pits Terry and Tarquin in a mutual-loathing competition. June is keen for her husband to attempt to get on with his neighbour, as she is becoming friendly with Melinda (Diana King). Inviting them around, Terry cannot hide his frustration at discovering that Tarquin is playing the role that he enjoyed doing in last year's production of Treasure Island for the local am-dram group.

Come the next morning and Terry and June accept the invitation to join their neighbour's in a spot of bird watching at a nearby sanctuary. Bored, Terry plays a trick on Tarquin by pretending to make the sound of a favourite bird of his snotty associate before the actual bird is heard. Snapping some photos, thanks to Terry, both Tarquin and his wife will end up in the river (making a change from Mr Scott). Sometime later, Tarquin calls in on Terry at home and is delighted upon seeing the photos. In the meantime, June and Melinda fall out.

Cast

Allan Cuthbertson...Tarquin

Diana King...Melinda

Episode five: *Tea and No Sympathy*

Terry surprises June by enjoying a day off and being resolute in not doing anything but enjoy his rest but we know that this will not be the case.

A new fitted wardrobe is to be installed, and the arrival of the three workmen causes Terry some consternation as they reveal that they are on strike! Sitting around the house until offering to do some odd jobs that Terry never got around to doing, he later decides not to tell them that their union rep reached an agreement to return to work some three hours ago. Only after they have completed the tasks does a worried Terry learn of one of the lad's bad temper. The rep turns up at the house and tells them the news. Terry gets a pipe wrapped around his neck by Trevor (Mike Lewin) for lying to them.

A trio of actors seen in this episode had featured elsewhere in Terry and June; Mike Lewin had been in Camping, Nicholas McArdle had acted in One Arabian Night / The Auction and that fine character man Colin McCormack was also in two other episodes: Uncle Terry, Auntie June and Flying Carpets.

Cast

Paddy Joyce...Arthur

Mike Lewin...Trevor

Nicholas McArdle...Forrest

Colin McCormack...Jack

Episode six: *Thanks for the Memory*

Terry. "Oh, I'll eat anything."

After not noticing June's new dress whilst at breakfast, Terry is off on a business trip to hopefully clinch a big deal for his company and a healthy commission for himself. Whilst on the train, he meets the attractive Liz (Sabina Franklyn) and chats with her via some innuendo-laden dialogue. Not initially particularly enamoured, as the journey passes, she becomes friendlier and agrees to his invitation for dinner (on a purely platonic basis). Taking her suitcase down from above the seats, it strikes him on the head and leaves him concussed.

At a police station, Terry is dealt with by an officer who arranges for June to collect him. He has no idea who she is and calls her "Joyce, Jenny, Jean, Jocelyn and Janet" in some very funny moments.

Returned home to bed, he doesn't even recognise friends Malcolm or Beattie. June feels like Terry is a stranger and undressing in another room, she returns to join him in bed but finds he is asleep.

Terry reveals to Malcolm that his memory has returned and did so last night. However, Liz phones to see how he is doing and June overhears the truth as Terry leaves the receiver in the bedroom off.

Thanks for the Memory proves quite an entertaining close to series six, after a couple of lacklustre entries. And the script has some interesting points to make, as Terry was going to meet Liz, despite being married.

Past Scott and Whitfield theatre colleague Colin Jeavons makes an appearance in this one after previously working on a 1976 episode of Happy Ever After and before that, three episodes of Scott On... Ms Franklyn had featured in a 1978 episode of Happy Ever After.

Cast

Colin Jeavons...Police Sergeant

Sabina Franklyn...Liz

Terry made a guest appearance on the boys' team of celebrity charades game Give us a Clue. Then hosted by Michael Aspel, he must have enjoyed himself alongside a host of light entertainment people.

The show was broadcast on 6 September and Terry was joined by the mighty Leonard Rossiter.

Remaining in September, Mr Scott was performing in the Ray Cooney farce Run for your Wife at the 1,348-seater Shaftesbury theatre in the West End. Cooney's eleventh play, it came under his fledgling 'Theatre of Comedy' umbrella, with the idea of utilising a stock team of creative talent and produce shows at the Shaftesbury. Plot wise, taxi driver John (played by Terry) lives with his wife Mary in their Wimbledon flat but simultaneously has a second spouse/ life with an unsuspecting Barbara in a Streatham flat. And with the whole kerfuffle takes place in one day and across two acts.

The idea for the play came after gestation for Cooney following his partnership with John Chapman on a number of projects. "Then John decided he preferred writing for television," offered Cooney, "I had been carrying around this idea of a guy with two wives, and how he would cope with that, trying to get out of that awful situation, if there was a danger of them meeting. I had made a few notes on bits of paper. When I got to about 100 bits of paper in my pocket, I thought "I'd better start writing this. One of the best professions for a bigamist would be a taxi driver, 'cause he's always running around the place late at night and getting up early in the morning and all that. It took me about a year to write it up in the attic where I go. I did what one usually does with the plays, I wrote it, left it alone for about a month; did a rewrite, and we had a play reading with my chum actors who I know from doing

Above: Terry with Bill Pertwee (top) and Eric Sykes in Run for your Wife! Photo courtesy of The Theatre of Comedy.

these plays. I did a rewrite after the workshop, then we tried it out at Guilford, another rewrite, then it came into the West End and it ran for eight and a half years.[10]"

Cast: Helen Gill...Barbara Smith
Anna Dawson...Mary Smith
Terry...John Smith
Eric Sykes...Stanley Gardner
Stuart Sherwin...Reporter
Bill Pertwee...D.S Porterhouse
Royce Mills...Bobby Franklin
Sam Cox...Det. Sgt Troughton

This particular production, directed by the author, had begun life at the Yvonne Arnaud theatre in Surrey some five months before opening here on 18 March. With panto replacing it in mid-December, Run! would transfer to the Criterion that same month but with a different cast. Terry played the lead in a role that would also see Robin Askwith, James Bolam and Richard O'Sullivan all step into at some point.

An astonishing seventh series of Terry and June commences at the end of October, with John Kane the scriptwriter for all the episodes except 2 and 3 which were created by Terry Ravenscroft.

Episode one: *Photo Finish*

Both produced and directed by Peter Whitmore, Terry looks to be quite stiff in his movements in this laboured opening instalment of the new series.

Above: Terry with Anna Dawson in Run for your Wife!
The pair had worked together previously.

Photo courtesy of The Theatre of Comedy.

Written by John Kane, it finds him spending a lot of money on a modern, high-tech camera and all its accessories whilst June splashes out on a new dress to wear to a dinner date engagement with her and Sir Dennis. Deadly serious in wanting to take a picture methodically, Terry gets talked into shooting an informal portrait photo of his chairman, in an attempt to show off his relaxed side.

Scott and Reginald Marsh always prove a fun combination and here they continue be so. Sir Dennis, whose role model is Churchill, often berates, belittles and reinforces other people's low view of Terry but he still uses him for whatever task is required. This often proves amusing, as Terry acts the fool around him and the two regularly come into conflict purely via the scriptwriter nurturing a constant state of confusion between the two men. June is often the mediator, but here she initially struggles to create the right ambience to allow Sir Dennis to be seen in a new light. Almost giving up, Terry manages to accidentally sit on a box of open chocolates, which all stick to his bum, resulting in causing much amusement to his chairman. June snaps away and the deed is done.

Cast

Reginald Marsh...Sir Dennis

John Warner...Rev Austin Doyle

Episode two: *One Little Pig*

Terry. Well I thought that churches were meant to be holey?

There are some entertaining elements in Terry Ravencroft's script which sees Terry and June peculiarly having to deal with a constipated young pig whom they believe to have innocently swallowed the diamond from her engagement ring. It is enjoyable to see June teasing Terry, with humour, as he goes from one catastrophe to another. Here he traces the animal that had eaten the slops provided by Reverend Austin (John Warner), namely Terry's inedible rock cakes and thinks that the £500 jewel will be retrievable once nature has taken its course! But in the world of the sitcom, things can never be so simple.

Taking the porker to the vets, the Medford's meet the friendly Mr Parkins (Derek Martin) and they will see him again, after his identity is revealed as a police inspector.

Having the embarrassment of reporting the pig's escape from their rear garden, Terry and June are laughed at by two constables at the police station. One of them is played by Terry's old mate Ian Masters. The Inspector calls in, having been involved in an accident involving the said animal and so June and Terry beat a hasty retreat.

This episode has an odd close, a bit like when a dancer has finished a soft-shoe shuffle with an open-palmed 'taddah!' But this is not unique to Terry and June, as often Hancock or Steptoe and Son episodes ended clumsily too.

Ian Masters returns as a friendly policeman after first working with Terry and June back in 1977 on an episode of Happy Ever After. He was also in two other episodes of Terry and June: Ill Met by Moonlight and Eyeball, Eyeball where he played another copper and a soldier. Daniel Hill, seen here as a colleague, also had a role in Moonlight. Derek Martin also returned after being in a 1979 episode.

Cast

John Warner...Rev Austin Doyle

Ian Masters...PC Williams

Raymond Mason...Mr Adams

Daniel Hill...PC Grout

Derek Martin... Mr Parkins

Episode three: In the Navy

Episode three: *In the Navy aka The Raft Race*

Sir Dennis. "What do you know about cupboards?"

Terry. "Old Mother Hubbard had one..."

Possibly the strongest episode in the series, we find Terry still driving an Austin Princess car and now favouring a cap to set off his suit, the Medford's are off to Ross-on-Wye for a business trip/ break. Terry is meeting Herbert (Terry's theatre co-star Dennis Ramsden), an old friend of his Chairman's, in an attempt to sell some fire extinguishers.

Chatting with some men in the hotel bar, Terry exaggerates his past in the navy and hears about an annual raft race that Herbert's company usually enter to drum up publicity for his business. Unaware until the following day that he is the man that he was sent to meet, Terry is obliged to take up the place of someone that dropped out after Sir Dennis threatens the sack unless he wins the race.

In truth, Terry Scott served on HMS Vanguard, serving his National Service amongst the 1600 men onboard a ship that was regarded as the Royal Navy's finest. Built during WWII, it was commissioned after hostilities had ended, due to structural plans being changed whilst Britain was at war. Whilst there, this took him on the royal tour of South Africa at Christmastime. Here he was involved with the ships entertainment arrangements, producing a pantomime, something never seen before in that particular country.

Opening on Christmas Eve, the Theatre Royal Plymouth pantomime Babes in the Wood chosen by Terry after spending part of his National Service days at Glenholt Signal Camp (which was situated outside Plymouth). But this time, demonstrating how far he had come, Terry had the honour of being entertained by the Commodore.

Written by the prolific John Morley and directed by Dick Hurran, its superlative cast of Carry On chums Terry and Bernard Bresslaw, alongside them was musical theatre veteran Dilys Watling and Norman Vaughan; both having worked with Terry before. Maggie Scott, Terry's wife, was the choreographer and Leon Greene was the Sheriff of Nottingham. A trained opera singer, Leon would link up again with Scott in a 1983 episode of Terry and June.

In a number of projects alongside Terry, 'big Bernie B' was a RADA-trained actor fondly loved by many British cinemagoers as a gentle giant. Like Terry, he recorded his own seminal song: Mad Passionate Love. Away from the popular comedy stuff, he worked with the Royal Shakespeare Company, made films, TV shows, plays and musicals.

The cast for Babes in the Wood was as followed:

Leon Greene... Sheriff of Nottingham

Liza Westcott...Maid Marion

Natalie Bayliss/ Samantha Keast...Tommy

Terry...Nurse Teresa

Dilys Watling...Robin Hood

Norman Vaughan...Norman the Gorm

Bernard Bresslaw...Bernie the Bad

Liz Kirby...Fairy Dove

Walter Plinge...The Black Raven

Ron Richards...King Richard

Simon Brotherhood...Little John

Paul Gurnett...Friar Tuck

Christopher Morris...Alan-a-Dale/ soldier

Michael Wyeth...Much the Miller's Son

Richard Earthy...soldier

Alex Starr...soldier

DUNCAN C. WELDON with PAUL GREGG & LIONEL BECKER
for Triumph Apollo Productions Limited
present

TERRY SCOTT
BERNARD BRESSLAW
DILYS WATLING
and
NORMAN VAUGHAN

in

a lavish new
production of

Babes in the Wood

with

LISA WESTCOTT

SIMON BROTHERHOOD   PAUL GRUNERT   LIZ KIRBY
CHRISTOPHER MORRIS   KEITH GILBEY   MICHAEL WYETH   RICHARD EARTH
THE CHILDREN FROM THE ANGELA COLLINS STAGE SCHOOL

and

LEON GREENE
as the Sheriff of Nottingham

Directed by
DICK HURRAN

Designed by Terry Parsons

Written by John Morley   Choreography by Maggie Scott

Musical Director Charles Miller

Theatre Royal Plymouth

Above: Terry in panto at the Theatre Royal Plymouth
(Courtesy of TRP)

Two Terry's came into contact with each during the war years, Messrs Scott and Thomas, in the most bizarre location, a sea fort on the Thames estuary. "[I] found that he was (unlike most comedians) an attentive and appreciative listener. Mind you, there weren't many other distractions...in the middle of the Thames. He laughed so much, when I told him some cockney stories, that I feared he was going to fall overboard...variations on this theme, all rendered in my usual posh, gap-toothed style, reduced Terry Scott to tears[20]"

That was how comedy bounder Terry-Thomas, writing in his amusing autobiography remembers meeting Terry. Built by 1942, the group of seven Maunsell sea forts were constructed of concrete and metal on long legs with the intention of attempting to reduce the Germans using the Thames as a navigational route to attack Britain. Created by Guy Maunsell, the man that devised the Mulberry harbours, it is unknown as to which one Terry would have been situated upon, as they each had different names and can only be described as inspiration for the Star Wars AT-AT vehicles: they were an amazing sight but by 2011, only two were left standing.

Back to the storyline, practicing, poor Terry falls into the river again and again whilst June watches on. Come race day, Medford starts in last place until he unravels his secret weapon: a motor! Eventually catching up and passing his competitors, the engine falters and Terry comes in last. Accidentally setting off the motor again, he zooms down the strong-flowing river before falling off his raft and into the water.

Cast

Reginald Marsh...Sir Dennis

Dennis Ramsden...Herbert Bell

Stuart Sherwin...Mr Adams

John Owens...Mr Parker

Christopher Morris...Bellboy

Dulcie Huston...Receptionist

Episode four: *Too Many Crooks*

Terry. "I'm putting loud speakers out in the garden."

Nora. "Loud speakers? Oh good, we can't stand people that mumble."

David Taylor directs another amusing John Kane which gives some moments in the spotlight to the dotty Dingle sisters, Nora (Patsy Smart) and Emily (Beatrice Shaw). Come the series after next, a certain Miss Dunwiddy would fulfil a similar role; that of the quaint eccentric, often confused by the simplest of information.

The viewer suspects that they are in for a fun time upon seeing Terry in cowboy boots and pyjamas in the opening scene occurring in the Medford's bedroom. It transpires that he is wearing them in anticipation of a Western-themed barbecue that the couple are throwing the next afternoon. Immediately you think, is it wise putting the self-proclaimed, accident-prone Mr Medford in such a precarious environment and of course, Terry manages to set the barbecue alight, along with the garden canopy above and a fence panel; all before the guests have arrived, except for the barmy Dingle girls!

Malcolm and Beattie turn-up dressed as Native Americans, after the latter misunderstood Terry's invite. And in a daft moment, Malcolm sets ablaze the beautiful, decorative feathers on his head-dress, whilst cooking burgers for Terry.

Oh dear, then it rains but Terry continues to cook the burgers on the outside grill only to be hugely disappointed after everyone has gone, discovering the snacks secreted all about the living room.

Past characters Malcolm, Beattie and Miss Dingle make a return in **265** this episode. Patsy Smart has been mentioned a number of times in the text, as she had acted in Happy Ever After and Hugh and I previously but this would be her first time in the role of Miss Dingle after playing to different characters in the show. The super Beatrice Shaw would act in two episodes of Terry and June, as different characters, after previously appearing in a couple of Happy Ever After episodes, also.

Cast

Tim Barrett...Malcolm

Rosemary Frankau...Beattie

Patsy Smart...Nora Dingle

Beatrice Shaw...Emily Dingle

Martin Wimbush...Nigel

Episode five: *Pardon My Dust*

Sitting at the breakfast table, Terry reads news of the death of his charismatic uncle Charlie. He and June travel to the funeral but manage to attend the wrong service before calling in the house of his Auntie Madge (Gwen Nelson); also there are his Uncle Bob (George A.Cooper) and sickly Billy (Ronnie Brody). Learning of Charlie's desire to have his ashes scattered across Piccadilly Circus, this is to cause Terry a great deal of trouble.

Returning home later that evening, Terry decides to complete the task in the early hours. However, some time later he returns home after being unable to do what was asked due to being arrested and the police analysing the ashes (thinking that they might be drugs).

George A.Cooper would feature in three episodes of Terry and June and he had already worked with Terry in another BBC comedy series: Son of the Bride. Another actor, Ronnie Broody, acted in a couple of episodes of Terry and June, Scott On Entertainment and Carry On Loving (1970).

Cast

George A. Cooper...Uncle Bob

Gwen Nelson...Aunt Madge

Ronnie Broody...Billy Weston

Stephanie Cole...Mrs Hunt

M.J. Matthews...Attendant

Episode six: *The Artistic Touch*

June." Hey, can you smell burning?"

Terry. "I think it's my brain overheating."

12 December marked the broadcast of this final episode of series seven and what a funny entry it was from a witty John Kane script.

It often proves to have Terry and June interacting with others and here proves a joy as plumbers call in to do a job at the Medford's home. Johnny Wade returns to the show after playing a chirpy milkman back in a 1985 episode and Gordon Salkilld is again cast after acting in Uncle Terry, Auntie June and he was in a 1978 episode of Happy Ever After. Terry's recent panto co-star Leon Greene, who curiously enough had also been in Carry On Henry, was in this one. Michael Sharvell-Martin would make a number of appearances in Terry and June and had acted in an episode of Happy Ever After.

Tasked with looking after a portrait of Sir Dennis, Terry manages to get it damaged by one of the workmen and tries to fix it before anyone sees it. Showing the results to Beattie, she describes it as resembling Frankenstein's monster before she and the Medford's dream up a ridiculous plan to allow them time to have it repaired. Involving staging a burglary, Terry and June enter the home of Malcolm and Beattie only to discover two actual burglars already there. Giving them the impression that the portrait is valuable, the crooks make off with it. Viewers would have to wait until September 1985 when the team would return.

Cast

Tim Barrett...Malcolm

Rosemary Frankau...Beattie

Michael Sharvell-Martin...Arnold

Johnnie Wade...Clive

Willie Jonah...Murphy

Gordon Salkilld...Man in Car Park

Brian Hall... Bernie

Leon Greene...Perce

Terry is in the cast of The School for Wives at the Yvonne Arnaud Theatre, Guildford, from Wednesday 30 May to Saturday 23 June 1984. This was then a new version of Moliere's play, written by the prolific Miles Maleson. With his recognisable, almost rodent-like face, Miles was also a supreme character actor and had appeared in films that Terry was also in, namely And the Same to You (1960), Double Bunk (1961) and I'm All Right, Jack (1959).

Taking its name from a French actress that made her home in the area, the Arnaud theatre opened in 1965 and in 2015 celebrated fifty years as a working venue, with tributes and thanks from both Judi Dench and Penelope Keith. Terry starred in the play alongside 1970s sexpot Madeline Smith in a comedy first staged in 1662. She and Terry both had roles in Carry On Matron (1972) with the former a new mother worried about her new son's 'tinkle' and Terry as the lascivious Doctor Prodd. Following that film, they had work together, more closely in an enjoyable edition of Happy Ever After.

The School for Wives was directed by Val May C.B.E, who became artistic director at the Arnaud theatre back in 1975 and who would remain there until 1995. His career in the theatre was extensive, previously fulfilling the same role at The Old Vic and at both venues many of the productions would transfer to the West End after being directed by the unflappable Mr May.

Mark Wynter originally found success as a singer and later became a stage actor across pantomime, musicals and Shakespeare productions. He appeared in a 1962 edition of pop show Thank your Lucky Stars alongside Terry. Aubrey Woods complimented the cast and the production was directed by Roger Redfarn.

Terry was at the Theatre Royal Plymouth from 22 November through to 1 December in the musical comedy The Wind in the Willows when it played there and then advanced to Bath's Theatre Royal from Monday 3 – 15 December, with tickets from £3.50 - £7.50. After playing there, the production moved on to the aforementioned Yvonne Arnaud Theatre, Guildford from 18 December 1984 and on into the new year (12 January).

Billed as "a spectacular musical for all the family," Terry played the role of a well-received Toad. Past co-star Patrick Cargill was Ratty, Donald Hewlett as Badger and Melvyn Hayes was Mole.

Based on the Kenneth Grahame story, music for this production was written by Denis King, with its book by Willis Hall and direction by long term collaborator Roger Redfarn. He has enjoyed an extensive career in theatre, encompassing musicals and more, worldwide. Back in March he had directed Terry in School for Wives at the Churchill Theatre.

Offering a large cast doubling/ tripling up roles Willows was a Duncan C Weldon with Paul Gregg and Lionel Becker show for Triumph Apollo Productions Limited.

Of Terry's pedigree co-stars, Donald Hewlett possessed what David Croft defined as "a delightful light touch with comedy" and had worked on Terry's Happy Ever After series all the way back in 1974. Melvyn Hayes and Hewlett had both been in It Ain't Half Hot, Mum. Written by Perry and Croft, both had professional associations with Terry, previously. Appearing in Willows meant that the cast all had to miss out on their usual panto appearances this year.

The musical consisted of seventeen pieces, with Terry featuring in 8 of them. A full Cast included Peter Wiggins, Malcolm Wood, Paul Ryan, Richard Tolan, Dee Robillard, Allan Stirland, Michael Boothe, Anthony Collin, David Dandridge, Deborah Goodman, Judith Street, Fiona Alexandra, Wenda Holland, Christopher Hood and Robert Aldous. The latter had been in panto with Terry back in 1974.

Competition for the money in your pocket came from the Gemini cinema, Little Theatre (then in use as a twinned cinema) and the ABC where Arnold Schwarzenneger flexed his muscles as Conan and Tom Hanks goofed about in Batchelor Party.

Terry participated in a "lunch and listen" event with a local writer before donning a face mask and period outfit, with the local evening paper stating "Terry Scott heads a sparkling cast as the affable, amiable and adventurous Toad." Judith Boyd, writing in the Bath and West Evening Chronicle, added, "This adaptation is crafted with a great deal of affection for the original, and meticulous care in making the end product look stunningly good. Terry Scott as Toad 'an animal who was pampered as a tadpole,' is a thoroughly watchable mixture of outrageous conceit and schoolboy guile."

At Christmas, Terry returned to the Theatre Royal, Plymouth, for a shortened run of Babes in the Wood. It started on Christmas Eve and ran through to 28 January, 1984.

THE WIND IN THE WILLOWS

Based on the Story by

KENNETH GRAHAME

TERRY SCOTT
As 'Toad'

PATRICK CARGILL
As 'Water-Rat'

DONALD HEWLETT
As 'Badger'

and

MELVYN HAYES
As 'Mole'

Book & Lyrics by	Designed by	Music by
WILLIS HALL	**FINLAY JAMES**	**DENIS KING**

Choreography by	Lighting by	Musical Director
MICHELE HARDY	**ANDREW A. GARDNER**	**BARRY WESTCOTT**

Directed by

ROGER REDFARN

A Theatre Royal Plymouth Production

Terry's poor health was by now worsening, with a creeping paralysis seeing him having to wear a neck brace when not performing and the feeling in his left hand and feet also fading.

However, he continued to perform, appearing in a tour of The Wind in the Willows, as it moved to Sadler's Wells theatre, London after recently being staged in Guildford. A Bedfull of Foreigners plays at King's theatre, Glasgow in July 1985.

As himself, Terry made a television appearance on the nostalgia-fuelled Vintage Quiz show on 22 January. That was before series eight of the long-running sitcom Terry and June returning with a bang: thirteen new episodes, commencing at the end of the first week of September and running until Christmas Eve.

Just like a pair of comfy slippers, Mr Scott and Ms. Whitfield slipped back into their roles of screen husband and wife with consummate ease with a great deal of verbal jousting from the scripts of John Kane, Colin Bostock-Smith, Eric Merriman, Greg Freeman and Terry Ravenscroft.

Now into his late-fifties it is noticeable that both Terry and June are wearing more make-up, their mutual comedic flair had not diminished. At least two out of the series can be classified as some of the finest Terry and June episodes.

Episode one: *Many a Slip*

Sir Dennis. "Of course, you are a crawler. So long as it's me you crawl to, I won't see you go under."

With June's mummy due for a visit, Terry is more pre-occupied by a desire to play in his firm's cricket team, if only a doubting Sir Dennis would allow it. In real life, Terry was a huge cricket nut but here, he is a terrible player in a smashing series opener containing some witty dialogue and comedy moments for June Whitfield to also shine. (The script finds her rhyming "googly" with "wobbly" but it is all done with such aplomb that the viewer cannot but go along with.

Seeing Terry in his new whites, pads and the latest protective helmet/ visor is an amusing sight, even before June's erratic bowling skills are amusingly demonstrated. Come the day of the match after Terry had been bullied into getting June to provide the customary 'teas' for the players, despite her protestations, Terry is disappointed when Sir Dennis orders him to roll the green and the game starts without him.

Terry is the thirteenth man and after last man Potter (Barry Woolgar) rushes off to be by his wife's side, he wants to bat and not concede the game, as Sir Dennis suggests.

With nineteen runs required, and facing a mean bowler, in slow motion we see the ball strike Terry on the head; luckily June had rushed on to give him his helmet moments before. "Run!" demands Sir Dennis from the other crease as we watch the ball fly in the air and embed firmly into a tree.

With a single run required, after Terry had run down the wrong end, the opposition manage to locate the ball and the bowler throws it towards the wicket. It strikes Terry on the head again after collapsing at the crease: and they win the match!

John Quayle takes over the role of Malcolm following on from Terence Alexander and the excellent Tim Barrett. John had worked with Scott and June Whitfield on a 1978 episode of Happy Ever After.

Cast

Reginald Marsh...Sir Dennis

John Quayle...Malcolm

Rosemary Frankau...Beattie

Michael Redfern...Bowler

Barry Woolgar...Potter

Episode two: *Unfaithfully Yours*

The opening credits to Terry and June remained the same for this new series; fluctuating between seeing Terry or June's chair collapsing or the oversized patio umbrella flopping over them or no misfortune befalling them. In this second episode, it is June's chair that collapses!

Just as Terry's home town Watford often received a name check, the Medford's fictional address of 71 Poplar Avenue, Purley, gets mentioned in Kane's latest script. Containing more amusing word play, affairs of the heart and naked ambition are on show, with Terry again lying badly on behalf of his lecherous friend and immediate boss, Malcolm. Here the latter is chasing after Lola (Julie Dawn Cole); a young woman at the office manipulating the likes of Malcolm and a smitten Sir Dennisy. Personally, I never understood why Malcolm chased other women when his wife Beattie, is an attractive woman.

It seems that the devoted Miss Fennel (an always-superb Joanna Henderson) has fallen for Sir Dennis (Reginald Marsh) and mistakenly believes that he is going to ask her to marry him: alas not, he is actually intending to replace her with Lola. A distraught Miss Fennel returns to the office drunk and emotional after the set back.

June is there and she tells Terry that she saw the younger woman in the cinema, where she was kissing a chap that turns out to be the new chauffer (Tony O'Callaghan).

She wants to inform Sir Dennis, who is keen to ask Lola for her hand in marriage, but Terry tries to prevent her from doing so.

June goes to him privately but Sir Dennis thinks that she is declaring her feelings for him and on behalf of his secretary.

The shrewd Lola denies everything and shows herself as a nasty piece of work; even Terry is warned off. Pushing him backwards, he accidentally activates the intercom which can be heard in the main office, where Sir Dennis and June are talking. The truth is revealed to him upon hearing Lola's derogatory remarks.

Martin Shardlow received a director's credit for this episode whilst Robin Nash was the producer.

Cast

Reginald Marsh...Sir Dennis

John Quayle...Malcolm

Rosemary Frankau...Beattie

Joanna Henderson...Miss Fennel

Julie Dawn Cole...Lola

Tony O'Callaghan...Chauffer

Episode three: *One Arabian Night*

Sir Dennis asks Terry and June to host Middle Eastern prince Abdul Aziz (played by Derek Griffiths, an actor known to Terry from stage farce Run for your Wife!) with whom he hopes to do business.

The visitor wants to experience life for a regular couple and so the Medford's are asked to entertain him for a few days. Abdul takes a shine to June but proves to be a social liability for Terry (who takes the violent repercussions). Scriptwriter Colin Bostock-Smith, enjoying quite a diverse career writing for children's TV and sitcoms/ satirical stuff, took on the creative duties for his underwhelming episode. He would also furnish the script for a later entry, Ill Met by Moonlight.

Cast

Reginald Marsh...Sir Dennis

Derek Griffiths...Prince Abdul Aziz

John Warner...Rev Austin Doyle

Nicholas McArdle...Mr Dobson

Ron Tarr...McMahon

Terri Fleeman-Hardwick...Girl in club

Dave Cooper...Guy in club

Episode four: *New Doors for Old*

Terry Ravenscroft provides the funnies in an episode which despite requiring Terry Scott to have to do a bit of lifting and running, he does not look too agile.

The focus here finds June wanting a new front door but finding Terry reluctant to spend £300 on doing so. Visiting a local showroom, a mischievous Terry has fun rapidly opening and closing doors before they eventually place an order.

Upon delivery, the door is too short but June has just given their old one to a couple of young lads for their bonfire so the couple set off to get it back! Youngsters Wayne and Shane, alias Paul Reynolds and Russell Lee Nash are amusing as the boys in question. A replacement is ordered and the whole fiasco is repeated; only after the new one is too long.

Cast members Johnny Wade and Michael Stainton had worked with Scott before on Happy Ever After and Terry and June.

Cast

Nick Maloney...Grant

Janet Davies...Customer

Adrienne Burgess...Receptionist

Johnny Wade...Milkman

George Waring...Friendly man

Michael Stainton...Taylor

Roger Walker...Black

Kelly George...Douane

Russell Lee Nash...Shane

Paul Reynolds...Wayne

Episode five: *Death of a Salesman*

June. "Oh Terry, don't tell me you're tiddly?"

Terry implements a fitness and healthy eating drive in this entertaining entry in series eight written by John Kane. A number of amusing characters return, including youngster Russell Lee Nash (seen in the last instalment) and the brilliant Patsy Smart.

The always selfish Malcolm often gets Terry to lie for him and in this episode that continues. Terry has a company medical and mistakenly forms the impression that he only has twenty four hours to live after overhearing the doctor speaking on the telephone (in actuality he was bemoaning a faulty heart monitoring machine). He believes it is true after the sudden death of a work colleague that had recently engaged on a similar health kick of his own. Malcolm and Beattie are also at the office and think it true, also. Terry, with great equanimity, asks them to carry on as normal and not to let on to June when they visit for dinner later that evening. Terry, in his own style, tells Sir Dennis what he thinks of him, labelling him a "silly old poop" before walking out.

That evening, the friends call around and embrace Terry whilst June looks on, completely bemused. Interrupted by a telephone call from the medic, Terry is amazed to hear that he isn't actually going to die after all!

In the meantime Sir Dennis calls in and instead of getting a rollicking, Terry is astounded to be told that his chairman wants him to remain with the company and that he can have a raise. All the time Terry is unable to get a word in to tell him the truth. A relieved June finally gets to understand as to why her husband had been acting so oddly.

Film director was Martin Shardlow and the episode was produced and directed by Robin Nash.

Cast

Reginald Marsh...Sir Dennis

John Quayle...Malcolm

Rosemary Frankau...Beattie

John Woodnutt...Dr Fletcher

Joanna Henderson...Miss Fennel

Patsy Smart...Miss Dingle

David Hatton...Wilkie

Russell Lee Nash...paperboy

Episode six: *A Question of Property*

Retaining the John Kane insignia following his smashing previous episode, June asks Terry to go to their shed and collect a box for the church jumble sale, where he discovers a rough sleeper. The Medford's having been told that he spent the night there, seek to find him a place in a local hostel and June gives the man some money to see him off.

Beattie and Malcolm call around, with the latter attempting to convince them to invest in a timeshare property, as he has.

Investing 3k in the venture, Terry is distraught upon reading that the company has collapsed and that he has lost all his money. Already upset, Terry spots the vagrant, Owen (Edward Phillips) returning to the shed and goes to challenge him after suspecting him of stealing a carriage clock that belonged to his uncle. (Owen had recognised its value just as they were about to donate to the church). Revealed as an experienced clockmaker, Owen had been returning it to the shed after repairing it as a thank you. It is revealed that its value is commensurate to the amount that Terry lost in the timeshare venture.

As an aside, Owen, was Terry's real first name.

Cast

John Quayle...Malcolm

Rosemary Frankau...Beattie

Edward Phillips...Owen

Patsy Smart...Miss Dingle

John Warner...Rev Austin Doyle

Episode seven: *Terry in Court*

A council refuse van backs into the Medfords' car with June in it but the council will not pay compensation, claiming that June was in the wrong, so Terry takes them to court. His witness is a forgetful old dear who has no recollection of what happened but fortunately the council driver admits that June was not to blame and the couple are awarded compensation. See Happy Ever After for a copycat episode.

Cast

Patsy Smart...Miss Dingle

John Barron...Judge

John Horsley...Mr Smith

Robert East...Mr Robinson

John Bardon...Mr Grubb

David Killick...Usher

Michael Bevis...Clerk

Episode eight: *The Sporting Life*

Austin asks Terry and June to help equip the church youth club, so Terry builds a table for use in table tennis. He invites Malcolm over for a game, which gets increasingly more competitive.

Terry beats Malcolm but jumps over the table to celebrate his victory, wrecking it in the process.

Cast

John Quayle...Malcolm

Rosemary Frankau...Beattie

Patsy Smart...Miss Dingle

John Warner...Rev Austin Doyle

Colin Ward-Lewis...TV presenter (voice)

Episode nine: *The Dish*

When colleague Browne impresses Sir Dennis with the fact that he has a satellite dish and watches European television stations for work purposes, Terry lies and claims that he has one as well. After Sir Dennis announces that he will be bringing a Swiss colleague to the Medford's to watch it, Terry has to borrow one from his workman's brother. A chapter of accidents leads to the dish careering off down the road and colliding with Sir Dennis's car. The storyline seems like a rehash of an older Terry and June storyline involving a VHS video recorder being the latest bit of tech.

Cast

Reginald Marsh...Sir Dennis

John Quayle...Malcolm

Rosemary Frankau...Beattie

Shaun Curry...George

Clive Panto...Browne

Joanna Henderson...Miss Fennel

John Arthur...Ron

Paul Humpoletz...Mr Baker

Josie Kidd...Mrs Carter

Episode ten: *Ill Met by Moonlight*

When Jack, the landlord of their local, is unwell and needs to rest, Terry and June agree to help out behind the bar despite Sir Dennis's rule that his staff should not take second jobs. Unfortunately Terry has accidentally revealed to his boss that Gower, a colleague, also works as a taxi driver so Gower takes Sir Dennis to the pub to expose Terry. However Sir Dennis is in a forgiving mood provided that he be allowed to take a turn behind the bar.

Ian Masters had been in a 1977 episode of Happy Ever After and this was his third and final Terry and June episode. Daniel Gower had been in a 1983 episosde, also.

Cast

Reginald Marsh...Sir Dennis

John Quayle...Malcolm

John Rapley...Jack

Daniel Hill...Gower

George Malpas...Customer in pub

Ray Gatenby...Customer in pub

Ian Masters...Soldier

Episode eleven: *Mistaken Identity*

To his horror Terry sees that he is the double of a handbag thief known as the Granny Grabber and his picture is on the front page of the paper. Although he goes to the police station to explain matters he has to attend a meeting and goes in disguise. However on the drive home he is stopped by police for a faulty light and his disguise falls off, leading to his arrest. Guest star Josephine Tewson makes her second and final appearance after working with Terry previously.

Cast

Rosemary Frankau...Beattie

Roger Sloman...Police Sgt

Josephine Tewson...Mrs Robins

John Gleeson...Traffic cop

Christopher Farries...Traffic cop

James Charles...PC

Paul McDowell...Newsreader

Episode twelve: *Lover, Come back to Me*

All the main characters return for this episode. After Terry has cancelled his and June's skiing holiday, June goes out to dinner with an old flame of hers from before her marriage, back from Australia. Finding a love letter from June to him but unaware it was written many years earlier, Terry allows Sir Dennis and Malcolm to ply him with Dutch courage and stalk June, finally gate-crashing a poetry reading meeting which Terry, listening at the door, has interpreted as a declaration of love for June by the vicar.

Cast

Reginald Marsh...Sir Dennis

John Quayle...Malcolm

Rosemary Frankau...Beattie

Patsy Smart...Miss Dingle

John Warner...Rev Austin Doyle

Joanna Henderson...Miss Fennel

Episode thirteen: *Pantomania*

"Last time I heard screeching like that was when we accidentally vacuumed the cat."

It is the dreaded office panto and thinking that he will be asked by Austin to be Father Christmas in the church hall, Terry declines getting involved. Upon hearing that Tarquin has been asked, all that is left for him, and June, is the pantomime cow! A fire alarm starts whilst they are performing and somehow the couple end up in a lorry on its way to another part of London. By the time that they manage to get back, Beattie and Malcolm have stood in for them in this smashing Christmas Eve special written by John Kane.

Cast

Reginald Marsh...Sir Dennis

John Quayle...Malcolm

Rosemary Frankau...Beattie

Patsy Smart...Miss Dingle

John Warner...Rev Austin Doyle

Joanna Henderson...Miss Fennel

Michael Sharvell-Martin...Butcher

Paul Kidd...Panto cow

June Kidd...Panto cow

Roy Heather...Deliveryman

Tony McHale...Reveller

Stan Young...Taxi Driver

Patricia Varley...Mrs Waverley

Gracie Cole...Pianist

Also on ITV on 30 August, Terry alongside June, was a guest on We Love TV, having to endure feeble impressions of them from unfunny duo Les Dennis and Dustin Gee in the process.

Away from the TV, Terry starred as Dame Trot in the panto Jack and the Beanstalk at Bath's Theatre Royal with June Whitfield. This particular version of the popular pantomime veered away from the traditions shown in the story, here replaced with a generous dollop of adult comedy across its eleven scenes. June was Sweetcorn, the Vegetable Fairy whilst Jeremy Connor and Jay Cross, in the guise of Daisy, the cow, managed to upstage many. Sixties pop star and panto veteran, Susan Maughan was Jack, whilst Avengers star Honor Blackman vamped it up in the role of Fleshcreep. Jeremy Connor, son of Carry On actor, Kenneth, was one half of Daisy the Cow.

Christopher Luscome, now a successful theatre director, was then aged twenty two, and understudy to Terry. He also had his own role, as Simple Simon, Dame Trot's other son. Working the audience well, whilst Sarah Price played Princess Melanie, in a lavish production at the Theatre Royal spoilt only by an elongated running time of three hours, with a forty minute interval still proving testing for children in the audience. Chris had been inspired by seeing Terry at the London Palladium and also had a role as his stand-in for an acrobatic scene in

the panto. Such was the scale of the production, that the star got not only his own dressing room but another one to house his twenty costumes utilised during the show!

Directed and choreographed by Michael Tye-Walker, this Jack was written by John Morley, a veteran panto scripter with more than a hundred to his name and an expert on the topic.

Back when a local paper cost 16p, Jack commenced its run on Friday 20 December and ran through to Saturday 1 February with advanced advertising enticing a would-be audience of "Terry Scott and June Whitfield in lavish new pantomime Jack and the Beanstalk".

It worked, as the show took in more in advance bookings than the entire of the previous panto could manage all season. Neighbouring theatre, the Bristol Hippodrome, had comedy double act Cannon and Ball providing the competition for West Country audiences this year. Another criticial appraisal was equally as positive, "Terry Scott as the Dame coped professionally with some unoriginal material while upstaging himself wonderfully with increasingly over-the-top Danny La Rue-style gowns and wigs." (David Symington, Bath and West Evening Chronicle, 21 December 1985). Whilst the Western Daily Press termed the show, "Family entertainment in the best sense of the word."

Next year, Terry, June and their TV co-star Reginald Marsh appear at the Yvonne Arnaud theatre, Guildford, in their panto offering of Jack and The Beanstalk for a season running from Wednesday 17 December 1986 through to 17 January 1987.

Top billed, Terry and June were joined by his Carry On Loving co-star Janet Mahoney, Christopher Luscombe and Aubrey Woods in a show directed and choreographed by Michael Tye Walker.

Sadly, in 1987 Terry was diagnosed with cancer, a disease that would eventually claim his life in 1994, aged sixty seven. However, he was still working and would be seen back on the TV for one last time in series nine of Terry and June. Fittingly, John Kane furnished the scripts for all seven episodes in the final series and directed by Martin Shardlow (except for the first entry, which was directed and produced by Robin Nash). The show began its run on 20 July and the last Medford adventure occurred on 31 August with the opening credits seeing Terry repeatedly falling into the river as the distinctly 1980s zooming titles are overlaid. Fans might recall that these moments came from the In the Navy aka The Raft Race episode from series seven.

Episode one: *Age Before Beauty*

Terry. "Today is the first day of the rest of my life."

Away from performing, Terry Scott would often engage in spurts of exercise and here we see his alter ego Terry Medford engaging in a similar health 'reboot'.

After being guided across a road by both an elderly lady and a couple of little scouts, and being called "granddad" by a cheeky paperboy, as a result, he begins to work on his fitness.

After being made to feel old and taking a good look at himself, he decides to get June involved in his new regime by buying a rowing machine meant for both of them to use, or rather for Terry to justify its purchase! There is a lovely bit of slapstick which sees him struck by a vase following his first attempt at using it in the living room.

"Every time he gets a health kick, he ruins his health," scoffs June to friend and neighbour, Beattie, whose husband Malcolm also returns.

At work, Terry begins his work-out, doing press-ups and skipping but he only manages to bring the ceiling down on boss Sir Dennis. Confiding his weight woes to him, the latter tells him of an instant solution: wear a corset.

Coming down to the kitchen before work, a restricted Terry creaks a lot but doesn't tell June that he is wearing one.

Off without managing any breakfast, problems soon occur in the car, now a Ford Sierra, I think, where the device comes free.

Annoyed at her husband's observation that they are not young at heart, June decides to make him see how it is okay to act your age. "Defrumped", she shocks Terry into rethinking his ideas, by presenting a new image, a sort-of demented punk look; complete with spiky wig!

Produced and directed by Robin Nash, Evie Garratt makes the first of her four amusing appearances as dotty, elderly neighbour and general nutcase, Miss Dunwiddy.

Cast

Reginald Marsh...Sir Dennis

John Quayle...Malcolm

Rosemary Frankau...Beattie

Evie Garnett...Miss Dunwiddy

Episode two: *The Mole*

A busy plot involves the top secret development of the 'Titan 2000', a new, talking fire extinguisher from Terry's company, with the 'mole' being a competitor wanting to steal the idea. Early on, Terry proves to be the top suspect after the product blueprints are stolen.

Away from the office, Roger Martin makes sadly only a fleeting return as chirpy nephew Alan, one step ahead of the bailiffs and in real financial difficulty, he once again asks auntie and uncle to store some boxes for him at their place. And this is where the storylines meet as Major Fawcett (John Ringham) arrives at the Medford's looking for evidence to support his case against Terry. However, Alan and June mistake him for a bailiff and so June makes up a story that Terry is a major drinker, hence all the boxes of booze stored in the hallway. Technology changes rapidly and is displayed here with young Alan using a new "mobile telephone"; the type of model that was the size of a house brick back in its day.

After Terry forgets his lunch, June comes to his office to bring it to him and sees Miss Partridge surreptitiously coming out of it before her. The latter is secretary to Malcolm, with the two engaging in a bit of an affair and the latter telling Terry all about it. Wife Beattie suspects and asks Terry if he knows anything. He doesn't exactly say so but she takes his response as meaning that yes, her husband is being unfaithful.

Meanwhile Sir Dennis and Major Fawcett instigate a search of all the offices and Terry is obliged to go along with the idea that he has a drink problem. Sir Dennis proves concerned and they manage to deflect the attention away from the blueprint being used as a tablecloth for his lunch. The episode concludes with Miss Partridge being revealed as the culprit and Malcolm feeling stupid although I never did understand why he sought attention away from his wife.

Cast

Reginald Marsh...Sir Dennis

John Quayle...Malcolm

Rosemary Frankau...Beattie

Joanna Henderson... Miss Fennel

John Ringham...Major Fawcett

Roger Martin...Alan

Christine Garner...Miss Partridge

Episode three: *They Also Serve*

Wives Beattie and June set-up a home-baking business called Cosy Kitchen Catering and seek to promote it at Terry and Malcolm's office. With Sir Dennis scoffing at his employees being involved in non-company endeavours, when Malcolm accidentally overhears his boss talking to Miss Fennell (Joanna Henderson) about sacking people, he assumes that he means Terry and himself. Malcolm forces Beattie to drop her involvement in the business, much to her distress, and there is a funny moment following this when she accidentally splashes June in the face with cake mixture.

Although it transpires that Sir Dennis is actually in need of their services, as he is entertaining Sir Arthur (a returning Ballard Berkeley) and his wife, at home. Another old face returns, Tim Barrett, earlier playing Malcolm but here as a stock comedy drunk butler whose wife has just left him. Unable to perform his duties, Terry is forced into doing his job at the bequest of Sir Dennis and June. Unbeknownst to the latter, he has just had a run-in with the guests at a nearby shop after June sent him out to get some emergency cream for the starters. Adapting the disguise of comedy bottle-top glasses, a blind Terry manages to slop soup all over the place in an awkward bit of slapstick.

Odd this in that Tim Barrett makes a welcomed return to the show but not as Terry's sycophantic co-worker but in the role of Mr Basingstoke in the same episode as another actor playing his original part of Malcolm! Ballard Berkeley also returns, after playing Colonel Culpepper back in a 1982 episode. This was his penultimate acting job. He died in 1988.

Cast

Reginald Marsh...Sir Dennis

John Quayle...Malcolm

Rosemary Frankau...Beattie

Joanna Henderson... Miss Fennel

Tim Barrett...Mr Basingstoke

Ballard Berkeley...Sir Arthur Forster-Carter

Madeline Newbury...Lady Cora Forster-Carter

Episode four: *The Eye of the Householder*

Malcolm and Beattie join Terry and June in a game of Trivial Pursuit only to discover that ancient neighbour Miss Dunwiddy has been troubled by a prowler. This prompts Terry to set up a Neighbourhood Watch scheme and his first discovery sees him finding a chap sneaking into a nearby home. Unfortunately, he is not a burglar but was having an affair with the lady of the house.

Visited by Superintendant Carter (Dennis Lill) the Medford's are spurred on to arrange a meeting for interested parties at the local church hall. In the meantime, the bogus officer takes part in burglaries of all the neighbour's homes, apart from Terry and June's place. This leads them to be the main suspects and Terry is taken to the station for questioning. Cast member Robert Dorning had worked with June and Terry on their earlier sitcom Happy Ever After. In a peculiar little twist, we see that Terry has a signed photograph of Anne Shelton in his bureau, and back in 1959, as a performer, Mr Scott appeared on her television show.

Cast

John Quayle...Malcolm

Rosemary Frankau...Beattie

John Warner...Rev Austin Doyle

Evie Garnett...Miss Dunwiddy

Robert Dorning...Mr Duffy

Dennis Lill...Inspector

Ken Wynne...Mr Morgan

Arthur Cox...Mr Drayton

Jeremy Gittins...Constable Davenport

Eva Lohman...Angela

Episode five: Bats in the Belfry

In this the best episode from the last series, June and Terry manage to get themselves locked in the belfry tower at their local church. Relying upon the peculiar Miss Dunwiddy (Evie Garnett on fine form) to come to their aid proves a mistake; funnily she thinks Terry's voice is "from above" and proves of little help. With the service over and the parishioners and priest all having left, Terry manages to wedge himself in the space meant for the bell ropes as lightning strikes and rain comes down. Accidentally loosening a roof tile, they get the idea to sound the alarm by lobbing them towards a passing police car and they are eventually rescued.

Cast

John Warner...Rev Austin Doyle

Evie Garnett...Miss Dunwiddy

Peter Joyce...Policeman

Episode six: *Of Human Bondage*

Terry. "I'm sorry, I can't talk now: we're suddenly very rich."

That was Terry answering the phone a moment after June has just informed him that his late Uncle Charlie's premium bonds given to him have come up a winner: for £250,000. The news was relayed to them in a most haphazard manner by his Auntie Madge (Barbara Miller), assisted by Eric (a returning George A.Cooper) and Bernie (John Barrard) all of whom had featured in Pardon my Dust from series 7.

Initially choosing to be discreet about their good fortune, Terry gets drunk at the office and lets it slip. When Sir Dennis hears of the win, he uncharacteristically fawns all over him; wanting Medford to invest in the company and help fend-off a prospective take-over bid. Soon everyone wants money from them: Beattie for her niece, Austin for the church and Madge and Co turn up demanding their fair share as 'family'.

After initially having the win verified, a stressed Terry and June aren't too disappointed when told that the bond is invalid. Despite being given to Terry in his uncle's will, it was only active until the end of the year following a death. Relieved in a way, the Medford's have to laugh when they come up winners in the little prize draw organised by dotty neighbour Miss Dunwiddy.

Cast

George A.Cooper...Eric

John Barrard...Bernie

Amanda Bellamy...Clarice

Jonty Stephens...Post Office assistant

John Owens...Under-manager

John Quayle...Malcolm

Rosemary Frankau...Beattie

John Warner...Rev Austin Doyle

Joanna Henderson... Miss Fennel

Evie Garnett...Miss Dunwiddy

Barbara Miller...Auntie Madge

Ted Valentine...Ted Norbutt

Episode seven: *The Family Way*

And so to the very last ever episode of Terry and June; after 9 series and much merriment provided by the pens of John Kane, Dave and Greg Freeman, Terry Ravenscroft and others across 65 stories.

Initially shown on 31 August 1987, June persuades Terry into employing a cleaner whilst he is more concerned with his new acquisition: a goldfish.

When the matronly Mrs Bunce (Zara Nutley) arrives and given the job, subject to the Medford's fulfilling her own criteria, Terry finds her domineering character bothersome.

Meanwhile he, having previously visited a pet store run by Mr Biggs (Ronnie Stevens on fine form), grows concerned with the health of his new arrival and returns to seek advice. Biggs informs him that he is in actuality a she and that she is pregnant, recommending that he buy a bigger tank.

Back home, Mrs Bunce overhears June and daughter Wendy (a returning Caroline Hadaway) discussing the latter's possible pregnancy. Beattie is then given the impression that it is infact June that is expecting and so calls Malcolm at work to share the news. He, Sir Dennis and Miss Fennell are all somewhat shocked and when Terry ads to the misconception, he thinks they are talking about his fish, the fiasco continues. It is also done with such fun that the viewer can simply enjoy the ride however ridiculous it all seems.

Terry returns home and upon seeing June, he thinks that she might be pregnant. Wendy's career-minded husband Roger telephones and he naturally extends his congratulations upon discovering that Wendy is the one that is expecting! It seems that Roger was unaware of the situation but finally warms to it. Actress Caroline Holdaway plays the Medford's other daughter, Wendy, in her only appearance across nine series. Jessica Turner, as the other sister, was only in two episodes; the second in series one and a later one in 1981. And there we have it, the final outing for Terry and June Medford.

Cast

Reginald Marsh...Sir Dennis

Ronnie Stevens...Mr Biggs

Zara Nutley...Mrs Bunce

John Quayle...Malcolm

Rosemary Frankau...Beattie

Joanna Henderson... Miss Fennel

Caroline Holdaway...Wendy Medford

The 'fast, furious and very funny" Run for your Wife! starts its summer season on 8 June at Bournemouth's Pier theatre, with Terry sharing equal billing with lovable comedy writer/ actor Eric Sykes. Both actors had played in the show more than once, previously. Also along for the duration was old hand Jan Hunt, who had also been in Foreigners with Terry, Ron Aldridge, Fred Bryant and David Morton (an actor that had played in A Bedfull of Foreigners with Terry previously) in a production directed by Paul Elliott.

A true British farce, Run! would also tour the Middle and Far East with Terry attached and it seems everybody appeared in this play over the years both before and after his involvement: including Les Dawson, Lionel Jeffries, Barbara Windsor, Amanda Barrie, Jimmy Logan, Bernard Cribbins, Richard Briers, Bill Pertwee, Carol Hawkins and more. Also this year saw Terry tour the Middle East with The Mating Game.

In 2012, a film version was made with the charisma-free Danny Dyer headlining the cast in Terry's role as "gullible, foolish guy" John Smith. The film is pretty terrible but is worth seeking out for its blink-and-you'll-miss-them cameos from many, many old hands that had worked with its writer, Ray Cooney (Jacki Piper, June Whitfield, Anita Graham, Bill Pertwee, Barry Cryer, Frank Thornton, Jeffrey Holland, Carol Hawkins; most waiving their fees to be given instead to a theatre charity. "In the beginning it did run nine years in London originally, 30 years ago," offered Cooney, still selling it at a film premiere.

It clearly had something to offer, as it would play in the West End from 1983 to 1991 after first being formed at the Yvonne Arnaud theatre, Guilford, in October 1982.

Terry played roles in the play across at least four theatres between 1983 – 1991; the Shaftesbury, Whitehall, Aldwych and Duchess. And sometime in between, he took it to Bournemouth, Canada and at the Mill, Sonnig (near Reading).

Playing at the Whitehall must have proven a bit nostalgic for him, as he had been involved in the Brian Rix farces there back in the early-1960s and other plays.

In December, Terry joined Jean Boht at the Ashcroft Theatre, Fairfield, Croydon for their pantomime Jack and the Beanstalk. Opening in the third week of that month, it ran through to 23 January. Terry was the Dame and Marsh, The Villain. The Ashcroft Theatre could then seat 763 and had originally opened on 5 November, 1962 by Croydon-born actress Dame Peggy Ashcroft, after whom it is named. Fairfield was opened in 1962 and there are effectively three 'halls'. These are The Concert Hall, the Ashcroft Theatre and Arnhem Gallery.

Below: Terry with some of his panto co-stars this year,
including Sir Dennis from Terry and June (Reginald Marsh).
Photo courtesy of the Ashcroft Theatre.

Above: Terry in full 'dame' costume, immediate right.
Photo courtesy of the Ashcroft Theatre

Head of Marketing at the Fairfield, John Spring, writes on the excellent website, http://fairfieldat50.ehive.com, "The auditorium, on two tiers with the stalls heavily raked. The front of the circle is unadorned and the straight walls have natural finishes. The stage, with false proscenium, is well equipped with 30 single purchase counterweight sets for flying, and an orchestra pit on a hydraulic lift which can accommodate up to 16 players.

Alterations to the forestage were undertaken to lessen the barrier provided by the original Juliet balcony and side door structures.

The theatre fell into decline as a proper theatre from about 1990 onwards. However the good news is that we have re-launched the Ashcroft Theatre over the last two years with regular weekly touring shows and our own productions."News of his sitcom Terry and June being cancelled this year after an impressive nine series, plays havoc with Terry's mental health and it is reported that he has a breakdown, partly as a result. It came a year after he had drunkenly blabbed to the newspapers, after having had a drink, about his affairs whilst appearing on stage in Run!

"Terry was an appauling big mouth," chuckles his representative Richard Stone in his book, "Let loose with a journalist or worse, on a live television interview, he would pontificate and talk the most abject nonsense whilst firmly believing he was uttering pearls of wisdom." And he should know, as he was also well-aware that Terry often told other actors how to act, "However, I loved him. Of all my clients, I think he had the greatest respect for my advice."

During a long career, writer/ actor Eric Sykes worked with a great many legendary names in British comedy; whether by writing theirs scripts and/or appearing alongside them, Oldham-born Eric has been there. He and Terry played in a revival of Run for your Wife! at Bournemouth and in the West End and hence Scott's involvement in Mr H is Dead, a half-hour, near silent TV comedy.

Made by Thames for ITV, Sykes wrote/directed and co-stars in an inventive little feature that included some sparkling names: Spike Milligan, Roy Kinnear, Richard O'Sullivan and people familiar to Terry, namely Jimmy Edwards and Bob Todd.

Terry makes his entrance into proceedings some 3 minutes in, as a besuited hearse driver being bothered by an officious traffic warden (Edwards). And out steps Scots piper Kinnear from his vehicle, whilst Sykes and co attempt to remove a body, the eponymous 'Mr H' from within a tower block. But first, they have to get the empty casket up the stairs, and due to a mix-up they assume the lift is out of order.

Eventually lowering the coffin down from the top of the building, it accidentally ends up on top of a removal van being driven by race ace James Hunt before Sykes chases after it in a lorry driven by Tommy Cannon and Bobby Ball (popular theatre and telly comics at the time)

As the rain lashes down, the group manages to re-collect the casket and decide to take a bus to the funeral. However, by the end, with the widow and presumably, mother, returning home, they discover that the late Mr H is still stretched out on the bed. It was shown originally on 15 February and is available on DVD.

Terry was due to play the Theatre Royal, Bath from 18-23 April 1988 as Roland Dickerby in a comedy production called Kindly Keep it Covered. Also in the cast was old mate Anita Graham, who had played in a number of theatre productions and in Terry and June.

He was top billed, then Robin Nedwell and Amanda Barrie in amongst a cast which also included John Pennington, Chris Sanders, Peter Mackriel and Andree Melly. Written by colleague Dave Freeman and directed by Martin Connor, all the advertising flyers had been printed in advance and the Bath one, featuring an illustrated Terry, still turns up for sale on Ebay. So? Well, he never appeared there in this particular show despite featuring prominently in the poster and programme. He was, instead, replaced by substitute and old panto colleague, Jeffrey Holland at the last minute.

Back in 1981 former Carry On star Barbara Windsor took a production of The Mating Game to Blackpool and again the following year with Terry associate Norman Vaughan, it played the Floral Hall Scarborough, a venue known to Scott.

By 1984 she was still in it, for a summer season in Jersey back in a decade when she struggled to get work other than from the odd theatre job.

The Mating Game was written by actor/writer Robin Hawdon, and proved to be his first commercial success as a playwright. "Set in a smart Mayfair apartment, full of gadgets with a mind of their own, the story concerns the frantic attempts of a trendy young TV personality, to both lose his virginity and avoid true love, whilst at the same time preserving his image as a notorious stud.

Despite poor initial reviews the play was hugely popular with audiences, became a regular on the British touring circuit for the next twenty years, and is still frequently revived abroad." That was the summary of the play detailed at robinhawdon.com and viewing his site you will see that he is still very much active, in the creative sense.

Returning to 29 May, 1989, and Terry was joined by Barbara Windsor in the latest version of The Mating Game staged at the Bournemouth Pier Theatre for a summer season. (The author had the pleasure of seeing the old Carry On stars and remembers the thrill of seeing them!) Also in the cast were Elizabeth Bradley, Janet Edis and John Williamson, whilst an earlier team had included Anita Graham and Tim Brooke-Taylor.

The original 850-seater Bournemouth Pier theatre opened in 1960 with Carry On Laughing (no connection to the films) and saw summer seasons from Sid James and Dick Emery prior to The Mating Game playing there in 1969, 1971 and this year. Designed to resemble an ocean liner, the theatre was found a little way down the pier which dates back to 1880. A concrete sub-structure had been built underneath the pier to facilitate the theatre building but by 2011 the present, let alone future, was not looking rosy for the Pier theatre. By then reduced to 650 seats, it had endured losses amounting to 300k in its last five years and simply could not turn the clock back to the 1960s and 1970s when it was well visited. Today, the building is still there but has been rebranded/ modelled as an adventure activity centre. However, should the future see resurgence for plays, the structure can easily be returned to function as a working theatre again; hope so.

Terry was playing at the Aldwych and Duchess theatres in the West End, in Run for your Wife! in July this year with the aforementioned Eric Sykes and Carry On at your Convenience man Geoffrey Hughes. The latter had worked alongside Terry had been in panto together at the Alhambra, Bradford back in 1976. Whilst at the Duchess, Terry was in amongst a strong and familiar cast, namely Ralph Bates, Windsor Davies (seen in the 1954 feature Murder Most Foul) and Carol Hawkins from the Bless this House (1972) film. **Below**: Terry with Run! co-star Helen Gill. Photo courtesy of The Theatre of Comedy.

Terry in the 1990s

Sometime in 1993, Terry had his bladder removed and replaced by an artificial one. But on Tuesday, 26 July, 1994, he passed away. On 29 August, the BBC, where he had made his name, screened the first ever episode of Happy Ever After in tribute to him.

Much has been said about him as a person, positive and negative, but as a performer, he could not be faulted. So let's leave the final words to his friend and colleague, Anita Graham.

"I first met Terry when I was given employment as understudy to Aimee MacDonald in The Mating Game at the Appollo Theatre – it would have been early 70's I think. I had been there a couple of weeks and when Aimee was taken ill, I had to go on for the Saturday matinee performance. It was quite a technical show and there was a bit where my character, Honey Tooks, was performing a cod striptease on the bed to seduce the character Terry was playing. We got to the bit where the bra came off and the bed was supposed to disappear into the wall with Honey as her bra flew over the top of the bed. Unfortunately the bed didn't disappear and I was left topless and Terry and I were hysterical and that had broken the ice.

Over the years he was extremely good to to me, giving me lots of work because we clicked onstage. I played Honey in several summer seasons and tours and also Simone in A Bedfull of Foreigners. He was a brilliant comedian and very generous on stage.

At the end of a summer season show it was usual for the leading man to have a chat with the audience tell jokes etc. One night he said he wasn't going to give the speech because I had asked to do it. Gobsmacked I stepped forward; couldn't think of anything to say so just told his usual last joke of the speech. He could have been furious but he laughed and gave me a round of applause: he was a very generous performer if you were on his wavelength and he trusted you onstage. He was also a terrific actor, most comics are; making people laugh is the hardest thing. He could also be very hard on people who didn't come up with what he wanted.

I learned a great deal from him about timing and stagecraft and he gave me many opportunities; a part in Terry and June – he offered me a part in another TV show with Jo Tewson which I couldn't do because I was offered a musical at Drury Lane at the same time. We did several Derek Nimmo tours of the far and middle east and I saw places I'd only seen on a globe before and had so much fun. He had a wonderful family: Maggie his wife and four lovely daughters. We had some great parties at his house in the swimming pool and outings when they came to visit when we were in Bournemouth or Torquay and Jersey.

He was very ill towards the end but never complained, he had bladder cancer and some big operations. Visiting him then, he said, "Dont give it up, there are not many of us left.

I'm sure lots of people will tell you he could be a bastard – he could – but he was a great friend to me and I miss him. The business misses him too."

294

References & Thanks

References 1-20 are quoted in the text

1. Crying with Laughter, an Autobiography, Bob Monkhouse, Century, 1993.

2. www.leicestermercury.co.uk

3. www.spapavilion.net

4. helenjamesproductions.co.uk, 2008 interview

5. A Jobbing Actor, John Le Mesurier, Elm Tree, 1984.

6. Entirely up to you, Darling, Richard Attenborough, Arrow 2009.

7. My Farce from my Elbow, Brian Rix, 1975, Secker and Warburg.

8. Liz Fraser….and other characters, Liz Fraser, Sigmun Books, 2012.

9. theguardian.com, 8/9/2001.

10. Terry-Thomas Tells tales, An Autobiography, Robson Books, 1990.

11. As 7.

12. Terry Scott obituary.

13. Obituary, Edward Seago, theindependent.co.uk

14. Film Night Special: Carry On Forever, 1970.

15. Simon Jenner, theguardian.com

16. Barry Took, Terry Scott obit.

17. It's a Funny Life, Jimmy Logan, with Billy Adams, BandW Publishing Ltd, 1998.

18. You Should have been in Last Night, an Unusual Agent Remembers, Richard Stone, The Book Guild Ltd, 2000.

19. Don Grigware/ broadwayworld.com

20. As 10.

I read a great many books/ articles relating to Terry as part of my research and below, in no particular order, is a list of particularly useful titles:

Thank God for a Funny Face, Hugh Lloyd, John Blake, 2002.
You Have Been Watching…The Autobiography of David Croft, BBC Books, 2004.

Blimey! It's the Sid James Book, Gary Wharton, Lushington, 2007.

Name Dropping, Michael Pertwee, Valery, 1974.

June Whitfield At a Glance, An Absolutely Fabulous Life, Weidenfield and Nicolson, 2009.

Will the real Ian Carmichael, Ian Carmichael, Book Club Assoiciates, 1979.

Mr Carry On, The Life and Work of Peter Rogers, Morris Bright and Robert Ross, BBC, 2000.

That's Entertainment – Theatres and cinemas of Great Yarmouth and Gorleston, Colin Tooke.

www.lowestoftjournal.co.uk

http://archive.thetablet.co.uk/article/28th-july-1973/13/theatre (Macbett play review).

296

Thanks to everybody that took the time to help; from answering my questions or loaning pictures, I did appreciate it.

Particular thanks go to Darran Sproul, stevelilart.co.uk James Bryce, Sue Hodgson, Christine: Bath Theatre Royal, Deb Boultwood, Ashcroft Theatre, Theatre Royal Plymouth, Connaught Theatre, Quintin 'Tiny' Butcher, Carole Owens, Anita Graham, Wayne 'Pickles' Norman and The Theatre of Comedy for use of the photos.

Some dates/ information might be incorrect in the text but due to the nature of time passing, this sometimes happens and I hope you will not be too critical.

Above: Terry with screen wife June Whitfield in their first full sitcom together: Happy Ever After. They would establish a long-stand relationship that would flow through to nine series of its successor, Terry and June.

Index

Roy Castle 134-8, 199
Don Chaffey 68
Cyril Chamberlain 22, 24, 31, 36, 69-70, 86, 123
John Chapman 64, 70, 73, 77-8, 80-3, 87, 98, 101, 110, 113, 124, 132, 179, 183, 185, 190, 220, 256
Jacqueline Clarke 106, 163, 205
Lena Clemo 184, 187, 199
Alma Cogan 25-6
George Cole 22, 24-5, 31-3, 34, 36-7, 39, 70, 121
Sid Colin 161
Kenneth Connor 11, 30-2, 67, 69-70, 114, 117, 152-3, 155, 161, 168
Kenneth Cope 57, 107, 109-10, 169, 171
Russ Conway 11, 35-6, 42, 88, 98
Darcy Conyers 51, 63, 72, 81-2
Beryl Cooke 183-4, 203
Pat Coombs 17, 19, 92, 106, 111, 119, 124, 179, 195

300 Ray Cooney 45, 48-9, 55-7, 64, 82, 117, 170, 179, 220, 256-7, 260-1, 286
George A.Cooper 174, 176-8, 215, 266, 284
Tommy Cooper 44-6, 139
Harry H.Corbett 177
Ronnie Corbett 125, 168
Billy Cotton 35, 104, 131, 311
Hazel Court 60
Michael Craig 57, 59, 84, 86
Bernard Cribbins 65-6, 139, 141, 286
David Croft 9-10, 42, 73,87, 98, 110, 114, 126, 132, 139, 146, 162, 169, 268
Barry Cryer 149, 169, 286
Roger Curram 214
Jill Curzon 77-80, 87-8. 90-1. 93, 106
Alan Cuthbertson 234, 247
Dana 181, 186
Windsor Davies 103, 105
Anna Dawson 114, 182, 194, 257, 259
Vera Day 32, 36, 44, 46
Denville Players, Jersey 5-6
Robert Dorning 100, 111, 184-5, 283
Wallace Douglas 70, 83, 113, 117

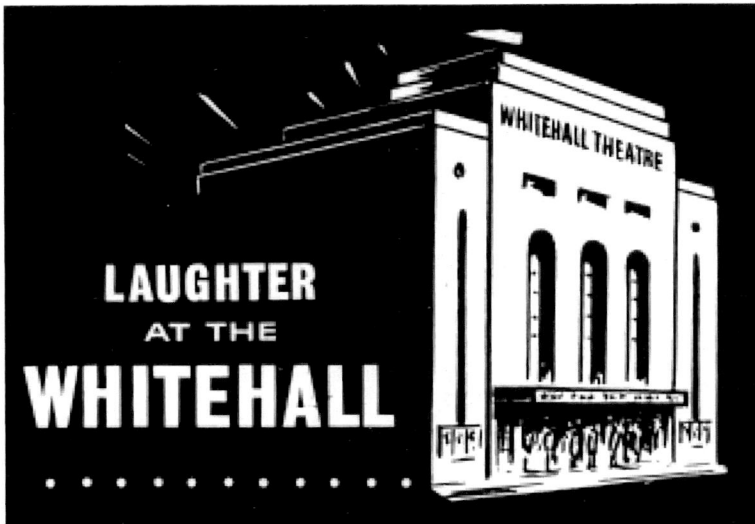

Theatre work

Lagoon Follies, Jolly Roger theatre, Clacton 8-9
Into the Sun, Newquay 12
Empire, Dewsbury 12
Jack and the Beanstalk, Worthing 12-13; Edinburgh 239-42; Bath 278-9; Croydon 287-89
Dick Whittington, Grand theatre, Brighton 13; Bristol 251-2
Out of the Blue, Southend 11, 14-15; Spa Pavillion, Felixstowe 19
Odeon, Romford 16
Sleeping Beauty, Leeds 16-17
Robin Hood, Finsbury Park Empire 19-20, 27
Robin Hood, Tooting Granada 25
Robin Hood, Slough 25, 33
A Season of Variety, The Prince of Wales, London 20
Chiswick Empire 21
Birmingham Hippodrome 25-6
Leeds Empire 25, 27
The Billy Cotton Bandshow, Pavilion, Torquay 36
Russ Conway Show, Glasgow Empire 37
Llandudno 37, UK tour 43
Make it Tonight, Floral Hall, Scarborough 42
Dickie Valentine Show 43, 44, 140
The Mating Game 45, 148, 161, 171, 186-7, 202, 233, 288, 290-3
One for the Pot, Whitehall theatre 54, 71
Babes in the Wood, Oxford 71, 180; Golders Green 88; Richmond 232; Plymouth 186-7, 233, 262,-3, 268, 290-3
Scarborough 25, 89
Spa Royal Hall, Bridlington 88
Let's Make a Night of It: Weston-super-Mare 97-8; South Parade Pier, Southsea 104; Winter Gardens, Margate 113-14;

Top: a gurning Terry in a publicity shot from the early-1950s

PAVILION THEATRE — WEYMOUTH
Director of Activities: PETER G. MADDOCK, F.IR. ENTS.
Box Office Tel. 783206

Commencing Monday, 14th July to Saturday, 6th September

Monday, Tuesday, Friday and Saturday at 8.00pm   Wednesday and Thursday at 6.00pm and 8.30pm
PRICES   -   £2.50, £3.00 and £3.50   Children and Senior Citizens 80p First performance only on Wednesday and Thursday
PARTY CONCESSIONS One in Ten for all performances (Except on reduced rates)

Stephen Bell Promotions Ltd. & Mark Furness present

TERRY SCOTT in

IN PERSON

ON STAGE

A BEDFULL OF FOREIGNERS

THE LAUGHTER HIT By DAVE FREEMAN

STARRING

JOSEPHINE TEWSON

BARRY HOWARD

FIONA DOUGLAS-STEWART

NICOLA HAMILTON

AND

PETER BYRNE

"...I've never laughed so much in all my life...."

Theatre work continued
Let's Make a Night of It:
Winter Gardens, Weston-super-Mare 104
Showtime '66, Wellington Pier, Great Yarmouth 122
Cinderella, London Palladium 125-6

Above: theatre flyer courtesy Deb Boultwood

309

Film appearances continued:

The Great St. Trinian's Train Robbery (1966) 24, 34, 63, 98, 110, 120-3, 125, 146, 187
Carry On Up the Khyber (1968) 99, 125, 133-9, 141, 146, 199
A Ghost of a Chance (1968) 139-41, 169
Carry On Camping (1969) 31, 137, 141-7, 155, 188, 244
Carry On Up The Jungle (1970) 117, 152-5, 165
Carry On Loving (1970) 31, 86, 114, 153, 155-60, 164-5, 172, 175, 199, 205, 266, 280
Carry On Henry (1971) 98, 110, 125, 164-69, 181, 201, 266
Carry On Matron (1972) 141, 161, 168, 171-4, 267
Bless This House (1972) 38, 78, 98, 144, 161, 163, 169, 174-7, 237, 292
That's Carry On compilation (1977) 199

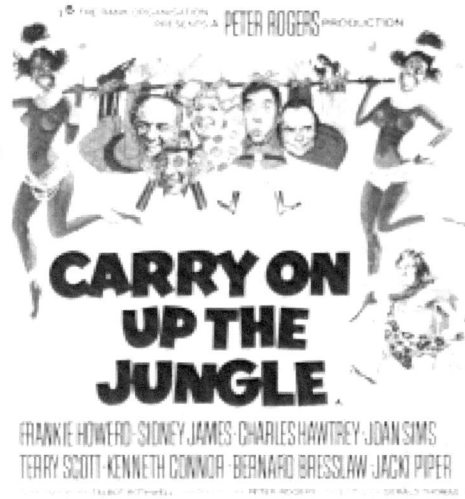

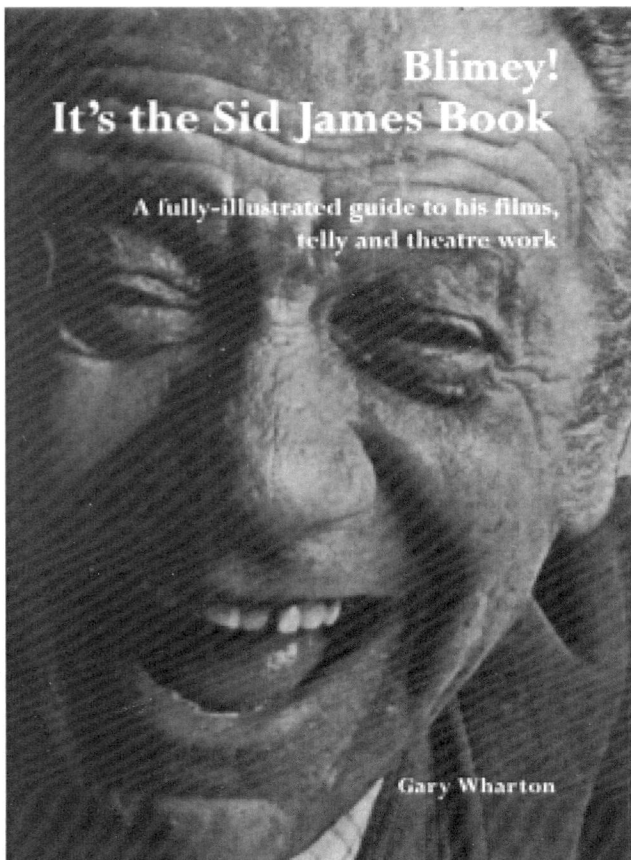

Blimey!
It's the Sid James Book

A fully-illustrated guide to his films,
telly and theatre work

Gary Wharton

Also written by Gary Wharton,
Blimey! It's the Sid James Book documents Sid's many
appearances across radio, film, television and theatre.
Detailed for the first time is his tragic death whilst on
stage at the Sunderland Empire in 1976, with new eye
witness accounts from those present that sad night.
Written by a fan, for the fans, the book is a marvellous
account of the career of a true comedy great.

ISBN 9780 954218744, 174 pages, illustrated

Order your copy via **sidjames_book@yahoo.co.uk**
See the Facebook page **@sidjamescareerbook**